LAST RITES
THE WORK OF THE MODERN
FUNERAL DIRECTOR

Glennys Howarth
University of Sussex, United Kingdom

Death, Value and Meaning Series
Series Editor: John D. Morgan

Baywood Publishing Company, Inc.
AMITYVILLE, NEW YORK

Library of Congress Catalog Number: 95-35982
ISBN: 0-89503-134-5 (Cloth)

Library of Congress Cataloging-in-Publication Data

Howarth, Glennys.
    Last rites : the work of the modern funeral director / Glennys
Howarth.
        p.   cm. - - (Death, value and meaning series)
    Includes bibliographical references and index.
    ISBN 0-89503-134-5 (cloth)
    1. Undertakers and undertaking.   2. Undertakers and undertaking-
-Social aspects.   3. Funeral rites and ceremonies.   4. Death- -Social
aspects.   I. Title.   II. Series.
HD9999.U52H69 1996
363.7'5- -dc20   95-35982
                                                                         CIP

To my father,
for showing me the mountains

Acknowledgments

A number of people have assisted me during the course of this project. First, I wish to thank Paul Rock for his encouragement, support, and guidance and for helpful criticisms on an earlier draft of this book. Steven Gallery gave assistance and made many suggestions for improvement of the manuscript. I am also grateful to two anonymous readers whose comments and suggestions have undoubtedly improved the quality of the text. My thanks also go to colleagues in the field of death and dying for their animated discussions of death, and especially to Peter Jupp for commenting on various chapters, and to Allan Kellehear for his enthusiasm for seeing the book in print.

I would also like to thank all the bereaved people who allowed me to observe their funeral rituals. The time devoted by deathworkers in demonstrating their work and in answering my questions is greatly appreciated.

Finally, I owe a debt of gratitude to the director and staff of "G. R. Stone" who gave so generously of their time in trying to help me to see funeral work through their eyes.

Cover photograph: Special thanks to Cribb & Sons for kind permission to use the photograph of their funeral premises in the 1920s for the cover of this book.

Contents

Introduction

This study began as an interest in the relationship between ritual and attitudes toward death. Having experienced bereavement I was disturbed and puzzled by the apparent lack of coordination between funeral rites and the "needs" of mourners. Equally, being at the grieving end of death, I could not understand why friends and neighbors found it so difficult to express the sympathy they undoubtedly felt toward me. Born of parents who retained the cultural traditions of their Victorian parents, death was a familiar talking point in my childhood in England during the late 1950s and early 1960s. When neighbors and distant relatives died, my siblings and I were not excluded from the discussion. Walks through the local cemetery were as much a part of the Sunday routine as Sunday School and a roast dinner. I recall when my mother assisted in the terminal care of an elderly neighbor she kept us informed of her condition and we regularly visited the woman as she gradually slipped into death. We shared the shocking news that Mr. Brown had "dropped dead" in the street and Mr. Evans in his armchair after a days work—all in the space of one unfortunate month. We drew our curtains as a mark of respect whenever a hearse arrived in the street and always stood in silence if we witnessed a cortège in the area.

Having accepted my family's behavior as the norm during childhood, my first experience of bereavement came early in adult life. By then, although I had been unaware of the transition, I could no longer accept the Victorian legacy which viewed death as a fact of living, as inevitable, and as something we should expect at any age. Bereavement can be painful and bewildering. This is not simply because of the trauma of grief but is also due to the way in which bereaved people are frequently treated by others. Avoidance is the usual strategy, but if chance meeting or protocol demand, a few mumbled words of sympathy and long embarrassed silences are commonly the norm. The solution, adopted by many of those who sorrow, is to keep their own company or that of those similarly "afflicted." With friends, work mates, and acquaintances one almost feels obliged to apologize for bringing fear and embarrassment to the social situation.

These personal experiences of bereavement suggested that there was often an inadequacy or deficiency of significant liturgy and I began to question the place of ritual in this crucial rite of passage.

In 1979 I moved to the heart of London's East End and was repeatedly struck by the sight of funeral processions. Having lived and experienced funerals in other parts of the country, the cortège in the East End was noticeably different—in part because it was so conspicuous. The number of cars, the abundance of floral tributes—often headed with the words "Mum" or "Dad" across the front of the hearse—and the slow, ceremonial walk of the conductor ahead of the procession, commanded the attention of passers-by. My curiosity was fired to know why the funeral ritual in the East End should appear so dissimilar to those in other areas.

The key to an explanation of these flamboyant ceremonies appeared to lie with the undertaker. In examining these rituals, however, my research soon became an exploration of funeral directing and an attempt to understand the undertaker's occupational role. Undertakers and undertaking are for most people in contemporary western societies, largely alien and unfamiliar territory.[1] Yet, exerting a powerful control over the after-death system, funeral directors are central to understanding many of our modern *post-mortem* rituals. By virtue of their directing role they liaise with all other agencies and coordinate the after-death system to provide a service which aims to resolve and dispose of mortal remains with the least amount of "fuss" and the maximum amount of "dignity." In this respect they can be interpreted as carrying out society's "dirty work" in that they release people from body-handling tasks and, by way of manipulation of mortuary symbols, deal with the practical and psychological requirements of bereaved people.

In selecting the East End of London as the focus for this research, the study provides a bridge between the small family business undertaker of the nineteenth and early twentieth centuries and the increasingly large depersonalized funeral chains fast becoming the norm in

---

[1] Studies of funeral directing have largely focused on North American practice [1-5]. Jessica Mitford's examination of the North American funeral extravaganza [5], which included a brief look at the British industry, is still often cited as the definitive account of funeral directing. The lack of recent research and, particularly, of studies of the British industry go some way to explaining this. It is to this lacuna that this book is addressed.

urban regions. Although in some ways the East End experience of "deathwork" is unusual, there are commonalities between "death-workers" which cut across British and North American cultures. Funeral directors maintain certain qualities of homogeneity and common cultural experience. They share a given status, similar values, knowledge, aims and objectives, and they supply a remarkably similar product—the funeral. Since the formation of trade associations, funeral directors have fostered an outlook which is identifiable in their codes of ethics, magazines and industry journals, conferences, and social events. Communication is achieved through a common register and an organizational structure that is peculiar to the industry. It is a kindred identity that enables undertakers to coordinate the duties of other deathworkers. Despite having a personality distinct from their "workselves," and irrespective of the intensity of their adherence to traditional funeral ritual and custom, their essential *sameness* to others in the business is indispensable if the trade is to function efficiently.

In carrying out the research I adopted an ethnographic approach. This involved a year of participant observation and in-depth interviews with funeral directors, embalmers, ministers of religion, coffin makers, nurses, doctors, police officers, grave-diggers, and many others. I was fortunate to negotiate a prolonged period of participant observation within a funeral company in the East End of London. This firm—which I refer to as G. R. Stone—was a traditional, small family business trading in a rapidly deteriorating urban area. The director and staff permitted me to witness, discuss, and participate in both "front" and "back stage" practice. This gave me insight into the work of funeral directors which was augmented by extensive observation and interviews with deathworkers in other areas and in related branches of the industry. The discussion here presents an ethnographic snapshot of funeral directing in this geographical region of London,[2] presenting a holistic account of the social structure of the group while capturing the richness and detail of their lives and values.

---

[2] As such it depicts the premises of G. R. Stone as dilapidated and undertaking practice as it was carried out in rather insalubrious back regions. The majority of the other funeral companies I observed, and certainly the more thriving businesses, were not operating from such run-down premises. Indeed, in keeping with the desire to achieve professional status, many were particularly concerned that their back regions should mirror those found within medical establishments. The analysis of the funeral director's purposes and procedures, however, are essentially true of undertakers throughout Britain, and indeed, within Northern Europe and North America.

ETHNOGRAPHY AND THE
DRAMATURGICAL METAPHOR

Ethnography or fieldwork is perhaps the most appropriate strategy when researching groups such as undertakers who possess an "outsider" status in society.[3] It has been defined as the "science of cultural description" [7, p. 112]; interpreting group dynamics from an "insider's perspective" by gaining fluency with the beliefs, values, and sets of knowledge characteristic of that community [8]. In so doing it helps us to gain, "access to the conceptual world in which our subjects live so that we can, in some extended sense of the term, converse with them" [9, p. 24]. This definition assumes a prior *inability* to communicate, a failure to comprehend, an ignorance of, and a desire to discover, the "cultural patterns of group life" [10]. Selecting a community for study, which is in some way alien to the researcher is instrumental to ethnography and this explains its traditional popularity with anthropologists and, more recently, with sociologists seeking knowledge of deviant subcultures particularly in urban settings [11-13]. Being a cultural outsider with little working knowledge of the undertaker's way of life, this study particularly lent itself to an ethnographic approach.

In accordance with much symbolic interactionist work, the analysis of this ethnographic data relies heavily on the dramaturgical metaphor [14, 15] which considers social life as analogous to the theater. This sentiment is captured most aptly by Jacque in Shakespeare's *As You Like It,* when he remarks:

> All the world's a stage,
> And all the men and women merely players:
> They have their exits and their entrances;
> And one man in his time plays many parts,
> His acts being seven ages.

This perspective regards the individual as a social actor playing a role and managing a character for the benefit of others. The role may be that of teacher, mother, or trade-unionist, played by separate actors or by one individual with multiple roles performed at different times, against distinct backdrops and for specific audiences. Actors alternate between being "on" for clients and being "natural" when relaxing in a group of people "of their own kind" [16].

The dramaturgical analysis has been successfully employed to examine the work of North American funeral directors [2, 17-19].

---

[3] For a detailed discussion of my methodology and experiences in the field see [6].

Although there are differences between morticians on either side of the Atlantic, there are two fundamental facets of their work which render dramaturgy the most appropriate analytical tool for interpreting their culture. First, undertakers are staging a ceremony, which like all its kind, requires a performance akin to theater. The interaction between undertakers and their clients revolves around language and objects designed to ensure the cooperation of all in sustaining the definition of the situation [20, p. 534]. The production requires the use of props, technical aids, costumes and make-up, rehearsed scripts, lead and minor roles, and audience, all necessarily caught up in the ritual. The traditional nature of the ceremony gives credence to the performance and usually ensures its success. Participants, especially those who arrive unrehearsed,

> ... play parts according to a scenario which they are in no position to modify because no one can escape the social roles he is obliged to assume [21, p. 82].

Second, in contrast to other industries whose services may only incidentally be interpreted in the dramaturgical manner, undertakers actually aspire to theatrical presentation. In attempting to protect customers from the horrors of mortality, they suspend reality, a basic tenet of theater. In this way, and with unwitting collusion, a more palatable version of death is provided which shifts from stark, cold permanence to a more gentle and temporary slumber. In this respect, the drama of the funeral operates as a device for making the unacceptable tolerable. For Duvignaud, who considers the distinction between society and the theater, death rituals are

> ... stratagems for averting or masking its hostile destructive force. In the theatre, death is something overcome and integrated, something that only remotely implies the real spiritual horror of actual annihilation ... [21, p. 86].

As we shall discover in what follows, Duvignaud's depiction of theatrical death is accurate. In his brief characterization of ritual, however, he fails to perceive the extent to which these stratagems are successful in disguising the "real spiritual horror" of mortality. In the production of the tragic ritual, funeral directors manipulate mortuary symbols in order to present a *dramatic representation* rather than the *disturbing realities* of death. The salience of the drama is its "respect" and "dignity." The corpse, centerpiece of the drama, is prepared and staged in a manner intended to resemble a peaceful sleeper. Props enhance the spectacle as shiny black limousines crawl ominously through the streets to the cemetery and coffins eventually disappear off stage as the final curtain falls at the close of the performance. Mourners are left to mumble *ad-lib* phrases as they admire floral tributes—the sole remaining symbols of death past.

A further explanation for the dramatic aspirations of undertakers stems from a desire to protect their professional status. The theater is shrouded in an air of mystery where only the initiated are privy to the secrets of production. Similarly the funeral trade closely guard the "professional" skills that metamorphose death's realities. The undertaker's magic transmutes the cadaver into a sleeping beauty; a modest room becomes a reverent chapel; funeral assistants, respectful footmen; and the director, the master of ceremonies. The more spectacular the show the more unlikely the profession will be plagued by impostors.

Industrial survival is a factor which perhaps is particularly relevant to the theatrical practice of undertakers in the East End of London. Here, staged displays are utilized as a means of advertising the quality of the service. Much of the funeral ceremony consists of scenes played out in public. For example, the coffin is typically laid in the hearse as it stands at the front of the undertaker's premises. Floral tributes may then be carefully placed around it. The bearers and drivers take their places in the vehicles and the cortège pulls away maintaining a "respectful" pace as it glides through the city traffic which is desperately and stressfully attempting to circumvent its mass.

One consequence of this ritual (responsible for sparking my initial observation) is its visibility. In British society where the advertisement of mortuary services is viewed with distaste, dramatic funerals provide businesses with a rare opportunity to promulgate their office. In this instance funeral directors' motives are more akin to the theater than to reality where,

> . . . the real difference does not lie in the simple contrast between real and imaginary experience. It rests on the fact that in the theatre action is *made for seeing,* and is, indeed, reconstituted *by* spectacle [21, p. 85 (author's emphasis)].

Undertakers are expert at making a drama out of a crisis and have devoted centuries of effort toward perfecting their art. Their justification is that the public, and more accurately the bereaved, need funeral rituals to assist them to overcome the trauma of personal loss. This interpretation coincides with that adopted by many religions, by bereavement agencies, psychiatrists, and other commentators.

"Without these customs," one undertaker observed, "it's like burying a dog in the ground." For a group who may still be heard to refer to themselves as "the last of the great showmen," this is fortuitous indeed. If the requirements for ritual disappear entirely in our fast-paced, high-tech, urban societies, undertakers and their dramatic personae will become things of the past.

THE STRUCTURE OF THE BOOK

The chapters that follow divide into two sections: the first examines death rituals and the social significance of undertaking in western society; the second presents an ethnographic account of funeral directing in an area of east London which, for the purposes of anonymity, I have called Easton. The discussion traces deathwork procedures from death to the grave. The aim is not to condemn undertakers nor to praise them, but to provide a critical interpretation of their role in the after-death system. As such, this book is concerned with undertakers' perceptions and organization of death rituals and with the way in which they make sense of their role.

Chapter 1 considers explanations for the existence of funeral rituals: social and individual needs, the desire to demonstrate a measure of control over mortality, and fear of the dead and of death itself. The question of how undertakers came to play such an important role in the after-death system is also addressed. Chapter 2 examines modern undertaking practice in the East End of London and compares it with funeral directing in other geographical areas. The next Chapter draws on fieldwork conducted in London's East End and introduces the staff of the funeral company at the heart of the study. The fourth Chapter considers the way undertakers learn their roles. Like medics, fire-fighters, and the police, funeral workers employ coping mechanisms to enable them to perform tasks which can be emotionally and physically distressing. The strategies morticians' adopt to counteract the stigma they frequently experience is contemplated alongside a discussion of the tactics they use to negotiate and manage the impressions others have of them.

A closer inspection of the undertaker's understanding of *post-mortem* requirements is best facilitated through a discussion of mortuary practice and Chapter 5 examines the range of contacts workers have with the dead body. Housing the corpse and accepting responsibility for funeral organization are presented by the trade as aspects of their work which expedite the mourning process. Chapter 6 describes the arrangements interview between the undertaker and the family of the deceased. The funeral director's use of personal front [15], spatial organization and communication format are outlined and their influence on the bereaveds' choice of goods and services assessed. Relationships with other deathworkers are addressed using the concept of the "closed network." Once the preferences of the relatives have been determined, preparation work on the body can begin and Chapter 7 focuses on the "scientific" transformation, or "humanization" of the cadaver. The use of embalming and techniques of theatrical presentation are elements of deathwork which have a significant impact on the ritual viewing of the corpse.

Chapter 8 is concerned with the drama of the funeral ceremony and considers the roles of conductor, funeral assistants, priests, cemetery workers, and mourners in the theatrical performance. The question of authority during the funeral ritual is an important one and the degree of control exerted by the undertaker, the priest, and the bereaved are central issues. The techniques used by undertakers to embellish the theatrical presentation while guarding against spoiled performances are important themes in this discussion.

The final Chapter reviews the development of the funeral industry and modern undertaking practice. A glimpse at the future of the small family business and a note of the fate of G. R. Stone, concludes this ethnographic account of last rites as they are performed by the modern funeral director.

REFERENCES

1. E. Waugh, *The Loved One: An Anglo-American Tragedy,* Chapman & Hall, London, 1948.
2. R. W. Habenstein, *The American Funeral Director and the Sociology of Work,* unpublished Ph.D. thesis, University of Chicago, Chicago, 1954.
3. L. Bowman, *The American Funeral: A Study in Guilt, Extravagance and Sublimity,* Public Affairs Press, Washington, D.C., 1959.
4. V. R. Pine, *Caretaker of the Dead: The American Funeral Director,* Irvington, New York, 1975.
5. J. Mitford, *The American Way of Death,* Hutchinson, London, 1963.
6. G. Howarth, Investigating Deathwork, in *The Sociology of Death,* D. Clark (ed.), Blackwell, Oxford, 1993.
7. H. Wolcott, Criteria for an Ethnographic Approach to Research in Schools, *Human Organization, 34*:2, Summer 1975.
8. D. M. Fetterman, *Ethnography, Step by Step,* Sage, Beverly Hills, 1989.
9. C. Geertz, Ritual and Social Change: A Javanese Example, *American Anthropologist, 59,* pp. 32-54, 1973.
10. A. Schutz, The Stranger, in *Collected Papers,* Vol. II, A. Schutz (ed.), Martinus Nijhoff, The Hague, 1964.

11. W. F. Whyte, *Street Corner Society* (3rd Edition), University of Chicago Press, Chicago, 1981.
12. H. J. Gans, *The Urban Villagers: Group and Class in the Life of Italian-Americans,* The Free Press, New York, 1962.
13. L. Humphreys, *Tearoom Trade: A Study of Homosexual Encounters in Public Places,* Aldine, Chicago, 1970.
14. K. Burke, *A Grammar of Motives,* Prentice Hall, New York, 1945.
15. E. Goffman, *The Presentation of Self in Everyday Life,* Doubleday, New York, 1959.
16. S. L. Messinger et al., Life as Theatre: Some Notes on the Dramaturgical Approach to Social Reality, *Sociometry, 25,* September 1962.
17. R. E. Turner and C. Edgley, Death as Theatre: A Dramaturgical Analysis of the American Funeral, *Sociology and Social Research, 60*:4, pp. 377-392, 1976.
18. D. Unruh, Doing Funeral Directing: Managing Sources of Risk in Funeralization, *Urban Life, 8,* pp. 247-263, 1979.
19. S. R. Barley, The Codes of the Dead: The Semiotics of Funeral Work, *Urban Life, 12*:1, pp. 3-31, 1983.
20. R. S. Perinbanayagam, The Definition of the Situation: An Analysis of the Ethnomethodological and Dramaturgical View, *The Sociological Quarterly, 15,* Autumn 1974.
21. J. Duvignaud, The Theatre in Society: Society in the Theatre, in *Sociology of Literature and Drama,* E. Burns and T. Burns (eds.), Penguin, Harmondsworth, 1973.

CHAPTER 1

Modern Death Rituals and the Undertaker

Almost every society transforms the disposal of human remains into a cultural ritual. These rituals, and the agencies and individuals dedicated to their maintenance, vary in complexity according to the place death commands within the social value system. In this chapter a variety of explanations are offered for the existence of modern death rituals. Those most commonly suggested revolve around social and individual needs to deal with loss, a desire to demonstrate some measure of control over mortality, and fear of the dead and of death itself. A combination of these led Michael Kearl to conclude that without funeral rituals,

> . . . bereaved individuals may be unable to function in their roles if overwhelmed by grief, incapacitated by fear, or unable to develop new relationships to replace the old [1, p. 481].

Let us consider each of the forces for ritual in turn.

SOCIAL AND INDIVIDUAL LOSS

The nineteenth-century anthropologist, E. B. Tylor, argued that thinking about mortality was a manifestation of nascent culture [2]. Our consciousness of the inevitability of death and the creation of sophisticated ways of dealing with it distinguish us from animals and from our former animal-like existence. Robert Hertz, a disciple of Durkheim, extended this analysis: people and animals die in an instant but because people are highly social beings, funeral rituals are created to enable others to adapt to the death of the *social* creature [3].

Participants in funeral rituals, however, often rationalize these rites by viewing them as being of benefit to the dead. In this respect we might consider the tendency to take great care of the way the corpse is dressed and coffined. This is conventionally explained by bereaved people as a desire to do one's best for the deceased—to "give them a good send-off." In pre-Reformation Europe and in some contemporary cultures such as rural Greece [4], funeral ceremonies may be observed as a means of assisting the soul on its long journey to the afterlife. In this context the pioneering work of Hertz discusses the practice of secondary-burial [3]. These rites are adopted as the means by which the soul is eventually released from the body after death. Similar customs are employed in the Neapolitan region of modern Italy where the inhabitants perceive exhumation,

> . . . as final proof that a soul has arrived safely in purgatory. This means that mourning can end. As the living resume normal life, so the soul starts its time in purgatory. In other words, the actions of the bereaved and the fate of the corpse and soul are synchronous and interdependent [5, p. 9].

Societies practicing secondary burials today tend to be small scale or rural communities and this accords with assertions made by Durkheim [6] and Hertz [3], and more recently by Blauner [7]. They argue that the key to understanding death rituals is contained in the distinction between simple and advanced societies. In simple communities, death has a profoundly disruptive effect on everyday life and is therefore accorded prominence in cultural behavior. As a society becomes more highly structured, death has less impact on the community as individuals perform a variety of social roles. Institutions and agencies evolve, such as experts in deathwork, to offset the more inconvenient aspects of mortality, thereby reducing the amount of time and commitment devoted by individuals to the loss of a family or community member.

On an individual level, it is often suggested that obsequies are employed as a means of consoling the living. Whether the rituals are seen as a method of coping with sorrow [8] or, alternatively, as a means of exorcising guilt [9], the periods and practices of mourning are, according to this explanation, primarily designed to help the bereaved to personally adjust to loss. Some studies concentrate on this aspect of funeral rituals, most notably Parkes [10]. This interpretation parallels that concerning the "emergence of civilization" as they both view the necessity for after-death observances as stemming from a social need to reconcile the loss of a community member.

CONTROLLING DEATH

A further explanation for the creation and nature of *post-mortem* ritual is connected with a need to exert some form of control over mortality. The Grim Reaper's arbitrary choice of victim has long been a problem with which individuals and societies have struggled. Death is the unknown quantity—not only are we unaware of what, if anything, lies beyond the grave, but moreover, we cannot with any certainty even predict the "where," "when," and "how" of its coming. The fact that life may be extinguished without warning and with no consideration for the victim's situation, fills the human heart with fear. It is for this reason that people have been at pains to exercise dominion over the chance nature of death.

Philipe Ariès, in his colossal history of western attitudes to death since pre-Christian times, believed that there was once a golden age of death when people were somehow alerted to its imminent arrival; felt little physical revulsion or alarm toward the act of dying or the subsequent corruption of the body; and had no fear of the terrifying possibility of the eternal night [11]. If such a disposition did exist, then it was in Christendom when people relied on God's mortal agent, the established church, to guide them through life and into immortality; the overarching purpose of death rituals was to demonstrate control over the condition itself. In previous era, and in other cultures, religion or other supernatural forms were invoked to influence the nature, frequency, and victims of death. In the contemporary western world the declining role of Christianity in providing a framework for (or means of making sense of) mortality appears to be directly proportional to the increasing influence of science. People have always desired control over death. Historically this was pursued through religious belief. In modern societies, science and technology have largely replaced faith *as a means of influencing mortality*—perhaps with the underlying promise of eternal life. Like the quest for the Holy Grail, which was itself essentially a desire for immortality, its elusiveness merely serves to fire the determination of those in pursuit.

FEAR OF THE DEAD AND
OF DEATH ITSELF

Psychologists and social observers frequently stress fear of the dead, and of death itself, as the primary motive for the introduction of death rituals [12-16]. Puckle explains all such rituals as originating from a universal fear of the return of the dead [12]. According to this analysis, people accept a responsibility to care for, respect, and honor their dead because they fear that their deceased relatives might otherwise return to haunt them. In arguing his case, Puckle, an early twentieth-century social commentator, traces the origins of many superstitious and idiosyncratic conventions. One interesting example he cites is the wearing of black mourning dress, sometimes known as "weeds." In medieval times, black was thought to render the wearer invisible to the dead and thus protected them from any unwelcome advances.

In some societies it may not be the souls of the dead that people fear so much as the physically and symbolically contaminating properties of the corpse. Such fear of pollution is discussed by Watson in his work on the management of death in Cantonese society [17]. In the communities he studied, the cadaver was perceived as a source of impurity. Death contamination, the Cantonese believed, was carried both through physical contact with the body and also through contiguity to the corpse or merely from inhaling the "killing airs." That is, simply being in the vicinity of the body could have dire consequences as the defiling effect was carried in the very air breathed. It was important, therefore, to minimize the risk of contamination and this compelled the employment of professional corpse handlers to wash, lay-out, and coffin the body. As a consequence of their work with the dead, these undertakers were excluded from residence within the village boundary.

In some respects the modern response to death resembles Cantonese death rites. In western societies, since the nineteenth century, a physical and symbolic separation has occurred which has divided the living from the dead and has encouraged the development of rituals which privatize dying, death, and grief. It was in the nineteenth century that the link between disease and hygiene was first established. Once uncovered it was not long before the proximity of the graveyard to the abodes of the living was cited as a source of pestilence: for example, one source of cholera was traced to water supplies drawn from local churchyards. Similarly, symptoms of ill health and, occasionally, sudden death among gravediggers were identified as stemming from malevolent bacteria associated with putrescence. In modern societies, dying people have become separated from the healthy and this has created an illusion of distance from death. The typical place for dying is in the hospital, and more recently the hospice, not the home among the living; the place for disposing of human remains is no longer the local churchyard but the cemetery or crematorium, usually located at a distance from residential areas. When mourning, few individuals wear black even at the funeral and people are expected to "pick up the threads" and "get on with life" within a few days. This privatization of death, typically occurring in an institutional setting, and of sorrow, restricted to the immediate family, has been described as an unhealthy aspect of modern living [18-20].

The link between death and disease (see Chapter 5 for a full discussion), combined with the modern proclivity to classify and separate, has contributed to a perception of the corpse as polluting and a reliance on undertakers to deal with its ritual purification. Yet as Douglas suggests in her discussion of dirt, fear of contamination is not purely physical but is primarily symbolic [21]. In a society which emphasizes the need for order, for everything to be in its right place, a fear of being defiled by the corpse is not necessarily a physical sense of revulsion for the body of the deceased but rather a cultural abhorrence of

> matter out of place. . . . In short, our pollution behaviour is the reaction which condemns any object or idea likely to confuse or contradict cherished classifications [21, pp. 35-36].

The dead no longer belong among the living and the proper location for the corpse is not in the home but in the funeral parlor or mortuary.

Like the Cantonese, the effects of the need for separation are felt by those who work with the dead. The repercussions for funeral directors of the symbolic contamination with death are two-fold. First, undertakers are stigmatized by the omnipresence of death in their work. This, as I demonstrate in Chapter 4, encourages deathworkers to adopt a variety of strategies to combat detrimental images of the funeral industry and, on a more personal level, which allow individuals to "pass as normal" members of society. Second, and perhaps an unintended consequence of the first effect, this symbolic fear of death, coupled with the fear of physical contamination by disease and decay resultant from putrefaction, enables funeral directors to practice their trade with relatively little outside interference. Modern funeral directors acquire control over the funeral service via their custody of the corpse. Care of the body of the deceased is delegated to them primarily in societies where the fear of physical and symbolic pollution is high.

Bereaved people might also suffer a symbolic contamination with death and some report feeling shunned socially. This symbolic defilement could be responsible for what one person has described as the identification of bereaved people as "diseased"; a state which can lead to avoidance behavior.

> . . . I felt totally alone with my grief. I felt as if I had some kind of disease. I imagined that people could see just by looking at me that I had this illness, that everyone was trying to keep their distance. So I kept my distance too, or at least tried to hide my disfigurement [22].

A further basis for such avoidance may stem from the loss of codes for public expressions of sympathy and this has left friends and neighbors embarrassed and bereft of social skills for communication with the bereaved.

It is this last explanation that has led to mounting criticism of the professionalization of dying and death and to calls for reform [23-26]. Modern "deathways" are being described as isolating and inappropriate and there are now increasing demands for individuals and families to exert greater control over dying and for more meaningful funeral rituals.[1] The growth of the hospice movement and the proliferation of funeral reform groups are symptomatic of this rejection of late twentieth-century approaches to dying and death.

These relatively recent trends toward reform might appear to contradict the thesis (set out above) of the dead body as polluting. It should be remembered, however, that the corpse is not primarily perceived as physically defiling but is *symbolically* contaminating when it is located in the wrong place. If the separation between life and death is an artificial one, reuniting the two, an apparent aim for many of the reform groups, will negate the social perception of the dead body as out of place in the home. If this should occur, the role of professionals or experts in the care of the dying and the dead will be open to further scrutiny and will be either transformed or eliminated.

In the case of funeral rituals, rejecting the role of the expert entails mourners organizing their own ceremony. This type of funeral often brings great comfort by enabling them to control the proceedings and play an active part in the rituals. At present, however, most people appear disinclined to make this kind of effort. Organizing a funeral requires confidence, time, forethought, resources and, above all, inclination. Some people may believe themselves too busy or too inexperienced (in part attributable to the undertaker as we shall see) to contemplate the management of death rituals. Other funeral arrangers may be prosecuting a duty rather than pursuing a desire. Many, perhaps those overtaken by sudden death, are too incapacitated by grief to plan and organize a "meaningful" funeral ceremony. Whatever the reason, it remains the case that for the time-being at least, the overwhelming majority rely on a funeral company to organize and direct their last rites.

Let us now consider some of the ways in which undertakers came to play such a significant role in the death rituals of modern societies.

---

[1] For an interesting discussion of the development of these critiques of modern deathways, see [27].

THE EMERGENCE OF THE PROFESSIONAL DEATHWORKER[2]

The character assumed by death is interwoven with its surrounding discourse and with the emergence and development of deathwork procedures. Identifying a social need to control death, for example, has crucial implications for the undertaker who has a key role to play in the ritualized disposal of human remains. Religion, with its promise of salvation, has long been a central plank of funeral procedure. Concomitant with the descent from Christendom has been the transfer of funeral preparation and ritual organization to the "expert" deathworker. The role of the priest, once central to the death rites, has declined. Medics have taken control over the dying process and funeral directors, emulating the scientific approaches of the medical world, have adopted pseudo-scientific treatments such as embalming. Succumbing to the professionalization of dying and death, is, in large part, a consequence of the scientific, rather than the religious drive to exert control over death.

The roots of the modern funeral director, however, lie in the medieval art of heraldry with its provision of funerals for the aristocracy. Created and evolving in Europe during a dynamic of the commercialization of death, undertaker-entrepreneurs seized power from the College of Arms and eventually supplied burial rituals for all social classes [28]. A subsequent pre-occupation with health and sanitation in the early Victorian period resulted in the creation of extra-mural cemeteries. The consequent requirement for transport to relatively distant burial ground augmented the undertaker's monopolization of increasingly flamboyant funeral trappings. In a detailed study of Victorian death rituals in Britain, Morley [29] quotes from *Cassells Household Guide, 1870* which describes the paraphernalia required for the "full" middle-class funeral.

> Hearse and four horses, two mourning coaches with fours, twenty-three plumes of rich ostrich-feathers, complete velvet covering for carriages and horses, and an esquire's plume of best feathers; strong elm shell, with tufted mattress, lined and ruffled with superfine cambric, and pillow; full worked glazed cambric winding-sheet, stout outside lead coffin, with inscription plate and solder complete; one-and-a-half-inch oak case, covered with black or crimson velvet, set with three rows round and lid panelled with best brass handles and grips, lid ornaments to correspond; use of silk velvet pall; two

[2] For a fuller discussion of the development of modern undertaking see Howarth [42].

mutes with gowns, silk hat-bands and gloves; fourteen men as
pages, feathermen, and coachmen, with truncheons and wands, silk
hat-bands, etc; use of mourners' fittings; and attendant with silk
hat-band etc. [30, p. 19].

The funeral industry in Britain, however, reached its profit-making
zenith in the mid-nineteenth century when it was subject to criticism
and censure from an influential reform movement. Since the turn of the
twentieth century, British undertaking has undergone radical transformation. Treated with scorn by some sectors of Victorian society and
the target of a reform movement, undertakers toiled to achieve respectability. Professionalization was the major strategy employed in the
quest for higher status for their beleaguered occupation.

Relinquishing the designation of "undertaker," and its gradual
replacement with the title of "funeral director" was part of this process.
By 1940, following the North American example, the term "funeral
director" had been adopted in most branches of the trade in Britain. In
1935 The British Undertakers Association became the National Association of Funeral Directors. The industry's journal, once "The B.U.A.
Monthly," simultaneously became "The National Funeral Director"—
simplified to "The Funeral Director" in 1953.

Professionalization, with the emphasis on education, was, for both
British and North American funeral directors, related to expansion and
was used as a method of excluding impostors from the trade [30].
According to Millerson, there are six essential characteristics which
distinguish an occupation as professional [31]. These are: skill based on
theoretical knowledge, training and education, demonstration of com-
petence by passing a test, maintenance of integrity by adherence to a
code of conduct, a professional organization, and the provision of a
service for the public good [32]. Throughout the twentieth century,
undertakers have systematically developed all of these attributes.
Professional organizations have been created which regulate the work
of their members through codes of conduct. Funeral directors promote
a view of their deathwork as a public service which protects the
bereaved. The level of skill in funeral work and the knowledge involved
in techniques such as embalming, require education and training and
courses have been introduced which lead to certification for the successful student.

The industry's pursuit of professionalism has been modeled on both
religious and medical vocations. In the early part of this century they
inclined toward religious association and undertakers adopted Christian symbolism to embellish chapels of rest and to replace items such
as coffins in window dressing. In contrast to North American funeral

directors, and as a consequence of the clergy's resistance, British undertakers were unable to persuade priests to perform funeral ceremonies on their premises. As the century has progressed, however, the accent on Christian practice has foundered and the demand for ethnic and religious minority funerals increased. Consequently, the crucifix has largely been replaced by flowers and undertakers now prefer to emulate the medical rather than the clerical profession. The earlier trust in religion has been eclipsed by resort to science.

One of the central planks of professionalization has been the acquisition of the "science" of embalming. *The Undertakers' Journal* in Britain commented in 1910 that the possession of professional skills had favorable consequences in that there was,

> . . . something very alluring in the prospect of rubbing shoulders on a basis of equality of status with doctors and parsons [33, p. 85].

It was Thomas Holmes who during the American Civil War revived an interest in embalming. As a result of his achievements, this technique of preservation was taken up and embalming schools began opening in North America [34]. It was not until the beginning of the twentieth century, however, that British undertakers began to see the potential of this technique, couched in terms of hygienic treatment and seeking only to delay decomposition of the corpse. For undertakers its principal benefit was that it gave them an advantage over non-embalming competitors. As early as 1910, when the British undertaker was busy fashioning a pseudo-religious vocation, Professor George B. Dodge, President of the Massachusetts College of Embalming, who maintained a regular feature in a British trade journal, was advocating embalming as the key to professional respectability.

> Why every undertaker in this country does not prepare himself to use these methods . . . is something that is very hard to understand. The reputation he would gain for keeping bodies in good condition would rapidly spread and give him a vast advantage over his competitors who do absolutely nothing to prevent those most disagreeable conditions [35, p. 6].

A further aspect of the pursuit of professional status was the provision of shelter for the corpse. In England during the 1920s, people were encouraged to make better use of public mortuaries as sanctuary for the dead. This innovation must be set in the context of growing concern with public health and an increasing propensity toward the distancing of death. Relocation of the cemetery to the outskirts of the city in the nineteenth century, together with a perceptible decline in infant mortality meant that people were more able to escape the constant reminders of finitude and decay. Moreover, there was a lack of time in rapidly expanding industrial societies—more concerned with life than death—to care "properly" for the body and hence the willingness to transfer the tasks to an expert. The latter was a phenomenon occurring in many fields and reflected the needs and demands of societies based on a more sophisticated division of labor. Undertakers' desire to utilize their newly acquired scientific, preservation, and restoration techniques, combined with the realization that the body was fast becoming the key to funeral rituals, meant that they were keen to take custody of the corpse. Providing a chapel of rest allowed them to do just that.

As the twentieth century has progressed, the undertaker's provision of shelter for the corpse has been elevated to the status of necessity. In addition to the reasons already outlined, a further explanation is that death now more frequently occurs in the hospital rather than the home. In a hospital setting the body is rapidly transferred from the ward to the morgue and from there it is a simple step for funeral directors to take custody and remove the deceased to their own mortuary or chapel. Seldom do relatives request return of the body to the home. If the home has escaped the contamination of death there is usually a preference that it should continue to do so. Inviting death into the house is generally avoided. Furthermore, modern housing design, bereft of a parlor where the body would once have lain, and in Britain, the popularization of the "through-lounge" are further factors providing a niche for the chapel of rest.

THE ROLE OF DEATHWORKERS
IN MODERN WESTERN SOCIETIES

British society is most similar in its funeral rituals to the practices in North America in that the preparations and ceremony are managed by professional corpse-handlers or funeral directors. American anthropologists, Metcalf and Huntington attempt to explain why people chose to relinquish control of the funeral to the professional [36]. In so doing they focus on two commonly accepted stimuli. The first is economic and stems from the professional interests of funeral directors, depicted as a powerful professional elite who successfully lobby for legislation favorable to their industry. As controllers of the disposal ritual they persuade the public of the efficacy of mortuary techniques as a means of comforting the bereaved. However, while it is true that funeral directors in North America are a relatively powerful group (for example, successfully attaining legislation compelling the licensing of embalmers and so excluding untrained individuals from the trade) and that in common with Britain undertakers they play a significant role in the management of death rituals (providing extensive services which stimulate demand), these deathworkers are not simply manipulating their clients into accepting predetermined customs of their own choosing. As the anthropologists hint, there is a symbiotic relationship between public ritual and personal sentiment, ". . . conventions condition feelings and provide a setting for them" [36, p. 206]. Hence, funeral directors' promotion of particular rituals can both stimulate *and* satisfy the needs of bereaved people.

The second incentive Metcalf and Huntington suggest for handing over control to the funeral director is that death rites are rooted in private fear and guilt. Bereaved people choose to employ a funeral director because they fear death. Yet they purchase luxury items (such as cushioned caskets) because they experience a sense of guilt toward the dead [16]. The choice of embalming, allowing the survivor to view the body in a preserved state, helps to assuage this fear by creating an illusion of victory over death. Metcalf and Huntington criticize this analysis by arguing that modern embalming has only a transient effect. Moreover, the public have no desire for a more durable protection from corruption and this they contend, is evidenced by the failure of the Cryonics[3] movement in the United States. The popularity of cremation suggests that their assertion is also true of British society.

Metcalf and Huntington also reject the assumption that fear and guilt are heightened by the decline of organized religion. They observe that secularization is proceeding apace in Britain but without a similar stress on, what they term, "death denying" rites. Their evidence is Mitford's study of funeral directors [5] which, after supplying a brief glimpse of the British funeral trade, concludes that viewing and embalming are relatively unimportant aspects of the industry. When Mitford conducted her research in 1963, although embalming had been available for more than half a century, the practice was yet to gain in popularity. By the late 1980s, however, it had become a central, and often routine, feature of the treatment of corpses in many parts of Britain. Embalming schools now exist and the British Institute of Embalmers offers diploma courses for the modern mortician. The funeral director's practical manual explains the benefits for the bereaved and advises methods of encouraging uptake. Trade journals

---

[3] This is an attempt to gain immortality by deep freezing the body at death. The aim is to release the person from suspension in a future time when a cure has been found for their ailments.

are replete with advertisements for embalming materials, cosmetic kits, and with accounts of undertakers whose provision of the chapel of rest is seen by their customers as indispensable. Mortuary practice in Britain is now similar (although not so publicly celebrated) to that in North America. Mitford's brief study of English undertaking, significant though it was in enlightening its contemporary public, bears little resemblance to the industry today.

Metcalf and Huntington believe that North American society adopts the science of embalming and lifelike presentation of the corpse as a form of collective representation of the "proper life." The key to this is the notion of fulfillment. They contend that society has not rejected mortality but, due to advances in medical science which prolong life and alleviate pain, people expect that death will come painlessly and at the end of a long and gratifying life. The presentation of the deceased in sleep (the aim of the funeral director's "humanization" work) epitomizes a lasting peace. This does not, however, answer the question: why, if they accept the realities of death, do bereaved people wish to have the body manipulated by the mortician into a form of icon which symbolizes their own aspirations for life? A more fitting explanation may be that the work of the mortician is in keeping with the need to demonstrate control over death. The undertaker's stress on presenting a body devoid of the scars of age contradicts the notion of the collective representation of peaceful fulfillment in old age. Furthermore, when viewing in the funeral parlor, visitors are quick to comply with socially prescribed behavior which requires that they remark on the *well being* of the corpse and not on how good it looks *in death*.

> . . . on entering, the mourner must first approach the coffin. There is little show of emotion, but afterwards it is appropriate to make some brief remark about how well the deceased looks . . . [37, pp. 95-96].

The preoccupation with embalming and reconstruction work appear to be more concerned with creating a sense of individual immortality rather than reflecting a practical truth. The requirement for this fiction may stem from the fact that secular society now regards *the body* as the site of the self. Greater value is attached to the condition of the physical body than was afforded in an era when it was considered a mere machine or vehicle for the soul. Synnott contrasts the beliefs of Plato, Saint Paul, Descartes, and Sartre in relation to the body—tomb, temple, machine, and self, respectively [38]. Sartre, the most contemporary of these, was sure that the self was inseparable from the body. "I *live* my body . . . I *am* my body to the extent that I *am*" [39, pp. 428,

460]. Although folk religion may continue, the decline of institutional-ized Christianity and the escalation of materialism and individuality, both strikingly apparent in the late twentieth century, combine to magnify the significance of Sartre's thoughts. If one cannot be certain of Christ's triumph over death and anticipate the joy of reunion with those gone before, one can at least control the interpretation of death by commemorating the life that was, and revering the body that remains.

This purpose shares some common threads with the practice of constructing effigies to substitute the decaying bodies of royalty and aristocracy in some medieval and traditional societies [28, 40, 41]. With the scientific technique of embalming, mortal and immortal become one and the need for the effigy can be discarded. Just as the effigy comes to represent the perpetuity of nation and kingship, the humanized and preserved body of late twentieth-century western society symbolizes the continuity of individualism and the victory of the self over the collective body. Walter argues that individualism, for which we strive in life, is lost in death because the corpse is subjected to the "conveyor belt" funeral service [25]. While it may be true that the cemetery or crematorium isolate and alienate the individual, it is not primarily through religious services that deathworkers endeavor to generate a sense of individuality but through the scientific advances of modern arterial embalming, "cosmetology," and reconstruction work. It is in the privacy of the chapel of rest that the memory picture is presented, the individual honored, and the symbol of immortality created.

REFERENCES

1. M. C. Kearl, *Endings: A Sociology of Death and Dying,* Oxford University Press, New York, 1989.
2. E. B. Tylor, *Primitive Culture: Researches into the Development of Mythology, Philosophy, Religion, Language, Art and Custom,* Vol. I (3rd Edition), 1891.
3. R. Hertz, *Death and the Right Hand,* R. Needham and C. Needham (trans.), Cohen & West, London, 1960.
4. L. M. Danforth, *The Death Rituals of Rural Greece,* Princeton University Press, Princeton, New Jersey, 1982.
5. M. Hutchinson, Making Time for the Dead, *The Listener,* p. 9, July 23, 1987.
6. E. Durkheim, *The Elementary Forms of Religious Life,* J. W. Swain (trans.), Allen & Unwin, London, 1965.
7. R. Blauner, Death and the Social Structure, *Psychiatry, 29*:4, November 1966.

8. B. Malinowski, *Magic, Science and Religion and Other Essays,* Doubleday, New York, 1954.
9. S. Freud, Thoughts for the Times on War and Death 1915, II. Our Attitude towards Death, in *The Standard Edition of the Complete Psychological Works of Sigmund Freud, Vol. XIV (1914-1916),* J. Strachey and A. Freud (eds.), Hogarth Press, London, 1957.
10. C. M. Parkes, *Bereavement: Studies in Grief in Adult Life* (2nd Edition), Penguin, Harmondsworth, 1986.
11. P. Ariès, *Western Attitudes Toward Death: From the Middle Ages to the Present,* Open Forum Series, Marion Boyars, London, 1976.
12. B. S. Puckle, *Funeral Customs: Their Origin and Development,* Lt. Werner-Laurie, London, 1926.
13. J. G. Frazer, *The Fear of the Dead in Primitive Religion,* Vol. II, Macmillan, London, 1934.
14. H. Feifel, Attitudes towards Death in Some Normal and Mentally Ill Populations, in *The Meaning of Death,* H. Feifel (ed.), McGraw-Hill, New York, 1959.
15. R. Kastenbaum and R. Aisenberg, *The Psychology of Death,* Springer, New York, 1972.
16. E. Becker, *The Denial of Death,* Free Press, New York, 1973.
17. J. L. Watson, Of Flesh and Bone: The Management of Death Pollution in Cantonese Society, in *Death and the Regeneration of Life,* M. Bloch and J. Parry (eds.), Cambridge University Press, Cambridge, 1982.
18. P. Ariès, Death Inside Out, in *Understanding Death and Dying: An Interdisciplinary Approach,* S. Wilcox and M. Sutton (eds.), Mayfield, California, 1985.
19. N. Elias, *The Loneliness of the Dying,* Blackwell, Oxford, 1985.
20. G. Gorer, *Death, Grief and Mourning in Contemporary Britain,* Cresset Press, London, 1965.
21. M. Douglas, *Purity and Danger: An Analysis of the Concepts of Pollution and Taboo,* Routledge, London, 1966.
22. R. Adams, 1 Person, *The Guardian,* May 1987.
23. N. Albery, G. Elliot, and J. Elliot (eds.), *The Natural Death Handbook,* Virgin, London, 1993.
24. J. Spottiswoode, *Undertaken with Love,* Robert Hale, London, 1991.
25. T. Walter, *Funerals and How to Improve Them,* Hodder & Stoughton, London, 1990.
26. P. Jupp, *Good Funeral Practice,* National Funeral College, unpublished.
27. T. Walter, *The Revival of Death,* Routledge, London, 1994.
28. C. Gittings, *Death, Burial and the Individual in Early Modern England,* Croom Helm, London, 1984.
29. J. Morley, *Death, Heaven and the Victorians,* Studio Vista, London, 1971.
30. R. W. Habenstein, Sociology of Occupations: The Case of the American Funeral Director, in *Human Behaviour and Social Processes: An Interactionist Approach,* A. M. Rose (ed.), Routledge & Kegan Paul, London, 1962.

31. G. Millerson, *The Qualifying Professions*, Routledge & Kegan Paul, London, 1964.
32. G. Mungham and P. A. Thomas, Solicitors and Clients: Altruism or Self-interest, in *The Sociology of the Professions: Lawyers, Doctors and Others*, R. Dingwall and P. Lewis (eds.), Macmillan, London, 1983.
33. *The Undertakers' Journal*, p. 85, April 1910.
34. B. Parsons, The Pioneers of Presentation: Their Problems and Successes, *The Embalmer, 38*:1, pp. 16-24, 1995.
35. *The Undertakers' Journal*, p. 6, January 1910.
36. P. Metcalf and R. Huntington, *Celebrations of Death: The Anthropology of Mortuary Ritual* (2nd Edition), Cambridge University Press, Cambridge, 1991.
37. V. R. Pine, *Caretaker of the Dead: The American Funeral Director*, Irvington, New York, 1975.
38. A. Synnott, Tomb, Temple, Machine and Self: The Social Construction of the Body, *British Journal of Sociology*, 1992.
39. J. P. Sartre, *Being and Nothingness*, H. E. Barnes (trans.), Washington Square Press, Washington, 1966.
40. R. E. Giesey, *The Royal Funeral Ceremony in Renaissance France*, Librairie E. Droz, Genhve, 1960.
41. E. E. Evans-Pritchard, *The Divine Kingship of the Shilluk of the Nilotic Sudan*, Cambridge University Press, Cambridge, 1948.
42. G. Howarth, The Professionalisation of the Funeral Industry, in *The Changing Face of Death*, P. C. Jupp & G. Howarth (eds.), Macmillan, Basingstoke, 1996.

CHAPTER 2

The Business of Funeral Directing

When the undertaker visited, I was impressed,
Even his hair was polished black,
and you could tell he was a master craftsman
by his elegiac voice . . . [1].

There are few funeral ceremonies today where mourners recognize the funeral director as a "master craftsman." Uncommon though they are in the late twentieth century the flamboyant funeral customs operated by some small funeral companies in the East End of London furnish us with a direct link to the past and an insight into a vanishing tradition where communities were once compelled to proclaim death and to bid farewell to the deceased in the most celebrationary manner possible. Flamboyance, however, is not necessarily the trademark of the typical modern East End funeral. Many families wish to dispose of their dead in a simple and private fashion. For them, the undertaker can arrange a basic funeral, the price of which includes coffin, hearse, and one mourning car in addition to mortuary services.[1] Alternatively, a wide selection of goods and services can be provided for those who seek an embellished ceremony.

In making preparations for a funeral ceremony, the question arises as to why one family may choose a simple funeral and another be more inclined to conspicuous consumption [2]. A combination of factors influence people's funeral choices, not least of which derive from class, ethnic, and religious preferences. The notion of "care," however, is of central significance in deciding the extent and nature of funeral goods and services.

---

[1] Mortuary services include: removal of the body; laying out; use of the chapel of rest; and the labor of the funeral conductor, drivers, and coffin bearers.

CARE

It is difficult to define exactly what is meant by the notion of care. The Oxford English Dictionary (1984) defines care as protection or feeling concern or interest for an object or person. When we think of caring for the living it usually betokens providing for the physical and emotional needs of the most vulnerable: very young, very old, sick, and disabled people. Additionally, we may care for an animal or for plants—both living things. We may also care for a valuable possession: a car, a trinket, a piece of furniture. The care in all these cases demands gentle treatment to prolong or improve life or physical appearance. The extent of care afforded may be gauged by assessing the number and quality of services pursued on behalf of that which is valued.

The concept of care, crops up repeatedly in discussions with undertakers and bereaved alike and is bound up with the familiar sentiments of "love," "respect," "decency," and "dignity"—the most frequently voiced idioms when talking about funerals. In assessing the needs of clients the funeral industry refers to a range of indicators to discover current attitudes to death, bereavement and funerals and to discern the appropriate style of care. Professional Associations, such as the English National Association of Funeral Directors (NAFD), monitor a variety of sources, disseminating information and policy directives through trade journals, magazines, and the *Manual of Funeral Directing*. They consult expert studies produced by psychologists, sociologists, social workers, and bereavement counselors. Media reports are regularly inspected as they provide clear signals of attitudes to death and to the funeral trade. Newspaper articles are frequently reproduced in their monthly magazines. A related source of information is the work of pressure groups or government agencies and committees who periodically conduct enquiries into people's experiences of bereavement and funerals. Education and training courses for funeral directors and embalmers teach about the requirements of the bereaved and appropriate conduct for workers.

The overriding determinants of undertaking procedure, however, are tradition and practice. The novice funeral director inevitably refers to the manual of funeral directing for detail but his/her approach to the job will largely be dictated by knowledge of local and company specific funeral traditions as they are taught by experienced colleagues. Once trained, undertakers justify their practice by resort to customer satisfaction—a concept whose parameters are rather difficult to define. In assuming that bereaved people require particular types of ritual, the undertaker is released from the near impossible task of endeavoring to assess each funeral in terms of its validity or acceptability for the participants. The after-death process is implemented using a package of trustworthy recipes. Like other expert groups, the funeral director,

> . . . does not search for the truth and does not quest for certainty. All he wants is information on likelihood and insight into the chances or risks which the situation at hand entails for the outcome of his actions [14, p. 94].

If no one complains, all must be satisfied. Client satisfaction is assumed by default. When customers do complain, their grievances can usually be traced to mistaken performances on the part of the death-workers or their associates. The upshot of this is that the structure of the ritual is not refined unless in so doing undertaking practice is perfected.

How do undertakers transform their perceptions of the requirements of the bereaved into caring deathwork? As in any rite of passage the subjects retain their status until they adopt a new one [3, 4]. For example, in contemporary western wedding ceremonies the man and woman retain their "single" status until pronounced as "joined together in matrimony." Similarly, when death occurs the individual does not immediately lose his/her social status within the family or community. Identification of the deceased as having passed into the realms of the dead is deferred until the body is interred or cremated—forever removed from the living, or until it becomes unrecognizable through the process of corruption. This may explain the distinction voiced in popular expressions between "dead and buried" and between being dead and gone. It is not the act of dying that immediately separates the deceased from the living; this distinction is achieved as a result of burial or other form of disposal. There is a transitory or *liminal* [5] period which lasts from the moment of death until after the funeral. It is during this phase that the bereaved adjust to the social transformation of the deceased from society or family member to the legions of the dead.

Disposal is usually organized by a funeral director skilled in the ability to temporarily arrest the process of decomposition. In this the mortician conspires with the tacit desire of the family to perceive the uninterred corpse as being in possession of human qualities and therefore entitled to human respect. To achieve this, morticians go to great lengths to "humanize" the body. It is during this treatment that they translate the ideology of care into practice: providing shelter for the corpse which they will also wash, dress, and lay to rest in a lined and pillowed coffin or casket.[2]

When death occurs in the East End of London, families customarily demonstrate their regard for the deceased through the purchase of goods and services. This practice is common throughout British and North American societies. Although there may be a significant trend in favor of simple funerals, the majority of bereaved people, in keeping with the consumer behavior of western societies, continue to require relatively elaborate funeral services. For their part the funeral company's pursuit of profit is seen as compatible with a show of respect for their clients. Within the ideology of care, two further factors are significant—first, the availability of goods and services and second, the historical significance of funeral rites in this area of the metropolis.

From the viewpoint of the supplier, the undertaker's continued provision of conspicuous merchandise further stimulates customer demand. Purchasing the undertaker's services is one way the bereaved can demonstrate the care they have taken to ensure the best treatment for their loved one. After a lifetime of selling funerals in East London, John Fry[3] was convinced that, despite protests to the contrary, people really did want the assurance of knowing that their body would be handled carefully and treated with respect. He explained,

> A lot of people say they'll go for the quick and easy way out, sort of business. People say, "Oh well, you can take me off in an orange box"! When the time comes they're different. People have a different attitude. They want somebody to take care. I mean, if they've got somebody that's close to them they don't want the orange box kind of thing. They want someone to take care. They want someone to do the whole thing for them. . . .

Until comparatively recently the high cost of funerals[4] meant that the urban poor were effectively denied elaborate disposal rituals.

---

[2] Coffins have shaped shoulders and caskets are rectangular and usually cushioned.

[3] All the names used in this book are pseudonyms, adopted to protect respondents' identities.

[4] According to *Cassell's Household Guide* (1874) the cost of a funeral in England in the nineteenth century ranged from £4 (exclusive of burial fees) for a member of the "labouring class" to between £200 and £1000 for the funeral of a "gentleman." "Persons of rank or title" might expect to pay anything from £500 to £1500 [6, p. 118]. In comparison with prices in the late 1980s, the Victorian ritual was considerably more costly. According to the 1989 Office of Fair Trading Report the average price of a funeral in 1987 was £586; the fees are usually slightly higher for burial and lower for cremation.

The "whole thing," referred to by John Fry, consisted of acquiring a combination of material commodities in pursuit of the "decent" or "proper" funeral—much sought after and eventually gained by the respectable poor in late nineteenth-century England. Appraisal of undertakers' experiences of sales and my discussions with bereaved people suggest that the basic ingredients for today's "proper" funeral encompass removal and custody of the body, laying out and careful presentation, dressing in "good clothes", and purchase of a quality lined coffin or casket. Transport for the coffin and at least one mourning car complete the package, the elements of which are coordinated by the funeral director's staff and usually supplemented by a religious service in the cemetery or crematorium chapel. For those who choose to view the body, the coffin or casket provides a further public indicator of the depth of love felt for the deceased—a cushioned casket, elm coffin or lead-lined box, being more expensive, are perceived by purveyor and client as registering higher on the care scale.

The concern to purchase a strong coffin has survived from earlier times when there was a genuine fear that corpses may be spirited away from their graves by bodysnatchers [7]. Wealthier people could afford strong boxes and double coffins (one of wood and another outer box of lead) but the poor had to take their chances with the "resurrection men" or resort to a night watch to protect their dead. A combination of reform, which succeeded in marginally reducing the flamboyance and hence the price of funerals, coupled with the newly acquired benefits of burial insurance meant that by the end of the nineteenth century the poorer sectors of British society were at last able to afford these accoutrements. Although there was no longer a need to secure the body in its grave, the strong coffin and its embellishments had become a symbol of wealth and status which the working class were not about to relinquish. Moreover, the coffin and funeral ritual signified the gulf between the respectable poor who were able to afford the security of a decent burial and those forced to suffer the degradation of the pauper burial.

This is a further explanation for the continuity of such practices in the more traditional sectors of modern working class communities. In the East End of London a concern for the strength, quality, and decoration of the disposal receptacle lingers on. John Fry described some of their requirements.

> When people come in here they can have everything from a very basic coffin up to lead-lined caskets—we sell quite a few here. Or the American style of casket—sprung mattress and everything else fitted in . . .

Again, in the East End a lot of people know what they want. I mean, we have people coming in and they'll say, "We want an elm coffin and it's got to be an inch and a half . . ." They used to go round looking at the thickness of timber.[5] If you can imagine an inch and a half thickness—it's a hell of a coffin! Weighed a ton! We got it made for them. No problem there. If it's what they want then that's it.

The most public expression of the care taken by both the bereaved and the undertaker is furnished by the spectacle of the cortège. Nowhere in the East End of London is the ostentatious in more demand than for the funerals of local celebrities. Whether neighborhood fame was achieved through good deeds or foul, or in some cases by meeting a tragic or untimely end, the display is an endeavor to demonstrate the love, comradeship, and esteem in which the deceased was held. Fry depicted such a funeral.

We do East End funerals with fifteen or twenty limousines. We did a publican's funeral recently where there was about eighteen limousines and there was three hearses—(one for the coffin) and the other two hearses were just loaded with flowers. And there was flowers lying on every vehicle and underneath. We just didn't know what to do with them, you know. And it was just one person and he was a publican. Well known—done the local boys boxing and things like this and just very likeable. That's the way people show their respect, with flowers.

. . . I'm not saying you do that many funerals like this but they're not unusual. You take the funerals we've had this week—there's been two where there's been six or more limousines. Now I mean, that's the East End. Outside, you go to other areas and they say, "Six limousines!" They just don't have it nowadays. But it's not unusual here.

For many working class people in this geographical region, the show and expense of the funeral were considered by participants and observers alike to reflect the extent of the love or respect felt for the deceased. In addition to the number of funeral cars the quantity of flowers received and displayed in and around the hearse was important. Undertakers also commented that it was fitting for their staff to mark their respect for the deceased with specific gestures at appropriate points in the ceremony.

---

[5] This preoccupation with the thickness of the coffin may also stem from a fear of decomposition and a desire to protect the deceased from the ravages of natural decay.

When we get flowers presented on the day of the funeral we still deck the hearse out. We have side rails and make the most of the flowers. So you really make a show. I suppose that's what it's all about. I mean, people buy these flowers so you make the most of it. And like with our staff—we always send a good size staff out so that the whole thing is carried off properly. The chaps can't just walk around they have to walk in and present themselves to the coffin. And it's just done with a certain amount of style.

It was once seen as a common courtesy for curtains to be drawn when a death had occurred in the house or for men to remove their hats when confronted by a funeral cortège. These are just two of the once familiar gestures of respect for the dead. Although their use has waned over the last twenty years, the more traditional undertakers bemoan their decline and insist on preserving similarly "respectful" gestures in their work.

FLAMBOYANT FUNERALS

The supreme in East End flamboyance, however, is the reintroduction by one funeral company of the horse-drawn hearse and carriage. As an alternative to the limousine they provide horse-drawn transport fully equipped with authentic or exact replicas of horse bits, velvets, plumes, bridals, and harnesses used in the heyday of Victorian mourning practice. Their reasons for resurrecting this mode of transport were based on the desire both to satisfy and to stimulate customer demand for the pre-war tradition and style of local funerals. The lengths that the company went to in order to achieve this were related by a member of this thriving family firm.

It was by request, in fact by local people who have a coaching firm. The old lady—just turned round and said, "When I go I want horses." It was just like that.

The funeral trade relied on horses from Holland—Friesian horses. . . . It was a horse that's really ideally suited for the funeral trade. And in fact when we started, about eleven, twelve years ago, doing horse drawn funerals again, nobody had this original set-up. So what we used to have to do was to use film prop companies. When they weren't doing funerals it was Hammer House of Horror type thing!

That was in 1973. Oh it was fantastic. I'll never forget when we did that first one. We loaded up and, oh, the local kids were there and they thought it was a princess and all this sort of business. It was great! Well nobody had ever seen it. Even now, I mean, people look at horses anyway. So now they're probably used to them round here, but people still stand and stare. You imagine, once they've got their plumes and these velvets which would hang down the side. And then on our horse drawn funerals the bearers that walk alongside will all carry a truncheon.[6] We have four men walking alongside with truncheons. . . .

That was our first one. And then obviously, like everything else somebody else saw it. And it may have gone a year before we did the next one and then we did two in a year. Next year we did four. Next year we did eight. But as we decided we were doing more and more, and my father's a bit of a perfectionist, he couldn't stand it. So we bought our own hearse and had it renovated—an old London hearse. Then we went to Holland ourselves and selected some horses and we imported those. Last year we did sixty odd. You know, it's gone on from strength to strength.

For dedication to the business of death this company was exceptional, but although neighboring funeral directors were less likely to offer such extravagant accompaniments to this final rite of passage they nevertheless prided themselves on the maintenance of tradition. Established traditions bestow meaning and purpose on human activity. Funeral ceremonies in particular reveal a great deal about the importance of the family and community and about the cultural significance of notions such as honor, decency, and respect. The proliferation of flowers and their careful arrangement, the highly-polished and respectful appearance of staff, the provision of immaculately presented quality vehicles and the preservation of customs such as the conductor walking ahead of the cortège, add gravity to this time worn ritual.

CONCLUSION

In this chapter I have discussed the unique character of funeral customs in the East End of London suggesting some explanations for the survival of much nineteenth-century mortuary practice. These revolve around the ideology of care which both the undertaker and

[6] Carrying truncheons was common among undertakers in nineteenth-century England. As the name implies the truncheon is a short wooden club. The origin of the practice is thought to stem from the need to protect the corpse from the bodysnatcher. It seems unlikely, however, that undertakers ever used the club as a weapon, particularly since the heyday of such artifacts does not coincide with that of bodysnatching.

the bereaved strive to demonstrate. For the former, this lies in the attention they devote to the preservation and preparation of the deceased; for the bereaved, care is shown in the purchase of material goods and services designed to enhance the funeral ceremony. Consumers of the more extravagant rituals tend to be those who have inherited the legacy of the Victorian middle-class funeral which was firmly denied to their ancestors, the nineteenth-century urban poor. Some funeral directors offer more elaborate services than others and the former often regard flamboyance as the key to the industry's continuation.

In the chapters that follow I shall examine the deathwork practices of funeral directors and present a snapshot of their lifestyle—captured in London's East End in the late 1980s. Although the company at the heart of the research was a small family business located in a rapidly deteriorating urban environment, it is clear from my contact with workers in other areas and also from literature examining undertaking practice [8-13] that funeral directors across western culture have much in common.

REFERENCES

1. S. Kantaris, A Dying Art, *Poems 1987,* Falmouth Poetry Group, unpublished collection, 1987.
2. T. Veblen, *The Theory of the Leisure Class: An Economic Study of Institutions* (New Edition), George Allen & Unwin, London, 1925.
3. M. Bloch and J. Parry (eds.), *Death and the Regeneration of Life,* Cambridge University Press, Cambridge, 1982.
4. R. Huntington and P. Metcalf, *Celebrations of Death: The Anthropology of Mortuary Ritual,* Cambridge University Press, Cambridge, 1979.
5. R. Hertz, *Death and the Right Hand,* R. Needham and C. Needham (trans.), Cohen & West, London, 1960.
6. J. Morley, *Death, Heaven and the Victorians,* Studio Vista, London, 1971.
7. R. Richardson, *Death, Dissection and the Destitute,* Routledge & Kegan Paul, London, 1987.
8. R. W. Habenstein, *The American Funeral Director and the Sociology of Work,* unpublished Ph.D. thesis, University of Chicago, Chicago, 1954.
9. L. Bowman, *The American Funeral: A Study in Guilt, Extravagance and Sublimity,* Public Affairs Press, Washington, D.C., 1959.
10. V. R. Pine, *Caretaker of the Dead: The American Funeral Director,* Irvington, New York, 1975.
11. R. E. Turner and C. Edgley, Death as Theatre: A Dramaturgical Analysis of the American Funeral, *Sociology and Social Research, 60*:4, pp. 377-392, 1976.

12. D. Unruh, Doing Funeral Directing: Managing Sources of Risk in Funeralization, *Urban Life, 8,* pp. 247-263, 1979.
13. B. Smale, *Deathwork: A Sociological Analysis of Funeral Directing,* unpublished Ph.D. thesis, University of Surrey, 1985.
14. A. Schutz, The Stranger, in *Collected Papers,* Vol. II, A. Schutz (ed.), Martinus Nijhoff, The Hague, 1964.

CHAPTER 3

Funeral Directing in Easton

The fieldwork for this study was carried out in an area of East London which I shall refer to as Easton.

EASTON

In 1724 Daniel Defoe marveled at the great number of carriages owned by the wealthy merchants of Easton. When, in 1840, the first undertakers established their businesses here the locale could still be described as a flourishing area and was popular with the wealthy middle classes. Prestige did not result in rapid urbanization as it was predominantly a residential district rather than an industrial base. Indeed, in 1903 Walter Besant, sketching the boundaries and character of East London, was delighted by this small semi-rural suburban village.

> There is one spot—before the place was built over there were many spots—where one may stand and, in the summer, when the sunshine lights up the stream, gaze upon the green meadows, the mills, the rustic bridges, the high causeways over the marshes, and the low Essex hills beyond. The Essex hills are always far away; there is always one before the traveller; if he stands on an eminence he sees them, like gentle waves of the heaving ocean, across other valleys . . . [1, p. 268].

The population of Easton was soon swelled by an exodus of the middle classes from the metropolis, keen to avoid the excesses and health risks associated with inner city life and eager to enjoy the proximity to the countryside afforded by this relatively unspoiled area. The population multiplied as trade and industry expanded, inevitably attracting rural migrants fleeing the unemployment generated by declining agriculture. In the twentieth century, during the inter-war period, the wealthier sectors of the community, now dissatisfied with their increasingly urban surroundings, were moving out to greener pastures. In the late 1950s and early 1960s, as Easton was finally engulfed by the London urban sprawl, the more affluent members of the working class followed them into the semi-rural surroundings north and east of the metropolis. The spaces they left were rapidly filled with migrants from crowded neighboring areas and ethnic minority immigrants new to the country and searching for prosperity in this grey land.

In the late 1980s the Victorian and Georgian houses, abandoned by the wealthy, remained. Most had been converted into flats and bed-sitting rooms. The main street, a rather scruffy shopping parade, provided accommodation in flats above the retail premises. High rise blocks, the architectural hallmark of the 1960s, were relatively few in number—some having been demolished—and much more common were the four story maisonettes popularized by the public housing designs of the 1970s and 1980s. White working class and a sprinkling of ethnic minority families had been relocated into these blocks following the demolition of slum housing. The older converted houses and flats above the shops were largely occupied by young childless people of all ethnic groups. Over 50 percent of households in the immediate area were either single or dual occupancies. There was a rich cultural mix in the area. Seventy-one percent of residents were born in the United Kingdom or Irish Republic; 23 percent were from the New Commonwealth and Pakistan; and the remaining 6 percent emanated from a variety of countries including Greece, China, and Vietnam. All competed for the insufficient space, resources, and available services.

A *milieu* of decay was readily perceptible. The streets strewn with debris were cleaned erratically; the sparse parkland and green areas had their seating vandalized; paintwork on houses and shop fronts was dull or peeling; shops specialized in cheap clothing or highly priced basic foods; bookmakers, fish and chip shops, and kebab take-aways enjoyed prosperity. In 1987 unemployment, in the order of 25 percent, was high among both young and old and this was easily observed by the number of men hanging around on street corners or whiling away their time in the "betting shops" and cafes. Primary occupations for those in employment were manufacturing for men and distribution and catering for women.

EASTON FUNERAL WORKERS:
THE FIRST MEETING

A cold, rainy, late afternoon in December found me standing outside the offices of G. R. Stone. The business premises were situated in

Easton High Street. The exterior of the building exposed the efforts of successive proprietors to cultivate a traditional ambience, symbolizing continuity with the past. White paint contrasted with the black tudor-style beams nestling under a gabled roof. The appearance of the building was starkly different from the refurbished (but now dilapidated) facades of the remainder of the shopping parade. Undertakers' shops have a specific style of window dressing. The window through which I peered was not frosted but contained memorial stones and photographs hung as mementos of earlier times when the horse-drawn hearse was the usual mode of transport to the grave. The raised window sills had their floors covered with the blue and white stone chippings commonly associated with the bed of graves. Through the glass-paneled door I could see a second entrance, leading, I correctly judged, to the inner sanctuary of the undertaker's office.

Opening the door I was greeted by a slim, red-haired young man wearing grey and black striped trousers, a white shirt, and waistcoat. "Am I expecting you?," he enquired with a quizzical look. I gave my name and his face broke into a wide smile as he extended his hand to introduce himself. My first batch of preconceptions were discarded on the doorstep—he was certainly not the rather sinister, dismal, elderly gentleman I had expected.

Adrian Stone led me through the internal wood-paneled door and into a small, neatly arranged office. Offering me a chair which he drew up to the desk, he sat opposite. The furniture was sparse—a desk, filing cabinet, three chairs, and a safe. Against one wall was an electric fire emitting a warm red glow. Whenever I visited the premises, winter or summer, this red light was always burning. I was told that no matter what time of year or how warm outside, "people always shiver with cold when they come in here." The light was an attempt to provide an atmosphere of warmth. Above Stone's head hung the photographs of his predecessors and they provided the starting point for our conversation.

Stone's was a small, but long-established family business, and Adrian Stone was the latest in a long succession.

It was started by my great, great granddad—George Robert the First. George Robert was a carpenter in Ralfston who made boxes for the local undertaker there. He moved down to here in 1840. That was the year that private cemeteries were first allowed because the churchyards were getting full.

So he thought, "nice little growth area," which of course was full of fields and there was nothing between here and the river at the time. He started up a business by taking over part of the stables of the coaching inn next door. He used them for his own horses and the carriage.

So that was a handy little place to start and of course, as it was a growth area he made a very good business until he died in 1870. It was then taken over by his son George Robert the Second who worked till he was seventy in 1920. The buildings and place were vastly renovated by *his* son who kicked out the horses and got in cars. That was about 1924—Daimler hearse. It was quite early to bring in cars but then again it was a growth area and he was making quite a lot of money. It was a successful business at the time.

It's been in the same family ever since 1840. We've been here all the time—grandfather was the last person to re-build this place and I'm still trying to do so.

The most significant change since the early part of the century was the fact that the business was no longer lucrative. This was reflected in the structural and decorative condition of the premises. Public areas were well polished and presented with an emphasis on tradition. The back-regions, hidden from the public gaze, however, were in poor repair with the rear office (sporting a *"Save fuel, get cremated with a friend!"* sticker) functioning as a rest room in addition to the proprietor's kitchen. The large garage space—once the stables—was used for coffin storage, embalming, and housing the vehicles.

A diagram of the buildings, highlighting the division between front and back regions appears in Figure 1. A back region is simply an area to which public access is restricted in the interests of sustaining a performance. The existence of a backstage is a common feature of many workplace situations and is particularly valuable to service industries which promote a carefully orchestrated front. Up-market restaurants exhibit this phenomenon: waiters produce impressive dishes that have been prepared by staff out of public sight in the kitchens (back regions) of the establishment. For the undertaker, aiming to present the bereaved with a stylized image of the deceased, maintaining concealed workspaces is essential.

Lefebvre, in his discussion of the meaning of space, distinguishes four varieties of space: accessible space, boundaries and forbidden territories, junction points, and places of abode [2, p. 193]. When applied to the undertaker's premises these distinctions provide valuable insights into the regulation and use of space. Each category is addressed as I relate details of the guided tour I received of Stone's workplace.

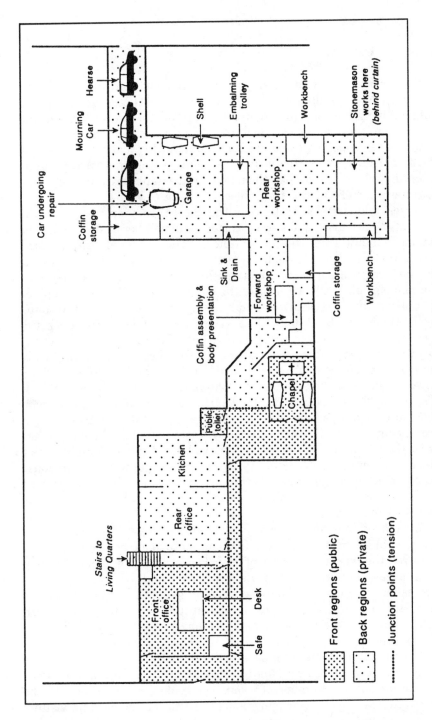

Figure 1. The funeral director's premises.

Front regions (public)

Back regions (private)

•••••••• Junction points (tension)

Hearse

Mourning Car

Car undergoing repair

Coffin storage

Garage

Shell

Embalming trolley

Workbench

Stonemason works here *(behind curtain)*

Rear workshop

Sink & Drain

Coffin assembly & body presentation

Forward workshop

Coffin storage

Workbench

Chapel

Public toilet

Kitchen

Rear office

Stairs to Living Quarters

Front office

Desk

Safe

41

Accessible Space

The front office has already been introduced and can clearly be described as accessible space. There was unrestricted access to the public during normal office hours but interaction between client and purveyor in these areas was governed by a set of established rules and patterns developed by the undertaker and quickly learned by visitors. These norms were particularly important during the arrangements interview which determined the nature and extent of ritual production (the operation of which is the subject of a later chapter).

When mourners came to view the corpse, they entered from the front of the premises and were escorted by a member of staff along the corridor leading from the public office to the chapel of rest, situated across the courtyard. An extension to the business in the late 1930s, this building was separate from the other front regions. In summer, as the photograph of the exterior of the chapel shows (Figure 2), copious shrubbery lined the pathway and hanging baskets adorned the route. Inside this small, brick-built chapel the stage had been carefully set in a conspiracy to assuage the effects of age and providence. The only furniture was an altar which directly faced the entrance. The white lace altar cloth, centrally positioned crucifix, candles, and artificial flowers can be picked out in the photograph of the chapel interior (Figure 3). The crucifix and bible-bearing lectern were religious symbols left over from an earlier age when the undertaker actively sought professionalization through religiosity. Installed when the chapel was first erected, these were regularly dusted but otherwise remained as a tokenistic gesture to Christianity. When the chapel was used to house people of other religious beliefs these emblems were left in place. One could speculate that the failure to remove the items was a reflection of their lack of significance.

Regularly housing two bodies, this edifice was cold in winter and summer alike. Having no windows or method of heating, it never captured the warmth or light of day. The prospect of spending more than a few minutes within its confines could be daunting. The inevitable chilled atmosphere surrounding death coupled with the necessity to store bodies at low temperatures meant that the experience of viewing the deceased may not have been an especially comfortable one.

In more luxurious funeral parlors the chapel, or "rest rooms" as they have become known, are usually integral to the premises and some companies boast a number of rooms set aside for the privacy of the bereaved. Having three or four rooms ensures that bodies and visitors do not intrude on each other's space. Modern viewing facilities are

Figure 2. Exterior of the chapel in summer.

normally heated and carpeted. Any window will be curtained—again for privacy—and the room usually bathed in subdued lighting with *boudoir* effect. This provides the corpse with a better appearance as dead bodies do not "look good" in natural light.

Boundaries and Forbidden Territories

Leaving the chapel we took a sharp right turn as the funeral director led the way along the passage and into the back regions. The walkway we used provided no shelter from the incessant rain. Making our way into the bowels of what was once the stables, I discovered that the deficiency of overhead cover was not an unusual feature of the workshop. Indeed, much of the roof was missing. The rain frequently intruded, miraculously avoiding the fluorescent strip lights which

Figure 3. Interior of the chapel.

clung at regular intervals to the remaining solid patches of ceiling, and finally coming to rest in large puddles which filled the well-worn hollows of the ancient flagstones. The undertaker appeared not to notice the rainfall let alone excuse the inconvenience. One side of the forward workshop was exposed to the thick shrubbery which marked the boundary between Stone and his neighbor. On the other side he pointed to the coffin assembly area. Leading me deeper into the workshop we passed a stack of variously sized coffins awaiting occupation. At the end of this narrow causeway the shop opened out into the wider area of the rear workshop where embalming took place. The space resembled a garage where vehicles were repaired rather than a private mortuary. Indeed, vehicles were housed along another narrow corridor which ran from a further stack of new coffins to the doors at the rear of the premises. They comprised a Rolls-Royce hearse, two mourning cars and, at the rear of the procession, a further mourning car in a state of disrepair.

A view of Stone's backstage would not simply have detracted from the illusion and drama of the funeral ritual but would probably have horrified the bereaved. In contrast to more modern and spacious funeral parlors, his premises were designed in the last century and, constrained on both sides by other businesses, the only available space for expansion had been used for the erection of the chapel—a progressive step in the days before "hygienic treatment" captured the imagination of the small English undertaker. Prohibiting the bereaved access to the back regions was, therefore, essential. The undertaker explained that reinforcing the division between private preparatory work and public display protected the client from distressing sights. The practice also permits the funeral industry to preserve trade secrets of the "humanization" process (the focus of discussion in Chapter 7).

Junction Points

A junction point is a place of passage and encounter [2]. In the context of the undertaker's premises the concept is used to describe the boundary between forbidden and accessible territories. These junctions are sites for potential conflict as public meets private—the bereaved confronting the mortician. In actuality, however, there is little tension and sophisticated exclusion techniques are unnecessary because consumers *collude* in the separation of the two areas. No reports of the bereaved demanding access to these hinter regions have been publicized. Indeed, studies of the funeral director in the United States remark on customer reluctance to trespass into private areas [3, 4]. It was this diffidence that allowed funeral companies like Stone's, at the poorer end of the trade, to continue to prepare bodies in the garage workshop. Years of experience had taught these traditional undertakers that clients were unwilling to enter backstage. Indeed, Stone's were so confident of the public's continued lack of curiosity that they had no compunction about laying-out and embalming bodies among this dereliction.

A junction point which did require policing was the passage to the backstage where it met the chapel of rest. Conscious infringement was unlikely, but the possibility that visitors might unwittingly stray into the back regions generated avoidance strategies. On an occasion weeks later, I was talking with Gordon, one of the undertaker's workers, as we walked from the back regions to the front. Reaching this junction we observed Roberta, the receptionist, posted sentry-like outside the chapel. My companion immediately fell silent and ushered me through the courtyard into the rear office. He explained that it was highly ". . . unprofessional to be talking near the chapel." Moreover, overhearing backstage colloquy could have serious implications for the funeral company. Assigning a member of staff to guard the chapel thus served two purposes. First, she/he acted as an escort for the mourners, ensuring that they did not infringe non-public space. Second, her/his presence was a signal to workers of the proximity of the bereaved and hence the need for cautious talk.

Places of Abode

This category may be used to interpret three exclusive backstage regions: the director's living quarters, the rear office and kitchen, and the corpse storage areas. Each zone was either a permanent or temporary place of abode.

Living Quarters

Adrian Stone lived on the premises and his apartment was situated on the first and second floors of the building. The area was clearly out of bounds to the public and could be interpreted as a back region within a back region as it was also off limits to the majority of staff. It was here that he relaxed, entertained guests and cultivated the necessary personal distance from his workforce to allow him to sustain the managerial role of funeral director.

Rear Office and Kitchen

The rear office was used for typing correspondence and consulting trade manuals, but the chief function of this room was staff relaxation. The office was untidy and the walls decorated with yellowing newspaper articles and cartoons, a local and a London-wide map, and photographs of the director and his friends. A large chipped mirror hung above the fireplace. On the mantlepiece stood a collection of "Thank You" cards from satisfied customers and an invitation to a Rotary Club dinner. Half empty boxes held a myriad of items ranging from car parts, magazines and old letters, to overalls, gloves, and a pair of shoes. At one end of the room was an electric typewriter and above that two shelves lined with trade manuals, lists of stockists, invoices, and stationery. In comparison with the public office it was cluttered and the furniture lacked coordination. A large wooden table, which was rarely cleared, was a rich source of lost equipment. Two swivel chairs and a makeshift desk top marked one section as an office. Two straight-backed, and two easy chairs—the latter unmatching and tattered—were placed near the fire, around which the staff huddled in the depths of winter. The overall impression was messy and disorganized, but when the workers assembled for a tea break and a chat there was a remarkably cozy atmosphere. In this space, between public areas and the hinter regions, workers could retreat from the ritual performances demanded by the bereaved, and, furthermore, they could escape the onerous tasks of bodywork.

Corpse Storage Areas

The final places of abode were those occupied by the cadaver. When the body was brought to the funeral home it temporarily resided in the removal shell[1] in the garage workshop. Here the body was laid-out and embalmed. When ready for dressing and coffin presentation the corpse was promoted to the forward workshop from whence it was transferred to the chapel of rest. In most cases the deceased had inhabited two temporary places of abode—the rear workshop and the chapel of rest, and dwelt in one transit zone—the forward workshop—before departing for its final journey to the grave. The body's transfer from the depths of the back regions to the heights of the front coincided with the stage reached in the process of decontamination and humanization.

THE SUCCESSFUL FIRM

The flourishing area discovered and exploited by George Robert the First in the 1840s no longer existed and the business was now struggling to survive. The trade that Stone was able to attract reflected the cultural make-up of the community. Funerals were undertaken for a range of ethnic and religious groups including Sikh, Muslim, Hindu, Jewish, Greek, Chinese, Vietnamese, Roman Catholic, Church of England, and a variety of smaller religious sects. Although the majority of funerals continued to be arranged for the white working class community this merely mirrored their numerical predominance and had relatively little bearing on the cultural preferences of most ethnic minority groups in the district.

The degree to which funeral companies prosper within an area is influenced by the vagaries of local custom and the requirements of individuals for more, or less, extravagant practices. Popular belief assumes that owing to the inexorability and inevitability of death the

---

[1] A fiberglass coffin which can be cleaned and re-used and is designed for the removal of bodies.

undertaker will never be out of work. Stone's averaged four funerals a week, two hundred and fifty each year. A small family business like this may conduct as many as eight funerals in one week then none for the following fortnight. The reason for this is that the frequency with which death occurs and the subsequent choice of funeral director is not so easily forecast. The disparity between profitable and struggling funeral establishments in a particular locale is primarily a consequence of consumer choice. For most companies, business is attracted by recommendations and previous personal knowledge, location of premises, advertising, and price. Let us briefly consider each of these in turn.

Recommendations

In their search for a suitable funeral company, bereaved people may encounter various types of recommendation. One source of suggestions may be friends or neighbors. It is pertinent to note that because most people seldom arrange funerals they have no precise yardstick to judge the standard of the work provided. Friedson argues that this is true of medical services [5]. Indeed, he considers it strange that people accept, rather than question, the judgment of experts.

> If one has never used another (*expert*), and no one else one knows has ever used him, he is an unknown quantity, even if he has the qualifications necessary for being hired by the group. The tried-and-tested is less uncertain than the merely professionally certified [5, p. 64].

It is probably for this reason that a firm of undertakers employed by the family on one occasion will be chosen again if their services were considered satisfactory. Furthermore, this lack of "expert" knowledge commonly results in the bereaved seeking advice from the funeral director as to the necessary requirements when arranging a funeral. As Adrian Stone explained,

> . . . a lot of people come along and say, "I don't know what I'm doing." My attitude is, no, of course you don't. You've only got two parents, you're only likely to do this twice in your life. I do it more than that in one week. So obviously I'm ahead of them all the time.

In advising the family of appropriate custom, however, the undertaker is effectively prescribing the limits of local practice.

Although not strictly classified as recommendations, if relatives are at a loss for the name of an undertaker, hospital staff, doctors, or the police may suggest one. The adroit businessman, Stone contended, would ensure that he was

> . . . known in an area as providing a reasonable service. I think the strongest recommendation you could have, say from the Registrars', would be, "Well you're in Mr. Hall's area, you're in Mr. Stone's area and they would actually direct you to where the building is, as opposed to telling you to "Go to Stone—he's great!"

Endorsement might also result from association with the Coroner's Office or the Medical Examiner. In cases of unexpected death[2] the body must be conveyed to the public mortuary for autopsy examination. The Coroner's Office employs an undertaker to transport the remains to the mortuary. The officer's choice of funeral company is influenced by availability, geographical proximity to the deceased, and sometimes personal preference. Having moved the body, and therefore being equipped with preliminary details of the case, this undertaker is likely subsequently to be used by bereaved people wishing to pursue an uncomplicated path to the funeral.

Location

A firm of undertakers may be approached by a client simply because of their proximity to the home or perhaps because they were the only firm the family were aware of. Unlike most commercial businesses which are situated in the High Street, people rarely windowshop undertakers' premises and therefore are not always aware of the range of companies available. A company whose shop front is striking in some way will fare better in this respect than the more anonymous one. Stone's facade was set with a large, accurate clock. Being situated directly opposite a busy bus stop, the clock was constantly used by the public and the nature of the premises widely known. This undertaker considered his location fortuitous.

Advertising and Price

In Britain and Canada, unlike much of the practice in the United States of America, advertising and business promotion for the funeral trades is publicly viewed as distasteful. Further, in the United Kingdom, funeral directors are loathe to advertise services and

---

[2] Unexpected death includes sudden or "unnatural" death such as murder, suicide, and road accidents, but also refers to unanticipated death and that where the deceased had not consulted a doctor during the previous two weeks.

especially *prices* as this is regarded by them as detracting from the image to which they aspire, that of public servant. A dominant cultural conservatism may partially explain this reluctance. The National Association of Funeral Directors' manual, for example, reminds its members that the funeral director is,

> . . . primarily a professional adviser and only secondarily a salesman. The funeral director should never forget that the main thing that he sells is service and that selling a funeral is not a simple trading transaction [6, 1: p. 2].

Advertisements in the British media reveal little about the price or quality of the funeral director's service and must adhere to the strict code of practice issued by the NAFD. This standard advises its members,

> (t)o ensure that advertising is always in good taste. No sensational, offensive or undignified advertising is permitted [6, 1: p. 2].

This directive generates rhetoric such as "Peace of Mind Day and Night," "A Complete and Dignified Personal Funeral Service," and in Stone's case, "Funerals Traditionally carried out with Thought and Care at Reasonable Prices." The reluctance within the industry to advertise funeral costs perplexed the authors of the 1989 Office of Fair Trading Report which remarked on the practice.

> The Office has little sympathy for the view, which seems to have become current in the industry, that there is something intrinsically indecent about advertising the cost of a funeral . . . [7, p. 29].

Stone's, however, prided themselves on their reasonable prices. Adrian Stone believed that he offered the best value for money in the area.[3] The reasonable price of his funerals was achieved by cutting down on overheads such as a separate embalming room and by employing the minimum of full-time staff. The latter were augmented wherever necessary with temporary employees. Paradoxically, unless clients have been referred by a friend or relative and supplied with information about costs, then undercutting competitors has little effect on an undertaker's ability to promote business as it is very unusual for

---

[3] Most small funeral companies own a hearse and two limousines. When more cars are required these are hired on a reciprocal basis from other small businesses. This exchange of vehicles and staff leads to a "friendly *camaraderie*" among funeral workers in a particular locale, and an insight into each others prices and methods.

funeral arrangers to shop around. People, in the throes of bereavement are unlikely to countenance the sort of investigation necessary to ascertain the foremost undertaker in the area for price and quality of service. Furthermore, funeral directors' themselves are not favorably disposed to quoting over the telephone, arguing that each funeral is unique and therefore requires individual pricing. Stone told me of a mistake he made when he first entered the business—that of giving telephone estimates.

> If people phone up and say, "Which is the cheapest form of burial you can do?" I can give them a figure. Then having done that somebody comes in and decides they want a church service and seven cars and the biggest casket you can have in a private grave. The price has gone five or six times as much. And they'll say, "Well that's not what you told me over the phone." So I got my fingers burnt having opened my mouth down the telephone. So now I don't do it.

This practice effectively precludes comparison as prospective customers find face-to-face interaction far more compelling than a short telephone conversation.

Having toured the premises and considered customers' choice of funeral parlor, we may now meet the staff of Stone's funeral company.

GETTING TO KNOW THE STAFF

A rapport was immediately struck between Adrian Stone and myself and as our discussion drew to a close at that first meeting, he invited me to observe a funeral the following week. I readily accepted. It was during the next meeting that he responded favorably to my proposal that I spend some time with the company—observing and participating in their daily routines. He clearly enjoyed demonstrating his skills and those of this staff and thought it quite novel to play host to someone with a keen interest in the funeral business.

The permanent staff at Stone's numbered four: Adrian, the owner-director; Roberta, the receptionist; and two male assistants, Peter and Barry. This number was supplemented by Ralf, a self-employed stonemason who contracted exclusively to Stone's and worked on the premises; Betty, a part-time cleaner; and three casual, but highly experienced operatives: Bob, the former manager; Gordon, a "Jack of All Trades"; and Alan, a personal friend of the director. Nine members comprised the team.

The Funeral Director

Adrian Stone was manager of the family business and performed the role of funeral director. The undertakers' sombre uniform of grey and black stripes failed to subdue his naturally warm personality. His sharp intellect was always alert to the possibility of acquiring a greater understanding of the human condition and he continually searched for the humor which he believed was present in every situation. Leisure time was predominantly taken up with visits to local public houses and dining out with friends. The fact that the family business had stood in this parade of shops for over one hundred and fifty years gave him a measure of respectability in the community which he was keen to maintain. He was strongly committed to the local Rotary Club and, in the capacity of treasurer, spent a minimum of one weekday evening on Rotary business. Participating in activities which stressed his similarity to others was one method he employed to manage the stigma of being an undertaker. (This, and other such strategies are considered in the next chapter.) His great love was piloting light aircraft, and weather and business demands permitting, he headed for the nearest airfield and took to the skies.

Although a family business, Adrian Stone, in his thirties, had only been actively involved in the undertaking industry for twelve years—a time during which he estimated performing over three thousand funerals. Previous employment spanned jobs as diverse as merchant seaman and computer programmer. His career in deathwork began when, during a time of unemployment, he was approached by his parents to help out as a driver for a trial period. He agreed to "give it a go" and after a brief apprenticeship took over the management when his uncle retired.

Analogous with other traditional style undertakers, Adrian Stone ran the company in a highly autocratic fashion. Every member of staff, whether permanent or casual took instruction from, and reported directly to him. There was no chain of command or pyramid structure of hierarchy such as that which exists in many other modern businesses. The head of the company was clearly the funeral director and all power radiated from him. In days gone by, I was informed,

> . . . the old undertaker didn't give any responsibility to his staff. He didn't say where you were going on a funeral, the address or anything like that. He just gave directions as you were travelling. If you asked the address he'd say, "Why do you want to know? Aren't you coming with us?"

Time has moved on and Stone's management style was not as extreme as the one cited. Nevertheless, depriving staff of information regarding destination or timing gave the director absolute control over the funeral ritual and the movements and behavior of his workers. One practical explanation for this (discussed in detail in Chapter 8) is that it was a method of guarding against spoiled performances [8]. To ensure a successful delivery of the rituals each operative deferred to the funeral conductor's commands. All participants might be experts in their own field but nothing moved without the express authority of the conductor. Only he could manage the funeral ritual. Relinquishing full responsibility to the conductor ensured perfect timing and harmony within the orchestra.

Stone's role as director entailed controlling both back and front regions of the undertaking stage. He coordinated the work of his staff as they busied themselves with the daily round of checking and polishing hearse and cars, preparing their uniforms, assembling coffins, engraving nameplates, and moving bodies. He adhered to the principle that to supervise people you must be able to acquit yourself well in their work. Living on the premises and being on call twenty-four hours a day often obliged him to work outside normal office hours to initiate or complete a job. Clearly, it was imperative that he possessed an intimate knowledge of all aspects of the business. In addition to his managerial and organizational duties he took sole responsibility for embalming and cosmetology ("beautifying" the body). Indeed, Adrian Stone was certain that he alone among his staff was capable of displaying the artistic skills required for such delicate and critical operations.

Unattached Workers

In this category I have included Allan, Gordon, and Bob—all casual workers—in addition to Ralf, the self-employed stonemason. Although Gordon and Alan shared a comparable position in terms of status, this derived primarily from their personal relationship with the director. The three men shared a substantial portion of their leisure time and common interests such as eating out and socializing in the "pub." Both these pursuits were considered paramount to the bachelor existence which Adrian and Gordon declared they enjoyed.

As owner of the second mourning car, Gordon's position within the company of freelance undertaker was sufficiently independent to permit him to feel in control, while simultaneously offering him the security of being first to be called upon when an extra car and driver/bearer were required. Gordon's casual or freelance status preserved his elevated position in the internal hierarchy. He was never approached to undertake direct bodyhandling tasks which (although he told of 15 years experience in the trade) he deemed beneath him. He regarded himself to be well and truly "in the driving seat." His connection with the trade originated through the car-hire business[4] and this type of work continued to make up a proportion of his income. He did however, consider himself to be one of a dying breed of "true" undertaker who were identifiable by the possession of the three qualities which he asserted were essential in an undertaker. First was the need to have "a strong stomach"; second, possession of a sense of humor; and third, was a liking for alcohol. That these stereotypical characteristics have traditionally been associated with undertakers stems from the unpleasant nature of their work with the body and the consequent need for a strong constitution, effective coping strategies and "liquid relief." Gordon bemoaned the growing trend to recruit "disinterested" or "inept" assistants, whom he saw as being forced upon the industry by the demise of the family business.

Alan's contact with the business, like his social relationship with Adrian Stone, was in decline. Although he helped out with evening removals when called upon, his role was a limited one. He maintained his high position in the social structure of the company because of his friendship with the director.

Bob was a short, elderly man. His status as marginal to both the higher and lower echelons can be accounted for by his one time role as funeral director and hence his "professionalism." For this he commanded the respect of all staff members but preferred to identify himself with the undertaker's assistants, possibly because 1) he now performed the work of an assistant, and 2) the assistants were older than Adrian and his friends and more inclined to the relatively sedentary life which Bob now enjoyed. As a blood relative of the manager, he was given priority when allocating work and recruiting additional helpers. Although he did not drive for the company and therefore was not competing with Gordon, whenever a bearer or "shoulder" was required, Bob was the first to be selected. As an old age pensioner, the extra cash-in-hand provided a welcome supplement to his state pension.

Ralf, a rather shy man in his mid-thirties, was another unattached worker. He spent most of his working day performing stonemasonry skills in the shop front. This area, directly to the rear of the large windows, was allocated by Adrian as a place where Ralf could work, distancing him from bodywork—of which he was quite squeamish—

---

[4] This is a trade with traditional links with undertaking and one which, as we shall see in Chapter 4, is often used as a euphemism for deathwork.

and at the same time providing a spectacle to attract the interest of passers-by to the premises. Whether or not the director was correct in his belief that people frequently stopped to watch Ralf at work was debatable. Social life for the stonemason revolved around his wife and child and although he was of similar age to the manager he did not choose, and was not invited, to share the latter's bachelor leisure activities. In his relationship with other workers he was closest to Roberta the receptionist, and Peter and Barry the undertaker's assistants. Given his self-employed status, he largely decided his own working days and hours. Preferring a late start in the mornings he was constantly teased by the others for laziness.

The Undertaker's Assistants

Peter and Barry were full-time, permanent members of staff. Both were in their fifties and married with adult children. Both came to the undertaking industry after the better part of a lifetime in other, unrelated trades but both hoped to remain in deathwork until retirement. This, however, was where the similarity ended as they bore no physical resemblance to each other and were quite different in character.

Peter was tall and slim with a perceptible stoop, possibly cultivated over the years by an attempt to compensate for his height when communicating with others. Balding with sharp features he was described by Adrian Stone as "an absolute diamond" and exuded a warm, gentle, guileless personality—the type of person it is extremely difficult to dislike. Peter was friendly with all of the company employees. He tried not to criticize anyone but nevertheless, found humor in some of the more scathing comments aimed at his colleague, Barry.

Barry was much shorter and rounder than his work-mate. Physical differences gave the pair a rather comic "Laurel and Hardy" image when they appeared together. Unlike Peter, Barry moved slowly but purposefully, betraying his need to consider the appropriateness of an instruction before he acted. He continually questioned the director's decisions and reasoning. His refusal to simply accept and carry out an instruction gained him a reputation among his peers and overseers as "dull." Gordon, in particular, relished any opportunity to present his employer with an example of Barry's inadequacies as an undertaker.

Women Workers

In common with many industries, female operatives in the funeral trade tend to be employed in office work and on other duties which reflect a traditional perception of women as domestic workers. Apart from typewriting and handling telephone enquiries, Roberta was engaged as receptionist on the understanding that she would deal sympathetically with the bereaved. "In some ways," Adrian Stone told me, "she can do the job better than I can because women are better at comforting distressed people. They're more understanding than men."

That the trade should maintain this sexual division of labor is peculiar for two reasons. First, given the "dirty" nature of the work and the ubiquity of allocating polluting tasks to women [9], it is curious they are not expected to have closer contact with the corpse, as they are in many other cultures [9-11]. The second factor is that until post-World War II, women in British society were commonly responsible for laying-out the body. The work was occasionally performed by female family members, or as Adams has illustrated in her study of Coventry, by neighborhood women recognized in the community as qualified for the task [12]. Subsequent to funeral directors provision of the chapel of rest, however, the position of women in the after-death system gradually eroded. Once in possession of the cadaver, undertakers initially contracted women to lay-out. Discontinuing this practice was, I suggest, first, a method of cutting overheads and second, it augmented the undertaker's control over the body and funeral preparations. Third, the exclusion of women from this role would have been further induced by the professional aspirations of undertakers.

It is well documented that the female layer-out was stereotypically subject to a denigrating image of her person and skills. Dickens, for example, derided the character of Mrs. Gamp whom he portrayed as drunken, dirty, degenerate, and ignorant [13]. These women were often untrained infirmary nurses and, although they were clearly expert in the tasks they performed [14], their lack of formal training did not endear them to the professionalizing undertaker. The latter's adoption of embalming was part of this drive for higher status and was marketed by the death industry as a scientific technique requiring education and skills. Perhaps inspired by the struggle of the male medical profession to control the work of midwives [15], undertakers resolved to remove these women from the trade. Coincident with the provision of the chapel of rest came countrywide criticism from the British Undertakers' Association of the role of laying-out women and of the need to exclude them from the profession. Transforming the perception of bodywork from menial to scientific, with the concomitant expulsion of women, served to mystify the after-death process and strengthen the occupational control of the modern funeral director.

By the 1960s most funeral establishments had succeeded in minimizing women's work with the body and restricting them to the role of receptionist and funeral arranger. Since the mid-1980s, however, the nature of women's participation in deathwork has begun to change.

Performing tasks from embalming to funeral conducting, women now constitute a small, but significant proportion of morticians. Two salient reasons emerge to explain their recent reassertion in the trade.

First, this development is demonstrably in keeping with the progress of women in other occupations previously restricted to men. It is pertinent to note that women are now demanding greater participation in the Church, the legal profession and the sphere of medicine. From trade and newspaper reports it appears that breaching the male enclave of the undertaker is less difficult for women whose forefathers were in the business. The number of small funeral companies is declining and, although figures are not yet available to endorse this suggestion, the loss of sons to other, more glamorous careers seems to have been compensated by daughters.

The second explanation for the readmission of women to the funeral trade derives from the public perception of women as carers. Because women are traditionally associated with caring [16], they are seen by some undertakers as having a greater capacity to be attentive to the needs of the bereaved. As one male undertaker told me,

> I have met a woman who was a conductor and she was absolutely excellent. You would say she looked the part and she handled people very well—probably far more compassionate than I would be.

Female undertakers encourage this view and are keen to reflect this persona in the redesign of their front stage. Mary Elements, a funeral director in Pinner, adopted the strategy of "feminization."

> Walk inside and the decor exudes "feminine"—pinks and subtle greys. . . . If you look into a couple of smaller side rooms, you can see telltale boxes of apricot and lemon tissues carefully placed on the edge of coffee tables. . . . Mary Elements had it totally redesigned. "It was very dark and closed in . . . I wanted to make it a private space . . . but I also wanted to make it light and airy" [17, p. 56].

It was an individual decision to re-vamp and "feminize" this funeral home to make it more user-friendly. The success of this tactic may in part be due to recent public clamor for reform. As noted in Chapter 1, funeral reform groups are stimulating change in the structure and image of the industry. Funeral companies, however, have not yet developed a formal, collective response to the criticisms of the reformers. The "feminization" of the industry is arguably a method of persuading consumers of their sincerity. By casting the undertaker as *female* and adopting the role of *carer* rather than *expert-advisor* the trade may be hoping to soften their harsh public image.[5] Mary Elements' approach to funeral directing illustrates this.

> Under Mary's supervision, the thinking behind Elements funerals has become less centred on logistics and timetables and more people-oriented. "Some funeral directors can seem rigid. I'm very attentive. If people are crying in the service, I'll put my arm around them."
>
> She also attempts to ensure her staff are aware of the needs of the grieving family. "I'll say to them, 'The widow was alone—why didn't you guide her in? She needed your arm.' People at funerals are lost, you can't communicate with them, but you can support them" [17, p. 56].

In sharp contrast to the feminization strategy is the response of funeral directors who argue against the reformers by insisting that people *need* the services of an *expert* to organize the funeral. Adrian Stone was one such funeral director. His nettled reply to the *London Evening Standard,* which had published an article on the benefits of the do-it-yourself funeral, noted that not everyone who required a funeral was physically able to organize it for themselves. On the price of funerals, an issue which undertakers have had over a century to consider, he pointed out that taking time and equipment into account, the do-it-yourself funeral was not terribly cost effective.

> I have no objection to people making their own arrangements for their relatives' funerals but will they stop shouting about it only costing £150 without including their own time at equity rates, including repeat fees, the time spent by their friends and the cost of the inevitable volvo. . . . Our profession is not only a service industry but also a High Street business, we have our rates and staff to pay on a full time basis. Unfortunately people do not always die at convenient times and places so there is also a 24 hour service to be manned.

Furthermore, he declared,

> I think it is about time that we cast aside that childish idea of the nasty man in the black hat who took Granny away. We provide the

---

[5] Changes in style and color of dress—from blacks to greys—may also be interpreted as part of this trend to soften the image of the profession.

community with an important service at a reasonable price and protect them from that which may offend.

Although I appear to have digressed from the sexual division of labor, it is apposite to note that funeral directors who adopt the second response to the reform movement, illustrated by Stone's correspondence, usually see no reason to welcome women into the bodyhandling areas of their trade. In these quarters undertakers may believe that women are more sympathetic than men but they are regarded as physically incapable of performing the work of the undertaker.

It's a situation where women generally are not as strong as men. (When) you're carrying you've got to look cool and calm and you've not got to complain that it's on your shoulder and it's getting heavier. You've just got to stand there and wait. And it hurts.

A further implication in their argument is that death is acerbic and the sight of the cadaver distressing. The public are perceived as requiring the services of an emotionally neutral professional undertaker to protect them. Their reluctance to involve female workers in bodyhandling activities they justify on the grounds that these women also need to be shielded from the distasteful aspects of deathwork. This form of rationalization is not new. The argument that women are delicate and emotionally and physically incapable of tolerating the stress associated with unpleasant or intellectually demanding occupations, has been widely used by the professions to prevent women from reaching their higher ranks. The medical profession, for example, barred women from its upper echelons and the academic profession excluded them from the universities with analogous sophistry [13]. In funeral directing, this belief has evolved into an ethic and in more traditional areas, such as the East End of London, operatives continue to refer to the trade as "a man's world." Women are thus largely restricted to aspects of the business which do not bring them into contact with the corpse.

G. R. Stone employed two women, Roberta the receptionist and Betty, the part-time cleaner. Roberta, in her late forties and mother of two teenage girls, had returned to work when her children reached secondary school age. First employed by Stone on a part-time basis, she became a full-time member of staff and was actively involved in the day-to-day running of the business. As such, she was integrated into the network and seen by other staff members as "doing a good job" on the administrative side. In her duties she had little contact with the corpse other than supervising viewing arrangements. This situation suited her as she said she preferred to remain working in the office as typist, receptionist, and funeral arranger, rather than encroach on bodywork which, because of its physically unpleasant nature, was seen by all involved as "men's work."

The firmest workplace friendship she had was with Ralf and this was possibly due to the fact that they were both distanced from the bodyhandling aspects of undertaking. Other workplace friendships were with the undertaker's assistants and with Bob, the former manager. Although she accepted instructions from the director, she was privately critical of his autocratic approach to the staff and could see no reason for his refusal to delegate responsibility.

Due to the part-time nature of Betty's job and the fact that her cleaning work was totally unconnected with the tasks of undertaking, she was rather distanced from the main body of staff. Like Bob she was an old-age pensioner and a blood relative of the manager. Constantly critical of the untidiness of the back office, she vainly attempted to bestow order but failed largely due to the inaccessibility of potential cleaning areas. Torpid and obviously painful movements told of her advancing years. Everyone agreed that she tried to "do too much" and should "rest more often." Some even felt that rather than coming into the office and working for extra cash she would have been "safer and happier tucked away in an old people's home."

Bodyhandlers and Professionals

In a small company such as Stone's there was little opportunity for social mobility. Indeed, apart from status gained through social contact with the funeral director, most workers occupied a similar standing. The differentiation which did exist stemmed from 1) the sexual division of labor and 2) the contact which each member of staff had with "dirty" or "polluting" bodywork.

In his study of rural Cantonese disposal rites, Watson argued that funeral specialists were ranked according to the extent of physical contact they had with the corpse.

> Geomancers, whose tasks do not require attendance at the funeral, rank highest. Lowest in the hierarchy are menial labourers employed to handle the corpse and dispose of clothing, bedding, and other materials most directly associated with death. These corpse handlers are so contaminated by their work that villagers will not even speak to them; their very glance is thought to bring misfortune [18, p. 157].

In British and North American society where deathworkers use the techniques of arterial embalming and where there is such stress on the presentation of the body, this analysis can be extended to include differentiation according to the *type* of contact the worker has with the body. The significant distinction here is that alluded to in the distinction between bodyhandlers and professionals.

Undertakers' assistants have direct contact with the "contaminated corpse." Required to act as bearers for house, hospital, and mortuary removals, they are on the front line of deathwork. Their duties may include washing the body and, once the embalmer has finished humanization work, the assistant may dress and place the corpse in its coffin. They will subsequently transfer the deceased from the premises to the hearse, from hearse to cemetery chapel and, in the case of burial, from there to the graveside. Their contact with the corpse can be reduced—apart from menial tasks such as washing and dressing—to a "hump and dump" role requiring little skill. In this work they suffer the sharp-end of death pollution as they collect, and are forced to handle, not only "ordinary" bodies but also the badly decomposed or severely deformed dead who make up a percentage of the undertaker's subjects. Similar to the laborers in Cantonese culture their contamination with death is the greatest of all funeral workers.

Both funeral assistants and embalmers confront bodily discharge. Blood, mucus, and excreta are perceived in many cultures, including our own, as a dangerous source of pollution [19, 20]. Assistants are exposed to these discharges in the "raw" sense—in removal work they are forced to tackle the most contaminating form of bodily waste: that which issues from the occurrence of death and the corruption of the cadaver. By contrast embalmers are tasked, not with handling the body or its waste, but with the *cleansing* of the corpse and the expulsion of impurities. Body fluids are replaced with formalin (embalming fluid) thereby neutralizing the harmful effects of decay and refashioning a "decontaminated corpse."

Thus, although embalmers have close contact with the cadaver, their work is conferred higher status within the industry than that of the assistant in virtue of the higher level of skill required. It is the professionals who "humanize" the corpse, preparing it in a manner that propels it from the world of the profane to the realm of the sacred. This is perceived within the industry as requiring training and professional expertise. This mortician does not physically maneuver the body from one location to another but transforms and preserves human remains in order that bereaved people may feel more comfortable in the presence of their loved one.

CONCLUSION

This chapter has introduced the funeral workers employed by G. R. Stone—the company at the heart of the research. Business success for a small funeral firm such as this one depends on a variety of factors including recommendations, location, advertising, and price. In Stone's case, although all these prerequisites appeared to have been met, the firm was struggling to survive. The company's predicament was related to the declining neighborhood in which it existed. Financial buoyancy was largely maintained by reducing overheads: for example, using the garage area for three different tasks and pruning the permanent staff.

The design of the funeral premises and the allocation of front and back stage regions as a means of avoiding potential conflict between bereavement work and bodyhandling tasks, have been examined. In discussing the different roles taken by the undertaker's staff, we have considered some explanations for the divisions of labor within death-work. The next chapter will consider funeral directing in more detail and will provide an interpretation of the way in which operatives account for, and manage, the identity of "deathworker."

REFERENCES

1. W. Besant, *East London,* Chatto & Windus, London, 1903.
2. H. Lefebvre, *The Production of Space,* Donald Nicholson-Smith (trans.), Basil Blackwell, Oxford, 1991.
3. R. W. Habenstein, *The American Funeral Director and the Sociology of Work,* unpublished Ph.D. thesis, University of Chicago, Chicago, 1954.
4. R. E. Turner and C. Edgley, Death as Theatre: A Dramaturgical Analysis of the American Funeral, *Sociology and Social Research, 60:4,* pp. 377-392, 1976.
5. E. Friedson, Medical Care and the Public: Case Study of a Medical Group, *The Annals of the American Academy of Political & Social Science, 346,* pp. 57-67, March 1963.
6. National Association of Funeral Directors, *Manual of Funeral Directing,* National Association of Funeral Directors, London, 1988.
7. Office of Fair Trading, *Funerals: A Report,* HMSO, London, January 1989.
8. E. Goffman, *The Presentation of Self in Everyday Life,* Doubleday, New York, 1959.
9. S. C. Humphreys, *The Family, Women and Death: Comparative Studies,* Routledge & Kegan Paul, London, 1983.
10. P. Metcalf and R. Huntington, *Celebrations of Death: The Anthropology of Mortuary Ritual* (2nd Edition), Cambridge University Press, Cambridge, 1991.

11. M. Bloch, Death, Women and Power, in *Death and the Regeneration of Life,* M. Bloch and J. Parry (eds.), Cambridge University Press, Cambridge, 1982.
12. S. Adams, A Gendered History of the Social Management of Death and Dying in Foleshill, Coventry during the Inter-War Years, in *The Sociology of Death,* D. Clark (ed.), Blackwell, Oxford, 1993.
13. H. Bradley, *Men's Work, Women's Work: A Sociological History of the Sexual Division of Labour in Employment,* Policy Press, Cambridge, 1989.
14. F. Thompson, *Lark Rise,* Guild Books, London, 1946.
15. A. Witz, *Professions and Patriarchy,* Routledge, London, 1992.
16. C. Ungerson, *Gender and Caring: Work and Welfare in Britain and Scandinavia,* Harvester Wheatsheaf, New York, 1990.
17. *The Sunday Observer,* April 14, 1991.
18. J. L. Watson, Of Flesh and Bones: The Management of Death Pollution in Cantonese Society, in *Death and the Regeneration of Life,* M. Bloch and J. Parry (eds.), Cambridge University Press, Cambridge, 1982.
19. M. Douglas, *Purity and Danger: An Analysis of the Concepts of Pollution and Taboo,* Routledge, London, 1966.
20. S. Laws, *Issues of Blood: The Politics of Menstruation,* Macmillan, Basingstoke, 1990.

CHAPTER 4

Becoming an Undertaker

This chapter enquires into the processes entailed in becoming an undertaker. Staff recruitment and the way funeral operatives are eased into the role of deathworker are considered. Accounting and neutralizing methods used by the trade to enable the performance of "dirty" work are addressed. A clear distinction is drawn between tactics adopted by "bodyhandlers" and those utilized by "professionals." These strategies are considered under six headings: *avoidance, dehumanization, distancing,* reference to the *essential nature* of the service, *professionalization* and accepting a *typology* of death. The funeral director's experiences of stigma are investigated and his attempts to "pass" [1] as "normal," scrutinized.

THE PROCESS OF "BECOMING"

All jobs have periods during which employees need to assimilate knowledge of the tasks involved and acquire communication skills for co-worker and, where appropriate, public interaction. There is much for the apprentice undertaker to learn in the process of career development. Removing a badly decomposed body, for example, is a tricky and unpleasant business. More significantly, the psychological and emotional adjustment that is called for when performing "dirty" corpse-handling work and when managing the pain and anger of others takes time to absorb. Because of the polluting nature of the work and the consequent stigma attached to the role player, deathworkers must adopt techniques that permit them to suspend personal prejudice and revulsion in the discharge of their duties.

There is a wealth of literature concerned with the process of "becoming" which adopts the concept of the "career" to understand the experiences, motivations, and perceptions of a particular group. This is used most notably by students of deviance and has been successfully applied to a variety of subcultures such as marijuana users [2], homosexuals

65

[3], nudists [4], and prostitutes [5] to interpret the way in which the novice is guided to maturity by veterans.

Although undertakers work within the law[1] and do not display socially unacceptable behavior in public places, they can, by virtue of their work with the corpse, be interpreted as constituting a deviant subculture not wholly accepted into mainstream society. Subcultural status emanates from their possession of the dead body. Modern society is in many respects far removed from the Merina culture in Madagascar observed by Bloch [6], but the essential characteristics of death pollution inform both cultures.

> Mourning in the Merina case involves the mourners taking on to themselves the pollution and sorrow of death, as though the mourners had to atone for the death of their kinsman. By taking on defilement the mourners clean the corpse and liberate it for its re-creation as a life-giving entity [6, p. 226].

We have no customs which construe the cadaver as a "life-giving entity"[2] but, as I argued in the previous chapter, its ability to contaminate those who care for it has been transferred from the women of the family to the undertaker. The funeral directors' dominion of the corpse releases the bereaved from death pollution but results in self contamination. Manipulating the body to restore the deceased's human qualities may explain the public characterization of the undertaker as "unnatural" or "unclean." Performing these tasks for monetary reward (in contrast to the family who are perceived as working from a sense of love or duty) amplifies popular belief in the immorality of the craft.

To perform decontamination work, individuals must suspend these preconceived notions inherent in the value system of mainstream society. It is essential that they construct a new morality enabling them to undertake work rejected and considered repugnant by the general populace.[3] The morality they devise is based on a set of accounting and neutralizing tactics which must be learned quickly and effectively if the novice is to adjust to deathwork. Jobs which disturb the psyche on the first occasion must not be allowed to continue to do so if the neophyte is to succeed in his/her chosen career.

---

[1] There is potential for law-breaking behavior in most walks of life. By cutting corners or taking short-cuts around the legal bureaucracy, undertakers may break the law.

[2] Except that is, in folk beliefs and popular superstition, for example, the adage, "news of a death—news of a birth."

[3] Weinberg for example, argues that nudists construct a new morality to make them secure in their deviation [4].

Furthermore, prospective undertakers must acquire the facility to cross back and forth between "respectable" and deathwork societies—the latter being regarded by the former as a strange subculture. Members of this outcast group perform a variety of mysterious tasks central to the production of the funeral and to the disposal of bodily remains. Because their industry is stigmatized they tend to be anonymous but are stereotypically perceived as sinister and mysterious with morbid tendencies or disturbing predisposition. Undertakers, however, live in mainstream society. The way in which they negotiate the conflict between their work and social roles will be dealt with later in the chapter. Let us begin by tracing entry into the career of undertaker.

ENTERING THE WORLD OF THE UNDERTAKER

In the late 1980s most undertaking establishments continued to be small family businesses. Many funeral operatives within them were absorbed into the work via the family. In this they may have much in common with people in other discredited trades, such as gelders and slaughterers. Heymowski, writing of the Swedish "tattare," for example, notes the inherited nature of their occupation and their deviant status in mainstream society [7]. If undertakers spend the greater part of their formative years in the environs of the funeral parlor, deathwork may be as familiar to them as the air they breathe. Where this is so, they may never recall a time when they considered undertaking to be at all unusual, strange, or disturbing.

Actually performing the role, however, necessitates a period of adjustment to the practical and psychological demands of deathwork. For Adrian Stone, starting in the family company at the age of twenty-six, the job was unfamiliar, difficult, and at first often extremely distasteful. Describing his apprenticeship he recalled being "thrown in at the deep end" and attending a funeral on his first morning with the company.

> Being the great, great grandson of the founder, I was naturally expected to be able to drive a Rolls-Royce and carry a coffin on my shoulder with no training whatsoever.

With verbal advice and practical guidance he successfully negotiated the role of driver and bearer. Following a short tea break he was rushed to a removal from a fourth floor apartment where the person had been dead for several days.

> Well as I saw it I would have to experience most things eventually
> and there is no time like the present so up we went with the
> shell . . .

> Not a pretty sight and the odor, even less so. I don't know how much
> help I was but I think I did my bit in getting the old dear into the
> shell, but I do remember the perspiration running off me and the
> occasional scurry outside for a breath of fresh (air).

Adrian continued to describe the experience of escorting the body
alone in the lift.

> During the next two or three millennia, I leisurely scout my present
> universe, a three by seven foot stainless steel box containing me, a
> glass-fiber box containing its unwitting occupant exuding unpleas-
> ant odors, a macabre spectre to my imagination. The other occu-
> pant chose this precise moment to move inside the shell. I spent the
> next eon telling myself not to scream, cry, panic, be sick or do
> anything else that might seem unprofessional and that somewhere
> in the other universe this had all happened before and that it was
> really quite normal. . . . With a lurch, the lift then started its
> downward journey and the light went out. . . .

Having the founder of the firm as his grandfather had evidently not
eased his entry into occupational responsibilities.

This undertaker's experience of confrontation with the cadaver can
be regarded as a form of reality shock and is suggestive of the accounts
given by medical students of their initial reaction to the anatomy
laboratory [8]. There are other professions which make similarly exacting demands on new personnel. Nurses, for example, face the trauma
of dirt, disease, and death from the very beginning of their training
[9]; "rookie" police officers do not usually have to wait long before
encountering their first road accident or victim of violence [10].

In contrast to the family member, some funeral operatives are
compelled by unemployment to seek what they would ordinarily regard
as rather undesirable work. Barry's introduction to undertaking was of
this type.

> It was basically a few weeks before Christmas and I thought I'd just
> take *any* job to be in work for Christmas.

Yet others experience a gradual induction into the trade. Engagement
as a driver or receptionist, for example, does not entail direct contact
with the corpse but these employees become increasingly involved if
they are called upon to perform bodyhandling work. Peter explained

that as an out-of-work market trader he had earned extra cash by working as a casual driver. Although he had no prior knowledge of the industry, having a brother-in-law in the trade meant that it was not altogether unfamiliar.

> All I used to do first of all was what they call a drive and a shoulder. . . . So obviously I didn't see nothing regards the making of boxes, people in the mortuary or anything like that.

The final source of deathworkers are those with no family connection with the trade but who actively wish to become undertakers or embalmers. A letter to *Funeral Director*—an English trade magazine—described the experience of a young hopeful.

> In my last letter I told you of the difficulties I had been experiencing in getting a vacancy with a Funeral Director. Not wanting to be disappointed, I was ambitious and determined to become a member of the profession. . . .
>
> Today I am a sixteen year old school leaver, unfairly rejected, disappointed and disillusioned by the profession I adore. Despite this I am still convinced that there is hope on the horizon, for I have just heard that there is a vacancy for me with a truly remarkable man who is by my way of thinking a true funeral director, friendly, helpful, sincere and genuine.
>
> I am again cheerful and looking forward to being both a successful Embalmer and Funeral Director . . . [11, p. 15].

That someone should desire to pursue such employment may, intuitively, seem strange in a society which stigmatizes people who handle the corpse. A reluctance to acknowledge workers as "normal" partially explains the success of Waugh's, *The Loved One* [12] in which he presents a sardonic but, nonetheless, scathing attack on American morticians, mocking their dedication to the task and leaving the reader incredulous that they should really wish to manipulate dead bodies and organize funerals.[4]

---

[4] This stereotype has implications for funeral directors when hiring staff in that they must assure themselves that the recruit does not have necrophiliac tendencies. To some extent this caution is exerted in interaction with all outsiders who demonstrate an interest in their work.

RECRUITING STAFF

Successful assimilation into the industry, some funeral workers argue, can only be achieved by a particular type of person with specific qualities conducive to deathwork. When recruiting staff, Adrian preferred to employ people with no previous experience of deathwork.

> I've only ever employed one person who has worked in the funeral industry before. I prefer my own man. When he makes mistakes he makes my mistakes.

The novice can be tutored in the traditions of a particular firm. A more experienced operative would arrive with preconceptions about styles of undertaking not necessarily suited to the current firm. This sentiment was echoed by other funeral directors. Fry's funeral company claimed to have solved this problem by employing school leavers, of whom John Fry declared, there was no shortage.

> I could take on staff every day of the week. I don't know whether it's the fact that there aren't many jobs about so they'll take anything or what. We have four local schools and we're on their careers program. They get day release. They can come in on work experience and we have a lot—girls and boys. It's great for them. They come in, at first I suppose it's a bit tongue in cheek, but they get into it. Then they really enjoy it. They come back and they're really keen on coming into the trade.

> We recruit from outside. We always have a proportion of the family but the others are all school leavers. We have a policy of just taking on school leavers because it suddenly occurred to us that the only way you're going to get people to do what you want is to take them straight from school. If you take on an older person they're already set in their ways. They already know what they want to do—you can't tell them.

A further criteria for recruitment was to choose a candidate with the "right frame of mind." This quality, not easily perceptible to the observer, was said to inhere in the applicant and was not something that could be adequately learned on the job. People with the "right" approach were thought to be introverted rather than extrovert characters.

> The sort of person I want to employ is that quiet, calm person who you'd really think wouldn't be able to do the job at all. I employed one man who was one of those "I've seen everything, I've done

everything" types. But when he was left to his own devices he couldn't do it. He was a big tough man but he just went to pieces.

And yet Peter, he's a delightful, soft, mild-mannered man but he's got his mind right. I think it actually comes from the attitude of, "this is a job and it's got to be done"—they're not going to get in the box on their own! That is it. You have to just have the attitude that waiting around isn't going to do it. You're there to do a job so you might just as well make the best of it and get it over and done with. And that's the sort of person that you want. The tough, brash one—the one who goes around telling everyone about it—it's as they all say, the bigger they are the harder they fall. And that is very, very true.

Adrian Stone actively sought to recruit people who he felt were capable of combatting the personal trauma which could easily be a consequence of the nature of the work.

Assuming the correct frame of mind, there is still a transitional period shortly after joining the trade when novices learn a series of tactics which enable them to adapt to, and account for, their assimilation into the role of dealing with the dead.

ACCOUNTING AND NEUTRALIZING TACTICS

In common with other occupations in contact with death and dying, operatives develop techniques to negate the distressing aspects of their work. Humor, for example, as we shall discuss later, is used by firefighters, ambulance staff, and the police to counteract the anxiety generated by death [10, 13]. In the case of undertakers, individuals adopt a method best suited to their deathwork roles. In doing this, some aspects of the job demand one strategy, and others, another. Picking up the victim of a road accident may primarily require an interpretation which quells the physical reaction to the task. Locating and making an incision in the carotid artery in order to pump preserving fluid around the body draws more on mental composure. Undertakers making funeral arrangements with a family who have suffered a tragic bereavement, such as the death of a young child or sudden or violent death, will probably require a technique which holds the emotions in check.

In my encounters with members of the industry I observed that workers utilized a variety of accounting and neutralizing tactics. I have classified these under six headings as follows: *avoidance* and *dehumanization*—methods predominantly employed by funeral assistants in their body removal role; *distancing* and stressing the *essential nature* of the service—strategies used by funeral assistants and funeral receptionists in meetings with the bereaved; and *professionalizing*—a technique utilized by the more skilled sectors of the workforce, especially embalmers. The final category is that which refers to the use of a philosophy or *typology* of death which is used by all workers to interpret, and so manage, the constant presence of mortality. Let us consider each in turn.

Avoidance

The type of neutralizing technique employed depends to some extent on individual character traits. More important is the physical condition of the corpse and the undertaker's responsibilities toward it. A technique which was used primarily by removal operatives was that of avoidance. This may at first appear contradictory as it was these workers who, at the sharp end of death, were least able to avoid contact with the polluting cadaver. This approach, however, is used to some degree or another by all people who undertake "dirty work"—from "housewife" to refuse collector. It requires that the worker devise methods whereby she/he can perform the task with the least physical contact. In practice this means that if at all possible, they do not look upon and do not touch the source of contamination. Hughes, for example, reported the views of janitors on their conception of dirty work.

> Janitors turned out to be bitterly frank about their physically dirty work. When asked, "What is the toughest part of your job," they answered almost to a man in the spirit of this quotation: "Garbage. Often the stuff is sloppy and smelly. You know some fellows can't look at garbage if it's sloppy. I'm getting used to it now, but it almost killed me when I started" [14 p. 50].

Adrian Stone described how awful the sight of a badly decomposed body may appear and the physical revulsion at having to handle it.

> Obviously we do actually see and have to handle some of the most horrific things that you could imagine. . . . Some people have died some months previously and have been left in a flat for some time and they're *horrible, disgusting*. And you don't want to touch it. So you work out a way so you don't have to touch it. And you don't actually look at the thing at all!

As a novice, Barry had been somewhat disturbed by the experience of seeing bodies at the mortuary. Peter, his more experienced colleague pointed out that the solution was not to look.

> B: On occasions when we go to collect one, the door into the actual mortuary itself is open and they normally work on, possibly three tables . . .
> P: But then again that doesn't involve us.
> B: No but you see it!
> P: You might see it—but you needn't see it.

Others found that they did look but didn't internalize the sight. ". . . It's like looking at a video—you sort of see it and then you blank your mind to what you see." This tactic was usually employed in the more unpleasant aspects of the job such as mortuary visits and removals of badly damaged or decomposed bodies. By reducing physical contact with the corpse, funeral assistants can believe, and can project the idea, that their involvement with the more polluting side of the work is minimal. If this method of physical avoidance is used in conjunction with the technique of emotional or psychological divorce or distancing (discussed later), operatives are usually successful in neutralizing the effects of deathwork behavior. In the final analysis they can claim that they suffer only slight contamination from their role performance.

Dehumanization

> You don't think of them as people, or anything like that. Once I've seen a body that's it. I don't treat them as if that was once a living person. To me it's no longer. It's just a shell.

It is somewhat ironic that an industry which prides itself on its ability to soften, by individualizing and humanizing, the face of death, should find that some of its employees use dehumanization as a method of enabling them to handle the disagreeable nature of the job. This is a technique which is also used by medics to assist them to focus their scientific endeavors.

> To be really scientific it became necessary for the doctor to impose an instrument of some sort between himself and the patient. The patient was ignored in order to obtain a coned-down view of a single part [15, pp. 125-126].

Although the consequences are similar, in undertaking circles this technique was employed predominantly by workers in the process of collecting or depositing bodies. Dehumanization of the corpse is a rationalizing and coping strategy frequently used during the initial phases of bodyhandling. In contact with badly decomposed corpses workers continually referred to the cadaver as "it" or "the thing." In a disagreement between Peter and Barry over the treatment received by bodies undergoing *post-mortem,* they only perceived of a cadaver as having human qualities when directly referring to Barry's late father.

B: See my old man had a *p-m* and I was on the understanding when he was in that chapel that he was complete.

P: Well they are complete. It all goes back into a person. They don't take it out and throw it away. . . .

B: But I've seen them in there with no lungs in haven't I? And all split open?

P: No, no, no, no. It's all put back, all put back. Yes, of course, it is. They don't just take something out and don't put it back. . . .

B: Just say for instance, they disconnect a heart and all. There's no point in putting it back unless it's all stitched back in. . .

P: Well we know that but I mean if they've got a bad heart or whatever, you've got to find out what was wrong with them. They don't take the heart out and throw it away. They take it out, examine it, see what the cause of death was and they put it back. I'm not saying they stitch it back up but it goes back in. They don't come out of the mortuary less a heart, or less a lung. If it's got two lungs when it goes in there dead, it has two lungs when it comes out!

A further method of dehumanization stems from a willingness to view the body as nothing but the discarded shell—all that is left once the spirit has flown. This was an approach that Peter had learned from a more practiced undertaker and one which he frequently adopted.

I'll never forget what the fella said to me when I first went on a removal. This was an old lady. She lived on her own in a house and there was a young woman next door who used to come in everyday to see that she was alright. This old lady had fell and she'd hit her head and when the young woman come in to see her the next morning, about half nine, she found her. In the night she must have got up or something, she fell and she hit her head and that's it. Now when that woman come in and found her she phoned up and we went to pick her up. And she was sitting there, this young woman, and she said, "It's a shame." She said, "Poor Mary, it's terrible that she's been lying there all this time and I didn't know."

And this fella said to her, "Well, you've gotta look at it this way dear. Although that lady has fell, she's died and she's been there a long while, really that is only the shell of a person. The actual person's spirit is not there. She's died and that is just really a shell."

Which is right really, isn't it? And in her heart the woman was choked that she'd been there so long. And she'd said, "That poor lady laying there like that and I didn't know." And he said, "Yeah, there's that way to look at it but then again, really its only the shell of a person and the actual person itself has left her." And I think that's right. That's the way I always take it. Although a person has died I don't think it's the person—it's just the shell of the person. So I don't take no notice of it, I don't.

During the early stages of deathwork the corpse can, indeed, be viewed as "just a shell" because it has undergone none of the humanization processes for which the mortician is trained. When the corpse is collected it is simply a body from which life has gone, leaving potentially diseased and polluting remains. In Chapter 7 I suggest that it is only when this "shell" has been worked on for some time that it once again takes on human-like qualities.

Distancing

To facilitate the execution of their duties, funeral directors separate their public image from their private face—front from backstage. As the earlier discussion illustrated, backstage is partially maintained to protect the bereaved from disturbing sights and sounds. It also enables workers to labor on the body unseen—thus hiding methods and covering mistakes. Furthermore, by creating areas for relaxation within the hinter regions and by isolating this space from that dedicated to bodywork, they are able to distance themselves from the deathwork role.

Similarly, argot operates to distance undertakers from the stark realities of their trade. The body, referred to in interaction with the bereaved as "Mr.," "Mrs.," "Mum," or "Dad," is often transformed into the "bod," "case," or "thing" when addressed in exclusively undertaking circles. Coffins are recast as innocent "boxes" and so lose their association with death and the corpse.

The strategies of dehumanization and role distancing, however, present risks for funeral directors and it is crucial for their public performance that they do not confuse rhetoric with argot. Moreover, emotionally divorcing oneself from the task in hand may detract from the quality of the work. Unless the actor is perceived as whole-heartedly embracing the role, the service will be discredited. Doctors, for instance, have been castigated for failing to address their patients as human beings. The problem often stems from detachment.

> This is postulated as an unintended effect upon attitudes towards patients as human beings which derive from the nature of the learning experience. . . . A thin line separates "objective scientific attitudes" from cynicism or loss of humanitarianism [16, p. 85].

The solution to the possibility of over-detachment is regarded as the implementation of "detached concern" [8]. Divorcing oneself from the patient allows the doctor to exercise objectivity and sound judgment. A concern for the patient's psychological well-being results in sensitive understanding and care.

For deathworkers, detachment or distancing is again a method primarily used by removal operatives to dull the impact of their work. These funeral assistants have very little contact or autonomy in their interaction with the public. The likelihood of their conveying an uncaring performance therefore, is slim. For those concerned, divorcing themselves from the more unpleasant tasks "makes the job possible." It was perceived, therefore, that the *only* way to proceed was to mentally distance oneself from the work. Furthermore, although other tactics may be deployed in conjunction with this, psychological distancing could not be practiced intermittently.

> If you're going to keep thinking about them all the time and it upsets you I'm afraid you're wasting your time. You won't be able to do it. So you might as well say goodnight. You're not going to do it.

Adrian described the approach of one of his workers as the only "healthy" way to proceed.

> He'll go out and move a little kiddy into the coroner's for a *post-mortem*. And he'll go straight home and put his little grandson on his knee and bounce him about without even thinking about it. Divorcing, absolutely divorcing work from his own home life. If you relate the two I think you'd be in the Happy Home very, very shortly!

Recognizing and maximizing the comic side of deathwork, as noted earlier, is a distancing technique utilized by members of other occupations such as doctors [17] and the police [10]. Funeral workers, when they are not cast as gloomy and sinister, are stereotypically renowned for their sense of humor. Lack of emotional union with the deceased and familiarity with the roles they play endow them with the capacity to recognize the hilarity of some death and funereal situations. Exploiting this ability to distance through humor serves to encourage obduracy.

Whilst the lads would laugh and joke at the most ghastly and bizarre occurrences and tasks required of them, there was a good feeling of care and respect for the dead at all times. The seemingly hard and heartless things are said in jest as an ego boost to overcome a difficult situation either for themselves or for one of their colleagues. Not having been to war, thankfully, I can imagine similar gruesome humour arising to cope with the awful scenes in the trenches . . . [18, p. 23].

Despite the risk of communicating a weak performance, distancing was operated by the funeral arranger or receptionist in face-to-face contact with the bereaved. Conversing with a grief-stricken relative can be a highly distressing affair which threatens the workers emotional stability. The technique is used by some nurses to counteract the distress they may suffer from losing a patient they have become attached to.[5] Mauksch, in a study of American mid-western hospitals, argued that the omnipresence of death forced nurses to maintain an emotional distance from their patients [9]. When asked how she coped with her first experience of a patient's death, one nurse reported,

. . . I remember I cried about it because, well, it's your first experience with death. That's the trouble: I get attached to people [9, p. 92].

Clearly the implication here is that it is not death but fondness which is the problem. Distancing oneself from the bereaved was regarded by funeral workers as protection against over involvement. Furthermore, it helped Roberta, the receptionist at G. R. Stone, to account for her ability to perform work which required such close contact with tragedy. Roberta talked of the coping strategy she used when dealing with grieving families.

Having to deal with upset families—that's another thing that comes into it. Having to try and not get too involved and too upset. You take things as they come and you try not to let things upset you too much. You try to keep things on an even keel. I find it a little bit upsetting when it's a child. If I'm feeling very upset I really have to bite my lip. But I manage not to get too involved. Some people do get extremely upset and it's very hard not to get upset yourself, especially when there's a child, it can be a bit distressing.

[5] The success of this method over the period of a long-term illness is debatable—see the discussion in [19].

In this case Roberta distanced herself by holding her emotions in check and "biting her lip." Although she acknowledged that it was sometimes difficult to create a distance from others' sorrow, she considered it essential for her own well-being that she should do so. The ability to perform her occupational role would otherwise have been undermined. Her way of accounting for her desire to administer such a role was by referring to the essential nature of the service—"It's a job that's got to be done and someone has to do it."

The "Essential Nature" of the Service

There are many occupations claiming to be essential to the smooth functioning of society. These range from the professions to refuse collectors. Deathworkers occasionally declared that if they failed to do their job the very fabric of society would crumble. Gravedigger's strikes have exemplified the disruptive potential of their industrial action. The image and fear of bodies "piling up" in the streets is quite horrific. The funeral directors with whom I had contact felt that they were like any other "professional public service" in that their work should entitle them to claim the status of essential workers. When a death occurred at home, family or friends urgently required the services of an undertaker. There is a public perception that the corpse cannot be left in the home for any length of time and it is no longer seen as the responsibility of any other public service—the hospital, for example, is reluctant to dispatch an ambulance if the "patient" has already died. The body has to be dealt with, however, and this was the emphasis which Adrian Stone attached to his job: "It may be unpleasant but it is a public service and someone has to do it."

Professionalizing

The funeral director's resort to the notion of "public service" is a central feature of any profession [20]. It is this aspect of their work that entitles lawyers, clerics, and medics to claim vocational status. For the embalmer, in contrast to the undertaker's assistant, the corpse was not viewed as repugnant. The distinction between the professional and the bodyhandler is due to the differences in status, skills, and goals. Hughes offers an insight into dirty tasks which are not regarded as such when performed by a professional [14]. I quote at length because his analysis is particularly appropriate to the demarcation of roles among morticians.

> Delegation of dirty work is also a part of the process of occupational mobility. Yet there are kinds of work, some of them very high

prestige, in which such delegation is possible only to a limited extent. The dirty work may be an intimate part of the very activity which gives the occupation its charisma, as is the case with the handling of the human body by the physician. In this case, I suppose the dirty work is somehow integrated into the whole, and into the prestige-bearing role of the person who does it. . . . The janitor, however, does not integrate his dirty work into any deeply satisfying definition of his role. . . . Thus we might conceive of a classification of occupations involving dirty work into those in which it is knit into some satisfying and prestige-giving definition of role and those in which it is not [14, p. 52].

For undertakers, the less skillful the contact with the cadaver, the more polluting it became and the more revolting was the task. Embalming, the experts insisted, involved an intricate and highly-skilled process, requiring education and training.[6] The operatives regarded themselves as professional technicians and this was the way in which they accounted for their role.

Adrian chatted incessantly throughout my first cautious observation of embalming. He indicated the places for incision, the way in which the body was drained, the fluids to be used, and drew my attention to the return of "human color" as formalin (a derivative of formaldehyde) was pumped into the arteries and make-up artistically applied to the face. Although I did not ask for an explanation of his ability to perform such work he—perhaps responding to what he assumed was an inevitable question—nevertheless offered one.

The only difference between what I do and what a doctor does is that I work on dead bodies instead of living ones!

In this way the embalmer explained his work by reference to his professional status. Furthermore, he asserted that his work really ought to be less disturbing to outsiders than that of the doctor or surgeon because no pain was involved for the "patient" and no risks attached to the unsuccessful operation. Although doctors aim to preserve or enhance the quality of life and the mortician merely manipulates the discarded body, embalmers rationalize their work as a process which transforms and facilitates viewing of the corpse. It is, therefore, perceived by practitioners as invaluable in enabling bereaved people to come to terms with their grief.

[6] Encompassed in this notion of the skill required of embalmers is the professional's ability to symbolically transform the corpse from profane to sacred.

Embalming can thus be distinguished from the work of the removal assistants by reference to "professional skills," designed to protect and console the bereaved. Accounting, for embalmers, is linked to the production of a body which belonged to *an individual* and which in virtue of their expertise, is seen to be "at peace." Adrian Stone believed this brought comfort to the relatives and played an active part in assuaging grief. Although he usually explained the practice to clients in terms of its "hygienic" or "preservative" qualities (language appropriated from the discourse of the nineteenth-century reform movement in Britain which stressed public health and sanitation), in exercising his duties the embalmer prided himself on his ability to produce a "life-like" appearance in the face and demeanor of the corpse.

A Typology of Death

A further mode of accounting for the omnipresence of death is to formulate a philosophy of death and this entails devising a typology. The typology recognizes different types of mortality and rationalizes its routine occurrence.

Funeral workers' typology of death differed from that utilized by mainstream society because it was based on the *dead body,* rather than on social, political, or moral knowledge of the deceased. Bodies collected and worked on by these deathworkers are rarely known to them. Information about the cause of death or social circumstances of the dead person is only available 1) with a little detective work, or 2) as a result of, what I referred to elsewhere as, "mortuary gossip" [21]: comments passed to undertakers by physicians, mortuary attendants, the police, and so on. Normally, undertakers have little desire to know details of the death. Distancing themselves from the social circumstances of the deceased was a method of coping with their work. Therefore, commonly acknowledged categories such as "the merciful release," have no place in undertaking society.[7]

Five classifications were employed by the workers in this study to interpret, make sense of, and adjust to the corpses they confronted. Although their interpretations are similar to (and indeed, based on) mainstream cultural classifications of death, there are differences which stem from their development and use. For funeral workers these categories are constructed solely on surveillance of the body, that is, with no knowledge of the social background of the dead person. As

---

[7] Although, this does not bar the worker from drawing upon the rationalization in other social roles.

such, workers are able to adapt stereotypical types of death to fit with their accounting and distancing techniques.

The old were seen as having had "a good innings" and their deaths were the easiest to mentally reconcile. People in mid-life were less fortunate and workers resorted to the exercise of luck, explaining their misfortune as "unlucky" or untimely. Death of the young was viewed with sadness but could be mitigated if the deceased had colluded in their downfall and "brought it on themselves." Deaths precipitated by drugs, violence, or by what workers perceived as sexual promiscuity, for example, dying of HIV-related illnesses, usually left tell-tale signs on the body. The deaths which were "unfair" and consequently the most difficult for undertakers to manage were those of young children. The final category, sometimes used in combination with another death type, was a belief that the deceased's "number was up."

In devising a philosophy of death the funeral director was able to smother some of the detrimental psychological effects of facing mortality on a daily basis. Some categories were more useful in this respect than others. There were situations in which the philosophy failed to mitigate the apparent injustice in death. When the funeral director repeatedly met with "unfair" death, for example, this frequently gave rise to failed accounting and their ability to handle clients in a routine fashion was impaired.

FAILED ACCOUNTING

Although a variety of coping strategies are available for rationalizing deathwork there are occasions when the attempt to cultivate apathy is unsuccessful. Accounting techniques are not easily internalized and as tactics for limiting the disturbing realities of death they are at times ineffective. The two clearest examples I encountered of their inadequacy were first, in relation to the death of children, and second, when the deceased was known to the worker. In both these cases Adrian Stone had been unable to make sense of the deaths involved. In the first case this was due to a prolonged and unabated exposure to "unfair" death—that of children. He commented on his inability to behave in a routine manner with these crises.

> One week all I'd done was small kiddies and it was beginning to wind me up, beginning to get to me. You couldn't relax and do your job in the normal manner.

> And I was just going out for a quick drink, Saturday lunchtime, and somebody came through the front door. And I sat there with them

for a couple of hours and we made the arrangements and after that
I didn't want to talk to anybody because it was another kiddie. I
just went out and started slamming things about, went down the
pub and poured alcohol down my throat! It just seemed unfair. You
know, couldn't somebody reasonable bloody-well die for me! It does
get to you.

Similarly, the death of an elderly lady with whom he had regularly
visited came as a personal blow to the director. His familiarity with the
deceased prohibited any attempt to avoid, dehumanize, or distance
himself from the body. As there was no one to view the body he decided
not to embalm. Although employing a "professional" approach to
this "essential" job he nevertheless experienced the distress of
grief. The way in which familiarity with the deceased can spoil a
professional performance was a theme which also arose in discussions
with ministers of religion. Many were reluctant, for example, to conduct funeral ceremonies for friends as they felt that their own sorrow
might affect their professionalism.

STIGMA

In common with people from ethnic minorities who report that they
have never encountered racism, there are undertakers who maintain
that they are not shunned or stigmatized by mainstream society. The
degree to which this reflects the experience of deathworkers is
unknown since a study investigating the incidence of stigma has yet
to be conducted. The purpose of this section, however, is to examine
the strategies employed by those who are aware of suffering
discrimination.

The preceding discussion of the psychological and practical
demands experienced by undertakers helps us to understand the types
of rationalization they might adopt. The need for workers to account
both to themselves and to others has been alluded to but not yet fully
examined. Most of the difficulties they face in relation to people outside
of the industry are rooted in the *stigma* apportioned to funeral operatives and their trade. Let us first explore the notion of stigma. Goffman
describes it as "an attribute that is deeply discrediting" [1, p. 95].
Stigmatization occurs when,

... an individual who might have been received easily in ordinary
social intercourse possesses a trait that can obtrude itself upon
attention and turn those of us whom he meets away from
him, breaking the claim that his other attributes have on us. He

possesses a stigma, an undesired differentness from what we anticipated [1, p. 15].

In common with many other deathworkers, the attribute possessed by undertakers that separates them from society or emphasizes their "undesired difference" derives from their proximity to death and their handling of the corpse. They possess an ability to handle and decontaminate the dead and, like workers in other societies who perform similar tasks [22], they are stigmatized. Furthermore, there is a general inability to understand their business practice. Although like other private businesses they are motivated by profit, making a living from disposing of the dead is often perceived as immoral or perverted. This interpretation of funeral directing leads to a belief that as a group, they are superficially sympathetic in their interactions with grieving relatives and profit conscious at their expense.

If, in society, there is a general reluctance to confront issues of mortality, then undertakers' close proximity to death will result in public rejection or condemnation of their role. For as I later argue, the deathworker represents or signifies death. The stigmatization of funeral directors has resulted in the creation of a stereotyped image of the group. This image with its stress on the sinister and money-grasping disposition of these workers appears to be overwhelmingly accepted by the rest of society who rarely find the means or the desire to check its validity. Heightened public awareness of the "true" character of the funeral director is, of course, hampered by the workers themselves who, in response to the stereotype and as an exclusion mechanism, hide their identity and mystify their practice.

THE MANIFESTATION OF STIGMA

Undertakers' experiences of stigma and the strategies they adopt to manage that stigma, are influenced by the extent of knowledge that the public have of their occupation and by social perceptions of death. Goffman makes the distinction between the discredited and the discreditable.

... when his differentness is not immediately apparent, and is not known beforehand ... when in fact he is a discreditable, not a discredited, person, ... (t)he issue is not that of managing tension generated during social contacts, but rather that of managing information about his failing. To display or not to display; to tell or not to tell; to let on or not to let on; to lie or not to lie; and in each case, to whom, how, when, and where [1, p. 57].

In "uniform," or known to others as undertakers, the workers are discredited. When people around them are unaware of their vocation they are discreditable in that they may continue to pass as normal provided they do nothing to arouse suspicion of their stigmatizing secret.

The way in which the discreditable manage information and the techniques they use to pass as normal will be examined shortly. First, it is pertinent to consider the tribulations of the discredited death-worker. The belief in the vituperate nature of the undertaker commonly manifests itself in three ways. These are through humor (derogatory jokes or cartoons), apprehension, and typecasting.

Humor

Members of western society have a proclivity to laugh at things which disturb and/or frighten in some way. Humor is thought to be a harmless demonstration of a tendency to stigmatize. Jokes, however, reinforce stereotypes. There has, for example, been much debate about the damaging effect of comedy which takes minority or oppressed groups as its target. The trend toward "alternative comedy" which does not rely on prejudicial images supports a conviction that jokes can stigmatize.

Humor aimed at morticians often makes reference to the "fact" that they will "never be out of work." At this level the practice is really no more than an irritation to funeral workers who dismiss the frequency with which they are subjected to time-worn jokes of "the dying trade" with comments such as,

> You've never heard all the jokes—"dying trade," and that sort of thing. It goes on constantly. You get totally fed up. You get totally fed up with the same old jokes.

In a more serious vein are the incidents of hoax telephone calls which can be categorized as "bad humor." The success of this practical joke is occasioned by the shock effect of a visit from an undertaker. A telephone call from a member of the public requesting removal of a body usually brings a funeral assistant to the home. If the call is a hoax, but the funeral director has been taken-in, the unfortunate victim may be emotionally disturbed by the incident. The hapless worker, as Adrian described him, may have to suffer the consequences.

> You'll find the most incensing thing which an undertaker will have is a hoax call because we actually have to knock on somebody's door and they open it. And you know very well at that minute—you

think, "I'm not really supposed to be here, am I?" And you're checking the address and all that.

I've actually been chased up the street in that situation by someone brandishing a large piece of wood. And I'm shouting, "Yes, I know what you mean! I know what you mean!"

Apprehension

The apprehension with which undertakers are received is related to the fear of death and a refusal to contemplate the disturbing details of physical decay. Contaminated by the body and associated with the finite, mortal aspects of humanity, undertakers are either avoided or compelled to refrain from discussing their trade among outsiders. Keith, a small-scale craftsman of caskets, children's coffins, and infant cribs, plied his trade in a country setting. He related encountering tremendous opposition from the local community after submitting a request for planning permission for his premises.

They didn't want my business in this area. I can't really explain it but it was as though they superstitiously believed that by my being here and making coffins they were putting themselves, or their families, at risk.

The superstitious belief that proximity to death may stimulate tragedy is a familiar theme to many who have brief encounters with death-work [23].

Typecasting

The third way in which the deathworker's stigma is manifested is through "typecasting" the discredited actor. This occurs in many different spheres of employment. The police and medics in particular, bemoan the fact that they are rarely allowed to be "off duty." The officer may be out of uniform but if recognized as a member of the police force she/he will be expected to behave in congruity with the role of law enforcement agent [10]. Funeral workers also find it difficult to step out of role. They may experience difficulty persuading acquaintances that, like people in other walks of life, they perform a variety of roles: a business person, an aviator, an amateur photographer, a parent. Undertakers, however, because of their trade in death, are believed to be distinct from other members of society and therefore it is difficult for the public to see them divorced from their occupation. Peter described the response of his son's work-mates when he first met them.

> When I come to work or go on a funeral it's natural that I wear everything that I should be wearing—smart trousers, proper coat, and tie. When I go away from here I wear the same as everyone else. But I'll give you an instance. My boy's a fire officer at a station right near to where I live and he said, "Come up to the station." So all I do is slip on a coat. I had my slippers on, I had a flat cap on and away I went.

> Went into the station and they're all sitting there. "Oh, hello Dad," he said, "been busy today?" I said, "Oh not too bad." So someone said, "What does he do?" And my boy said, "He works in the funeral trade." So he said, "You can't believe that. He works in the funeral . . . dressed like that." So they accept that because you work in a funeral parlor you're gonna be dressed like it all the time.

On a more pernicious level, typecasting can cause funeral directors some distress. Adrian Stone recalled an incident outside his shop. A middle-aged woman had been hit by a car while trying to cross the road. Although not badly injured, the gathering crowd insisted that she lay on the pavement until the ambulance arrived. Having witnessed the accident the funeral director rushed upstairs to his flat to get a pillow and blanket for the woman. When he subsequently appeared at the scene in undertaker's garb, he was perturbed by disapproval among the assembled crowd and mutterings suggesting he was there awaiting business.

STRATEGIES FOR MANAGING STIGMA

Although those engaged in deathwork may be stigmatized (or regarded with circumspection) by friends and sometimes even family, it is much more evident from strangers. The most frequent barrages come from the media. In some ways, media attention, which is rarely flattering, is relatively simple for funeral directors to cope with. They can rationalize negative reports of the industry by dismissing them as founded on prejudice or ignorance. Disparaging "insider" accounts are explained as attempts by disgruntled workers to gain some form of revenge on their former industry. John Fry illustrated this point.

> More often than not the media coverage that you get is a bit sensational. They had some bloke who was a driver giving his story on what he thought of the funeral trade and how it rips off people and one thing and another. I mean, there's an old boy who's got a chip on his shoulder. I think he'd gone through all these years of the funeral trade and obviously not made enough at it!

They done a half hour program on the bad aspects of funeral directing but you could write an epic on the bad side of any job. There's some people that are in it for the money, there's some people that are ruthless, and sure, they're there but I'd like to think they don't hang around long. Our particular profession is (based on) the family firm where you're not just here to have a funeral this week, you're hopefully here for generations to come. It's all very well taking money off somebody now but you offer a service and you get paid for it. If you do your job properly people will come back and you build up a business.

Apart from the occasional flattering narrative, media analysis is seen by funeral workers as undeserved and illegitimate. The organizations best placed to counter this poor image are funeral directors' professional associations. Although these associations do not respond to every negative journalistic salvo, they do devote time, effort, and money to improving public perceptions of their industry. In Britain, the National Association of Funeral Directors (NAFD)[8] hired a firm of public relations consultants to deal with press and television coverage and to train individual funeral directors to handle media stories "in a positive manner." The consultants were happy to take on the task and reported that they were,

> . . . delighted to have been given the opportunity of promoting the NAFD and we do not underestimate the problems. For too long the public have been in ignorance of the problems facing funeral directors. All around the country, day in and day out funeral directors provide a highly professional and sensitive service to the community, and it is time that this was recognised by the community in return [24, p. 22].

Press attacks are usually against the industry as a whole and only rarely do they center on an individual company or operative. Although media coverage of the funeral trade can be irksome to individual workers, the disturbing repercussions of stigma are magnified when encountered on a personal basis.

The main concern of funeral directors' is the reception they receive from clientele. The views of the local community, however, will be influenced by the stereotypes, reproduced and flourishing in the media. Undertakers work hard to counteract negative images by nurturing alliances in the neighborhood. Adrian, for example, was an active

---

[8] Since the fieldwork was carried out, there has been a proliferation of professional associations created to serve the needs of various sectors of the funeral trade.

member of the local Rotary Club and spent much of his spare time organizing and supporting charity events. The operatives at Fry's also sought to promote an image of their business as a traditional part of the community with the accent on a friendly welcome, a chat, or a cup of tea for visitors.

Instances of the way deathworkers experience community stigma have been discussed. In the account of the injured woman, the undertaker could do little to combat the stigma so obviously attached to his role. The encounter was brief and it would have been inappropriate for him to attempt to justify his actions. Furthermore, he felt angry that he had been placed in such an invidious position. The problem, he was sure, lay in the prejudiced minds of those present and it was therefore *their behavior* which required correction.

PASSING

All members of stigmatized groups who have contact with "outsider" society develop mechanisms for passing [1]. Encounters with outsiders in which morticians are discreditable rather than discredited permit the application of mechanisms which they hope will enable them to "pass" as "just another ordinary human being."

> . . . Because of the great rewards in being considered normal, almost all persons who are in a position to pass will do so on some occasions by intent [1, p. 95].

Not surprisingly, undertakers consider themselves to be essentially the same as everyone else. As Peter remarked, "I'm no different to them and I'm no different because I work in a funeral parlor." At the end of the working day they wish to shed their undertaking mantle, socialize, and be accepted among other human beings. Accomplishing this goal, however, often compels them to adopt techniques which will qualify them to pass in everyday social situations. The methods used are fourfold: distortion, omission, evasion, and nurturing the stereotype.

Distortion

In seeking to "pass," workers habitually distort their role. The actor so emphasizes one aspect of the job that the others are denuded of significance. A frequent gambit was the car hire business cover.

> You never ask what people do for a living because if you do then they ask you. And if they do ask, you lie—"I do a bit of car hire.

Here's a picture of my Rolls Royce." So you can substantiate something which is half truth. You do tend not to tell anyone.

A variation of this theme was used by Barry's son to explain his father's trade.

> My son won't tell his friends what I do. I said, "Well, what do you tell people then?" "Well," he said, "I just tell 'em that you drive a Rolls Royce." But he doesn't tell 'em what I drive it as—in a funeral parlor. Because he can't accept that that's a normal type of job.

Omission

Omission entails failing to relay any information about one's occupation. As the earlier comment illustrates, it is not common practice for undertakers to apprise strangers of their profession. The effectiveness of this strategy, aimed at avoiding discrediting, relied on a lack of curiosity among those encountered. With any form of "passing," however, there is a risk of exposure. Adrian told of an incident in which his omission had been detected and his secret exposed.

> I did that wonderful trip to Cairo by Concorde and it was fantastic, it really was. Because we were delayed leaving we sat down and talked to this elderly gent and his daughter. And we kept bumping into each other because there was only a hundred of you on the trip anyway. So you bumped into people all the way round the whole thing. It's a whistle-stop tour. And at the end of it we were sat down having lunch on this beautiful river boat on the Nile. And there were people talking about this, that and the other. And something just came up in conversation and this man's daughter said, "Sssh! Don't bring up the subject. Don't!" And I just looked at him and I said, "You're not are you?" He looked at me and he said, "Do you know out of all the people on this plane you're the only person who hasn't asked me what I do for a living."

It was the fact that *both* men had been implementing the technique that had led to their mutual discovery. As Goffman notes, fellow sufferers are alert to techniques of passing.

> The presence of fellow-sufferers (or the wise) introduces a special set of contingencies in regard to passing, since the very techniques used to conceal stigmas may give the show away to someone who is familiar with the tricks of the trade . . . [1, p. 107].

Evasion

This method tended to be more popular for deathworkers who considered themselves to be in a fairly stable home relationship which customarily consisted of parents, children, and possibly grandchildren. It was additionally important if operatives had joined the funeral industry after having spent some considerable time working in an unrelated occupation and so known in the outside community in the guise of a different occupational role. As is usual among friends or acquaintances, people ask and are informed of any changes in employment. Others may be aware of the career move into the funeral world but after initial surprise, disbelief, and questioning, the deathworker would no longer be asked on any regular basis the familiar question—"how's work?" For their part workers might feel it inappropriate to make any mention of their day-time business. In this way social relationships survived by avoiding discussion of a topic which outsiders considered unpleasant. Peter, a comparative newcomer to the trade evaded discussion of his work when with friends of long standing.

> I've known people here for twenty years. I used to have my own stall in a market. When people say, "What are you doing now?" I tell 'em. And they say, "No! I don't believe that. How can you do that?" I don't know what they're imagining. Perhaps they're the sort of people that couldn't do it. But they say, "I don't wanna know." So you don't talk about it.

Nurturing the Stereotype

Undertakers are stereotypically renowned for their love of money, alcohol, and possession of a sense of humor. The extent to which any of these characteristics can be said to apply depends entirely on individual personalities. In terms of humor there are deathworkers who adopt a sense of humor as a means of nurturing the stereotype in order to pass in the wider community. An active member of the local Rotary Club, Adrian was unable to conceal the nature of his occupation at Rotary functions. Instead, he attempted to pass by indulging in humor based on stereotypes of his industry.

> They all know I'm an undertaker but that doesn't bother them. We have a laugh and a joke and I threaten to measure them up if they don't behave themselves—but it's all light-hearted.

When undertakers emphasize the comical rather than the gruesome, they attempt to do three things. First, they are demonstrating their sensitivity by displaying a need to evolve strategies (such as humor) to cope with deathwork. Second, making people laugh is a way of nurturing friendship and identifying common ground. Finally, the humor which they use often relies on stereotypical images of the role. In kindling the conventional stereotype of the funeral director they both reinforce and distance themselves from it, appearing to step back and ridicule the tasks involved. If the strategy is successful they may be regarded by outsiders as different from other undertakers and hence more like themselves.

CONCLUSION

This chapter has examined the concept of "becoming" in relation to funeral workers. In considering the problems which confront the novice in "coming to terms" with the unpleasant aspect of the work six accounting techniques have been defined: avoidance, dehumanization, distancing, stressing the essential nature of the service, professionalization, and reference to a typology of death. Identifying these strategies has sharpened our focus and understanding of the way deathworkers assimilate and adjust to their role. The distinction between body-handlers and professionals, for example, has implications for the accounting tactics each employs. The section concludes with a discussion of failed accounting, most common when the worker had known the deceased in life, or when the death was considered "unfair."

The stigmatization of undertakers is manifested in a number of ways. Workers may be the brunt of prejudicial humor; acquaintances may be apprehensive of contact with them; the public may typecast them, refusing to release them from the deathwork role that they perform. The methods which undertakers employ to control or negotiate these forms of stigma conclude the chapter. In attempts to "pass" as normal, funeral workers regularly use the strategies of distortion, omission, evasion, and nurturing the stereotype.

Morticians' marginal status in mainstream society stems from their proximity to the corpse; their public association with death marks them as signifiers of mortality. The physical and psychological pollution surrounding the body is scrutinized in the next chapter.

REFERENCES

1. E. Goffman, *Stigma: Notes on the Management of Spoiled Identity*, Prentice-Hall, Englewood Cliffs, New Jersey, 1963.
2. H. S. Becker, *Outsiders*, Free Press, New York, 1963.

3. K. Plummer, *The Making of the Modern Homosexual,* Hutchinson, London, 1981.
4. M. S. Weinberg, Becoming a Nudist, in *Deviance: The Interactionist Perspective* (3rd Edition), E. Rubington and M. S. Weinberg (eds.), Macmillan, London, 1978.
5. J. H. Bryan, Apprenticeships in Prostitution, in *Deviance: The Interactionist Perspective* (3rd Edition), E. Rubington and M. S. Weinberg (eds.), Macmillan, London, 1978.
6. M. Bloch, Death, Women and Power, in *Death and the Regeneration of Life,* M. Bloch and J. Parry (eds.), Cambridge University Press, Cambridge, 1982.
7. A. Heymowski, *I Samhällets Utkanter: om "Tattare" i Sverige,* Ingvar Svanberg, Chur, 1987.
8. H. I. Lief and R. Fox, The Medical Student's Training for Detached Concern, in *The Psychological Basis of Medical Practice,* H. I. Lief et al. (eds.), Harper & Row, New York, 1964.
9. H. O. Mauksch, Becoming a Nurse: A Selective View, *The Annals of the American Academy of Political & Social Science, 346,* pp. 88-98, March 1963.
10. A. Niederhoffer, *Behind the Shield: The Police in Urban Society,* Doubleday, New York, 1969.
11. *The Funeral Director, 63*:11, p. 15, November 1983.
12. E. Waugh, *The Loved One: An Anglo-American Tragedy,* Chapman & Hall, London, 1948.
13. D. Joyce, Why do Police Officers Laugh at Death?, *The Psychologist,* pp. 379-381, September 1989.
14. E. C. Hughes, *Men and Their Work,* The Free Press, New York, 1958.
15. E. H. O'Neill, An Experiment in Medical Education, *Medical Social Work, 2,* pp. 125-136, October 1953.
16. S. W. Bloom, The Process of Becoming a Physician, *The Annals of the American Academy of Political & Social Science, 346,* pp. 77-87, 1963.
17. H. S. Becker et al., *Boys in White: Student Culture in Medical School,* University of Chicago Press, Chicago, 1961.
18. J. M. Watson, *So Far, So What: Tales from Beside the Grave—An Undertaker's View,* unpublished paper, 1991.
19. D. Field, *Nursing the Dying,* Tavistock Routledge, London, 1989.
20. G. Millerson, *The Qualifying Professions,* Routledge & Kegan Paul, London, 1964.
21. G. Howarth, Investigating Deathwork, in *The Sociology of Death,* D. Clark (ed.), Blackwell, Oxford, 1993.
22. J. L. Watson, Of Flesh and Bones: The Management of Death Pollution in Cantonese Society, in *Death and the Regeneration of Life,* M. Bloch and J. Parry (eds.), Cambridge University Press, Cambridge, 1982.

23. S. Boston and R. Trezise, *Merely Mortal: Coping with Dying, Death and Bereavement,* Methuen, in association with Channel Four Television Co., London, 1987.
24. *The Funeral Director,* November 1983.

CHAPTER 5

The Contaminated Corpse

Previous chapters have noted the relationship between death and disease and the effect of this on understanding the corpse as the site of death and source of pollution. This chapter traces the way such a perception of the corpse assists the undertaker to achieve custody of the body. The social status of the body is considered and the reasons for its allure for the undertaker probed. The discussion of conventions governing the removal of the cadaver concentrates on the funeral director's justification for this practice. Believing that bereaved people find contact with the corpse distressing, undertakers rapidly collect the body, and, out of sight of the relatives, take with them material reminders such as dirty linen. The process "decontaminates" the home and family and allows them to regain a semblance of "normality." In transporting the body, funeral operatives consider they have a responsibility to protect the public from the sight of death—symbolized by the contaminated corpse—and so hide the occupied shell in "closed" vehicles or disguise the removal van with a coat of white paint, a red cross, and the word "ambulance."

DEATH AND DISEASE

Lindsay Prior traces the root of the relationship between death and disease to the development of the science of pathology—a discipline created at a time of increasing concern with health and sanitation.

> . . . in its search for the causes of death, pathology conflated a number of diverse objects; and so disease, the body and causation itself, overlaid one another in a physicalist account of the human condition. Death and disease were to be located in the human body, diseases caused death, and the causal sequence which linked the one to the other were made visible in human organs and tissues [1 p. 9].

If the cause of death is located within the human organism—and this is the rationalization for autopsy examination—then the lifeless body is not simply a consequence or by-product of death but is at once a source of disease and a signifier and symbol of mortality.[1] Care of the body of the deceased, sacred in life but profane in death, is transferred to the mortician. Prior to the establishment of the chapel of rest the corpse would have lain in the home, physically and figuratively polluting those closely associated with it. As a repository for disease, the family was obliged to inform outsiders of its presence in the house. More recently, however,

> . . . (i)n our culture, the attempts not to know about death, not to be reminded of it are predominant. The house of a deceased person no longer is marked in any way, no drawn blinds, no indication of recent death. The bereaved rarely wear mourning clothes or any other outward sign [2, p. 253].

The body is no longer welcome among the family who are usually eager to relinquish their custodial burden to the "expert."

If, as will be argued, bereaved people do not know what to do when confronted with a corpse, they are also unaware of their rights regarding care and disposal of the remains. In a time of crisis people look to the behavior of others as a guide to action. In other words the individual response is steered toward contracting a funeral director because this is the course of action adopted by the majority. It is the "done thing." If survivors are immobilized by the severity of grief they are unlikely to rationally consider alternatives. Furthermore, bereavement literature either actively advises, or, takes for granted, that relatives will contact an undertaker [3-5]. The situation is a *fait accompli,* the relatives rarely questioning their ability to do otherwise. The lack of information about alternative approaches to funeral arrangements is viewed by many modern reform groups, for example, the Natural Death Movement, as "dis-empowering" bereaved people [6]. As noted earlier, they believe that the undertaker is predominantly responsible for the professionalization and alienation of death, and so, they urge people to keep the body at home and make funeral arrangements themselves. The extent to which bereaved people wish, or are equipped, to retain custody of the body and deal with funeral preparations await research.

---

[1] In murder cases it is difficult to press a charge unless the body is available. The corpse is the chief evidence. Without the information it possesses—accessible through *post-mortem*—the crime may go undetected or unproved.

Whatever the reason for the surrender of the body, its removal decontaminates the survivors, liberating them from the obligation to publicly disclose death. For Pincus, transferring the corpse to the funeral home, and the failure to display traditional signifiers, is tantamount to a conspiracy to conceal mortality [2]. Such contempt for customary death mores, she believes, deprives the bereaved of valuable support mechanisms.

Undertakers' willingness to accept this defiling object is explained insofar as herein lies their source of power—the possession of the body. There is no legal recognition of ownership rights over the corpse. The nearest legal imperative is that of the Medical Examiners' or Coroners' commission to enforce *post-mortem* and inquest procedures which reinforce their claim to the body. In all other circumstances, rights over, and obligations toward, the *reliquae* normally fall to the next-of-kin who is entitled to dispose of them according to conscience. In most instances this will result in a prompt call to the funeral director who will swiftly arrive to remove the body. Given that the funeral is the modern undertakers' *raison d'être* and that this ritual cannot be enacted without a body, taking custody of the corpse empowers them to pursue their trade. They justify dominion of the cadaver by reference to the distress and ineptitude of the bereaved.

> . . . the utter finality of death still grips the heart with fear. It is this fear which sends out a cry for help to the funeral director. . . . He must be prepared to carry out the duty which is the fundamental core of his responsibility, namely, to take into his care and charge the body of the deceased . . . [7, p. 41].

This need to protect clients is an echo of other professions who argue that they provide a public service [8]. Indeed, it is remarkable when examining the funeral director's rhetoric how closely it resembles that of the learned professions. The language is the language of altruism which constantly refers to public protection, willingness to serve, and the need for consumer trust.

NEWS OF A DEATH

Nowadays, when a death occurs at home, people are generally at an immediate loss to know what to do. The advice of available literature distinguishes between the correct death and disposal procedures and processes [9, 10]. Figure 1 is reproduced from one such guide. It can be seen that what may have superficially been thought of as a simple process can turn into a formidable series of bureaucratic encounters

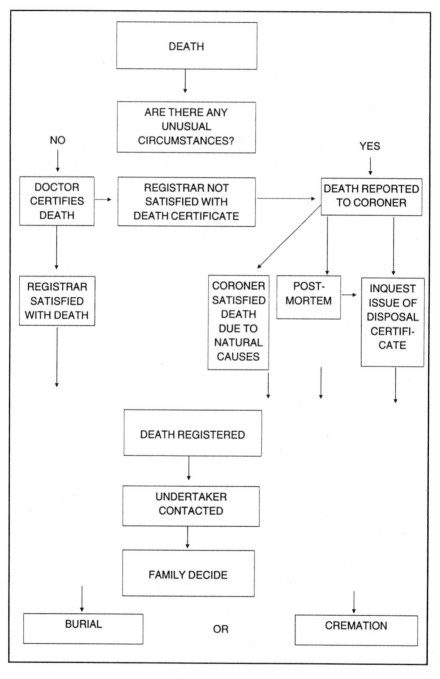

Figure 1. What to do after a death [10].

with medics, the Coroner, Registrar, Department of Social Security, and undertakers. The family cannot choose to deal with death in an absolutely private fashion. Agencies have to be informed, bodies examined, certificates obtained, and the death registered. All this is to be accomplished before the question of disposal can be contemplated. It is not surprising that the uninitiated resort to expert assistance to guide them through the tangled jungle of legal and social procedures. Consequently, when death occurs, people tend to enlist help from an outside agency which can flag legal obligations, make preparations for the funeral, and take custody of the body. In the immediate aftermath of death, when looking for a service which will help them, most choose between the hospital, the general practitioner, the police, or the funeral director.

THE MEDICAL PROFESSION

The Hospital

In Europe and North America it is estimated that around 75 percent of all death occurs in an institutional setting: hospital, hospice, old people's home, and so on. As a result, having only minor contact with the dead body, survivors suffer minimal contamination. By comparison, a death at home is aberrant or unconventional.[2] Despite criticisms of the institutional setting for death, the tribulations of facing a relative's death without the assistance of experts to manage the passage can be daunting. As Pincus in her study of *Death and the Family* discovered.

> When talking to the relatives, it often became clear, however, that they had willingly colluded with the hospital staff because of their own fears of what the encounter with death would mean to them [2, p. 253].

Consequently, the hospital is commonly the first port of call when death is imminent or has recently occurred. There is an element of security in the rationale of hospital procedure. It produces a sense of quiet, calm, control which protects the participants from the unbridled display of emotion.

A call to the hospital, however, is likely to be fruitless if the person has already died, as hospital managers point out, they deal not with the

---

[2] Although hospice care is increasingly helping people to die at home, those so enabled still comprise a small minority.

dead but with the living. If the ambulance does call to collect and the person is dead when she/he reaches the hospital, then she/he will be classified "B.I.D." (Brought In Dead) or "D.O.A." (Dead On Arrival) and transferred from the casualty unit to the mortuary. From here matters proceed as they would for a hospital death.

The Doctor

Since the Reformation, when medical practitioners wrestled control of the death-bed away from the clergy [11], physicians have accepted responsibility for structuring and corroborating the fact of death. Today the doctor is required to issue a death certificate (without which disposal cannot proceed). Most people are aware of this regulation and this explains the approach to their general practitioner. Furthermore, family doctors are conventionally relied upon to offer support in times of crisis. Their comfort and counsel in the after-death procedure is generally received with gratitude.

LAW ENFORCEMENT AGENCIES

Unless foul play is suspected, the bereaved usually only call the police if they have no inkling of the appropriate agency to call, or if they are unable to summon medical assistance. Once contacted, the constabulary are obliged to make further enquiries and visit the home. A policewoman who worked in the area under study described the procedure.

> People often ring the police when someone dies suddenly. We arrive at the address usually finding relatives or friends and usually they don't know what to do. First we get them out of the room where the body is. It's most often in bed or, if they're old, on the toilet. We get everyone out so that we can check there's no knife or blood or anything. Then we check to make sure the person's dead—like if the body's freezing and solid.

> Then we radio it through to HQ as a dead body and ask for the coroner to be contacted and the police surgeon, or if relatives know the deceased's doctor then their own doctor should be contacted to issue the death certificate.

If the doctor is unable to issue a death certificate, either because there are suspicious circumstances or because the deceased had not seen a physician during the two weeks preceding death, the body is taken to the public mortuary and is subject to a *post-mortem* and coroner or medical examiner's investigation. Once these officials are involved they will approach an undertaker who will be dispatched to collect and transport the body to the public mortuary.

> The coroner will ask if they want the body removed and usually they do and as soon as possible. So an undertaker is called for them from the list which we keep. The undertakers arrive in a white van and the body is removed by the pin-striped men. If a *post-mortem's* necessary we don't go into much detail to the family as it's unpleasant to say that their friend or relative will be dissected.

THE FUNERAL DIRECTOR

Where death occurs at home, the undertaker may be telephoned at the same time as the doctor. Few families in Easton preferred to keep the body at home. An urgent call to the funeral director is almost certainly a petition for the removal of this ignoble reminder of death. Protocol aside, there may be practical reasons for desiring its prompt collection. Adrian Stone explained:

> Generally they do like to see somebody come round. The daughter might have been called up in the middle of the night by the doctor and come out from Chelmsford or somewhere like that. And then they do want to see something happen because they want to get back to Chelmsford. They have their own children who have to go to school in the morning. It's all very practical. Life has to continue and we're here to make that easier.

People call in the early hours of the morning, at weekends, and even on Bank Holidays which further convinces Stone of the public demand to be rid of the corpse at the earliest possible opportunity. He did recall one exceptional occasion when eighty-year-old Mrs. Jones agreed to allow her husband's body to remain in her home overnight.

> I remember one time it was snowing like hell and this little old lady phoned me up and I went round to see her but I just couldn't get anybody to help me. So I put my shoes on and trudged up the road.

> And I said to her, "You can see the trouble on the roads and I wouldn't actually like to ask one of my men to drive into work at four o'clock in the morning with all this fresh snow. Is it alright if we leave him there until the morning?" She said, "Yes, I suppose so. I've slept with him for thirty-five years and another night's not going to make any difference."

> But that was her attitude and a very refreshing one too! Although I
> would have been quite happy to help him through into a chair in
> the living room so that she could have the bed.

Presumably this woman's telephone call to the undertaker in
the early hours of the morning reflected her expectation that the
body should be taken away. Her easy acquiescence with Stone's request
for it to remain suggests that she might not have really considered the
implications, or was not convinced of the need, to relinquish the body of
her husband. Advanced age could hold the clue to her behavior in that
the routine surrender of corpses in modern society has spanned little
more than fifty years. Her early encounters with death[3] would
have been at a time when it was common practice for the deceased
to remain in the home until the day of the funeral. The family would
either lay the body out themselves or employ a neighborhood layer-out
to do it for them. The role of the undertaker was much more concerned
with the organization of the funeral than with the care of the body.
This elderly widow was perhaps less apprehensive about the sacro-
sanct nature of the corpse and therefore more amenable to extend its
sojourn.

Undertakers are convinced, however, that the Mrs. Jones' of
this world are rare. The majority of bereaved people are reluctant to
countenance a lengthy period at home for the deceased and this
prompts them to contact their local mortician. Identifying a feeling
of abnormality among the bereaved, Adrian Stone perceived the
desire to have the corpse removed as an attempt to regain a sense of
"normality."

> So you go round and pat people on the head and tell them they're
> actually quite normal really. People have this funny attitude that
> they're abnormal. Somebody's died and we're not normal. I think
> people like something to happen. They want somebody to come
> round and make them normal.

If one interprets this "abnormality" as contamination—brought about
by the physical proximity of the corpse—then, by taking the body into
their custody, undertakers are effectively decontaminating the home
and its occupants.

---

[3] The mortality rate was much higher in the early part of this century than it is today.
It is likely therefore, that, in contrast with later generations, she would have experienced
the death of others long before approaching old age.

DECONTAMINATING THE BEREAVED

In accordance with his evaluation of the needs of the bereaved, and like most urban funeral companies, Stone offered a twenty-four-hour service. Death may occur at any time of the day or night. Outside normal office hours it was usually Adrian Stone who received and acted upon the request for removal, arranging for a colleague to assist him if required. After checking that the caller had contacted the medic, the funeral director took it upon himself to advise the family of what to do next. Even if they appeared to be clear about the procedures involved he would recount all the requirements pertaining to their legal obligations. Being fully conversant with the legal and social requirements of death registration and corpse disposal he is uniquely situated to guide his clients through the after-death network. For those unaware of the appropriate steps his advice was indispensable.

> What happens is people go to one place and then they get a signpost to the next one. It's always—"What do we do now?"—"Well you go to so and so." They *always* get a signpost to the next place. But I assume that even when people think they know what to do I'll always tell them where they've got to go.

After ensuring that the call was not a hoax[4] and having recruited assistance, the undertaker sets out to collect the body.

I have argued that removing the body from the home decontaminates the bereaved. Paradoxically, although the relatives have contacted an undertaker and are expecting one to call, she/he may still face an inauspicious welcome.

> They know they've died and they know they've got to go out. The worst is that people burst into tears when they actually see you coming in with the box.

As noted in the earlier discussion of stigma, both undertaker and coffin, analogous with the body, are signifiers of death; indicators because of their inseparability from their purpose. Their presence, therefore, brings stark awareness of the actuality of human loss.

Home removals are perceived by undertakers as requiring "sensitivity" and "efficiency" and their practice has been tried and tested over time to ensure that deathworkers disturb as little as possible. In

---

[4] Hoax calls are not unusual. Callers are commonly adolescents seeking amusement. Occasionally malice is intended. The hoax call is difficult to detect and most undertakers, at some stage in their career fall foul to some such deception.

pursuit of a smooth performance they must initiate only minimal communication with the bereaved. Consequently, they supply a service which purports to guarantee the minimum intrusion in this intensely traumatic period: speed and expertise in handling the corpse, and compassion and discretion in verbal interaction with the bereaved. The funeral assistants must operate within these prescribed boundaries in their work to procure the body. Perceiving one of their roles as that of protecting the bereaved from undue distress, they commence the operation by ushering relatives out of the room occupied by the body; maneuvering the corpse into the removal shell, or onto a stretcher, can be a clumsy and awkward operation requiring much pulling, pushing, heaving, rolling, and a generally undignified manipulation of the body. If the family are present, the difficulties of the task are compounded as workers, wishing to avoid the charge of brutality, struggle to protect the feelings of the bereaved. Furthermore, there is an accent on speed and silence. Excluded from the death room and not privy to the maneuvers executed on the other side of the closed door, the bereaved's anxiety and skepticism will alight on the undertakers. If they take time to achieve an ostensibly simple operation, or are noisy workers, a client's imagination may run riot.

When the job is finished there should be few remaining signs that death occurred in the room. Stained linen and crumpled sheets are commonly wrapped around the body as it is stowed in the fiberglass shell. Having exerted control of the situation (by virtue of greater experience) the workers hide the cadaver from the family and leave with the "contaminated corpse." The justification for excluding the family—that it would be distressing for them to witness the undignified exit of their loved one—remains pertinent to the process of removal.[5]

REMOVAL FROM AN OLD PEOPLE'S HOME

An extreme example of belief in the necessity to shield mourners from witnessing the removal of the corpse was illustrated by an occasion when Adrian, single-handedly, extracted a body from a local old people's home. He was a familiar face in the home and well known among the inhabitants. In his role as Rotary Club activist he had played Father Christmas at Yuletide celebrations. Standing in a queue at a do-it-yourself store on Bank Holiday Monday with his portable

---

[5] Although funeral directors thrive according to the rate at which they process bodies and, therefore, have an *arrière-pensée* in encouraging the bereaved to yield their dead, most, nevertheless, sincerely believe that their actions reduce distress and that they are thereby providing a valuable service to the community.

telephone slung over his shoulder he received a request for removal from the home. Unable to summon assistance, he mentally devised a method of carrying out the removal alone.

> I phoned up the old people's home and said, "When do you want me to come? Before lunch? Lovely." So that they can work their own little spot and not have too many people going about and seeing various coffins. Or if they are having lunch you can skip out of the back with nobody seeing—which is nice. It's all a bit like Burke and Hare but with the best will in the world.

It is not usual for the funeral director to arrange a time for collection of the body. In the case of this residential home the practice was designed to enable the staff to ensure that residents were out of the way when the undertaker arrived. Adrian went on to describe his method.

> I actually took the coffin out of a window which was set between two common rooms. The Matron calmly walked in the room where everyone was and closed all the curtains. I walked up to the window from the outside, stood on the shell, got through the window and hoiked it (the shell) through. I hopped on the bed, straight in with the body, and out the same way.

> They still talk about it up in the old people's home but nobody saw it. They were all sitting there having a little cup of tea and Matron—jolly Irish woman—went in and said, "Ah you can't be watching the television with all this, I'll shut the light out for you." And that was it.

> I didn't want twenty or thirty residents all watching tele' and saying, "There goes Ethel." Because they all stand up and look out of the windows.

In effecting this minor miracle the funeral director, in common with many other workers (including care staff) assumed that elderly people do not wish to be reminded of death. This belief is based on an implicit premise that relationships in institutional settings are not significant enough to warrant the opportunity to enable those involved to bid farewell to their companion. On the first point it is certainly true that there are old people (as there are young people) who greatly fear death and shun any contact with it. This is irreproachable. Denying them information about the death of another, however, does not address their distress. In some ways it compounds their fears when they realize that it is only a matter of time before they too are bundled, unceremoniously through a window or back door.

Grief is an exacting emotion which may be exacerbated by the knowledge that one's own demise is imminent. Failing to identify the bereavement of other residents can compound their sorrow, frustration and fear as they are denied the mourning rituals and bereavement counseling around which to structure their grief. Facing an empty chair and a wall of silence cannot bring solace to residents of old people's homes.

MANAGING POLLUTION: HIDING DEATH[6]

From the beginning of their relationship with the body until the point of display, funeral directors place great importance on the need to hide or disguise the body of the deceased. At the removal stage, this can be seen most clearly in the way in which the corpse is covered and transported. Journals of the undertaking trade are filled with advertisements for transport aids. Bodies can be removed from the place of death in a wooden coffin, in a fiberglass shell, or on a plastic stretcher. The latter is a fairly transparent attempt to emulate the ambulance service and to give the impression, at first glance, that one is dealing with the sick, rather than the dead. In similar vein, vehicles which transport the body to the mortuary may resemble an ambulance. Indeed many have the words "private ambulance" printed on the sides. Passing such a vehicle in the street, or even being next to one in a traffic jam would not arouse curiosity or hint that death was in attendance. Other vehicles used to transport the dead body place emphasis on the need to hide rather than disguise their cargo. The transit van, referred to as the "handy," is frequently employed and the shell is tucked away to the rear, remaining unseen throughout the journey. This was the method used by Stone's—the removal shell often vying for position in the old blue transit beside shovel, spade, planks of wood, and sheets of tarpaulin. The van's uses were multifarious as the vehicle's contents betoken.

A further method, used regularly by some undertakers (and occasionally by others when circumstances demand) is for the hearse to become the removal vehicle. Waiting outside a church one day while a lengthy funeral mass was being performed, Gordon showed me the shelf which lay hidden beneath the deck of the hearse. The space, he

---

[6] The discussion here is of the techniques used by the funeral director to hide or disguise the cadaver during transportation. It is not only this deathworker who strives to conceal the body. When death occurs in the hospital it is transferred to the mortuary—an area either removed from the main buildings or situated in the hinter regions. Sudnow discusses the secluded location of the mortuary in the hospitals he studied [12].

explained, was used for one of two purposes. First, when two funerals were tightly scheduled, in order to avoid a time-consuming trip back to the shop, they would simply carry the coffin for the second funeral in the unseen cavity and release it onto the platform shortly before arriving at the home of the deceased.

The second purpose was to house the removal shell. Although Stone's preferred not to use what was essentially a ceremonial (and valuable) vehicle for such a mundane task, if the "handy" was out of action or otherwise engaged the hearse was an effective substitute. The removal shell would never have been displayed on the platform as it was not in keeping with the tone and purpose of the vehicle. This space was reserved for the dignified and "decontaminated" body which issued from the humanization process achieved on the undertaker's premises.

ARRIVING
AT THE FUNERAL PARLOR

Until the body has undergone a process of "humanization" it is afforded no privilege. When Peter and Barry, the funeral assistants at G. R. Stone, returned from a "pick up" they entered from the rear of the premises, unloaded the grey plastic shell from its grimy surroundings in the aging van and carried it, without decorum, past the funeral cars and into the garage workshop. Here it was deposited in the place reserved for the shells, close to the store of coffins and conveniently situated near the drain and sink to accelerate laying-out. Unless the receptacle was required for another removal (and small companies usually keep two) the body remained in the shell until the embalmer found time to deal with it. In winter this may take longer than in summer when the corpse cannot be left for long before noxious odors remind workers of its presence.

It was some time before the cadaver was promoted from the status of contaminated corpse to the rank of central character, lying in state in the chapel of rest. Its progress through the decontamination process and the level it had reached could be assessed by reference to its physical location in the funeral company's premises. Transit through the building—from rear to front—corresponded with its acquisition of human-like qualities. A further examination of the diagram of the premises in Chapter 3, p. 41, illustrates this point. The contaminated corpse was unloaded from the transit van and entered through the rear of the building where it was left on cold flagstones among the empty coffins and vehicles to await funeral preparation. Following laying-out and embalming, reconstruction, and cosmetic work, the body was transferred to the front workshop where decontamination and humanization work (the focus of Chapter 6) was completed by dressing and presenting the deceased in the newly constructed coffin. Resembling a former self the deceased was laid in the chapel of rest to be visited by admiring mourners. When the day of the funeral arrived the sealed coffin was installed in a Rolls Royce hearse and parked briefly at the front of the shop where it was adorned with floral tributes before leaving with the cortège to the funeral service.

CONCLUSION

This chapter has focused on the practice of removing the body from the home to the undertaker's premises. I have suggested that the association between death and disease inevitably intensifies the perception of the corpse as contaminating. Furthermore, in the absence of popularly recognized *mememto-mori,* the corpse, as the physical manifestation of death, becomes the symbol of mortality. As a signifier of pollution and a symbol of death, bereaved families concede its custody to the funeral director. Deathworkers welcome possession of the cadaver because herein lies job security. Without the body, undertakers cannot be assured of control over the funeral. The rationalization for the practice of removal, however, is that it releases the bereaved from the onerous tasks of laying-out the body and allows them to regain a sense of "normality"—sentiments which I have interpreted as "decontamination."

In effectively removing the body from the home the undertaker is careful to shield the relatives from disturbing sights and sounds. The incident involving the removal of a corpse from an old people's home illustrates the lengths to which deathworkers will go to avoid "upsetting" the bereaved.[7] In any setting, however, institution or in the home, such furtive action may not be in the best interests of the residents. The resort to subterfuge by hiding or disguising the cadaver during its transportation to the mortuary further reduces the possibility of public recognition of the polluted corpse. Having arrived at the funeral home, the cadaver is delivered to the rear entrance and its movement *in transitu* through the premises is charted with reference to the processes of decontamination and humanization—to be explored in detail in Chapter 6.

---

[7] And perhaps in the process, upsetting themselves or making their work more difficult.

Undertakers take custody of the body in anticipation of organizing and directing the funeral. The arrangements interview where the bereaved make decisions which authorize the company to begin funeral preparations are the subject of the next chapter.

REFERENCES

1. L. Prior, *The Social Organization of Death: Medical Discourse and Social Practices in Belfast,* Macmillan, Basingstoke, 1989.
2. L. Pincus, *Death and the Family: The Importance of Mourning,* Faber and Faber, London, 1976.
3. E. Rudinger (ed.), *What to Do When Someone Dies* (revised 9th Edition), Consumers Association, London, 1986.
4. HMSO, *What to Do After a Death in Scotland,* HMSO, London, 1994.
5. J. Green and M. Green, *Dealing With Death: Practices and Procedures,* Chapman and Hall, London, 1992.
6. J. Spottiswoode, *Undertaken with Love,* Robert Hale, London, 1991.
7. I. Bennett, *Attitudes to Life and Death,* E. Hillman (ed.), conference paper, Report of North East London Polytechnic Seminar, London, 1978.
8. G. Mungham and P. A. Thomas, Solicitors and Clients: Altruism or Self-interest, in *The Sociology of the Professions: Lawyers, Doctors and Others,* R. Dingwall and P. Lewis (eds.), Macmillan, London, 1983.
9. Department of Social Security, *What To Do After a Death,* HMSO, London, 1990.
10. M. Wright, *A Death in the Family,* Optima, London, 1987.
11. R. Porter, Death and Doctors in Georgian England, in *Death, Ritual and Bereavement,* R. Houlbrooke (ed.), Routledge, London, 1989.
12. D. Sudnow, *The Social Organization of Dying,* Prentice-Hall, Englewood Cliffs, New Jersey, 1967.

CHAPTER 6

Making Arrangements

This chapter examines the practical and symbolic significance of the interaction between the funeral director and the bereaved in negotiating a contract of disposal. Deathworkers' perceptions of their roles and responsibilities toward the bereaved are investigated and the mechanism of the "closed network" that sustains their monopoly of disposal services is considered.

During the arrangements interview, funeral directors adopt a specific manner and appearance (a personal front). This, combined with the spatial organization of objects and bodies in their public office (the setting) and the patterns of talk they employ, enable them to define the situation and to structure the interaction according to their agenda and within strictly demarcated boundaries. An in-depth discussion of the arrangements interview explores the factors which affect consumer choice and highlights the practical and allegorical implications of their decisions.

PRACTICAL CONSIDERATIONS

In Chapter 5 I maintained that removing the defiling body decontaminated the bereaved. Removing the body with minimal communication with the relatives suggests that undertakers believe that there is a short period when distress is most intense. Thus, a time lapse between visiting the home and the arrangements interview is regarded as allowing emotional adjustment to the death (facilitated by taking control of the body). When a degree of composure is recovered the bereaved are ready to face decisions pertaining to funeral preparations.

The arrangements interview is both a practical and symbolic progression from the surrender of the body. The focus of the negotiation between the undertaker and the next of kin[1] is a material one where relatives typically wish to dispatch their loved one in a well-made coffin which is transported to the grave in a gleaming hearse, marshaled and escorted by professional staff. Through the eyes of the undertakers, the arrangements encounter is the time when, having already relieved the bereaved of the body, they are now able to deliver them from the exigencies of funeral organization. Once the death has been certified and registered, the bereaved are able to hand over all remaining preparations to the expert. Discerning their role as protector of the bereaved, undertakers are keen to assume responsibility for the practical organization of the funeral. Moreover, they are confident that this is what their customers both need and desire. Lack of knowledge about the process involved combined with a diminution of emotional composure, would, they believe, render funeral organization something of an ordeal. Relinquishing responsibility for disposal reduces the burden and expedites the grieving process. This, after all, is the funeral director's business. The arranger's motives are perceived to be in harmony with their own in that she/he seeks to commission the funeral company to administer the necessary procedures culminating in the disposal of the body. Delegating the minutiae of preparations to the expert frees the mourner for other pursuits during the two to five days before the funeral.[2]

THE SYMBOLIC TRANSFORMATION
OF DEATH

Only a few days before my husband died we were worrying about money—how we could afford one thing and how we could pay for another. The problem always seemed to hinge on the fact that there simply wasn't enough money coming in. Before the week was out he was dead. He died suddenly. And I realized just how stupid it all was. We'd spent such a large part of our last few hours together thinking and arguing about things that were really quite irrelevant and trivial.

And I could see other couples around me doing the same thing. I wanted to stop them and tell them not to argue—life's too short, enjoy each other while you can. It's only when you lose someone

---

[1] That is, the person who arranges the funeral and/or settles the bill.

[2] For the most part, undertakers have not addressed the criticism often leveled at them, that in taking control of funeral organization they have stripped the bereaved of any meaningful activity during this initial period of grief.

though that you really understand what is and what isn't important in life.

Death can come as a dramatic reminder that life, though quintessentially priceless, is ephemeral. Grief frequently takes the form of anger, fear, or shock as the bereaved, perhaps for the first time in their lives, are compelled to consider a world in which material satisfaction—the everyday basis of life in western consumer societies—appears to be meaningless. On a symbolic level, however, the arrangements interview can be interpreted as a mechanism for transforming death from an unmanageable specter into a collection of material goods and services. The interview is centered around the necessity to make choices pertaining to the preparation and conduct of the body in relation to the funeral ritual. The business transaction induces a perception of death in terms of material units (coffin or casket, shroud, vehicle hire) and professional services (embalming, liturgical minister, administration, conductor). Thus the occult character of mortality is transmuted into concrete, controllable elements which are subject to choice and manipulation.

This transformation is exacted during the arrangements interview which the funeral director conducts with the next of kin. The director's practical intentions are to elicit sufficient information from the client to enable him/her to proceed with funeral preparations. This purpose is greatly assisted if the bereaved regard funeral directors as experts and defer to them for guidance.

> It's horses for courses. You don't go to me and ask me for a whipped ice-cream because I wouldn't know how to work the machine! If you could afford to do everything yourself and work out how to do it you'd need at least three score years and ten to do the same amount of work. So obviously this is why you pay a professional.

The funeral director is undoubtedly an expert in human disposal and as Adrian Stone pointed out above, it would take considerable time and training for an untutored novice to become conversant with the intricacies of the after-death system. If clients appreciate this, the exchange is accelerated as undertakers are able to utilize their own well-rehearsed agenda for the interaction. In this their purpose resembles that of "professional" situations where purveyors rely on clients to accept their authority. That most people acquiesce with the expert's definition of the situation stems from the distinction between "lay" and "professional" judgment. The latter is perceived by customers as having "sapiential authority" [1] and so they defer to a greater wisdom.

A further critical aspect of the meeting is that, as far as possible, the bereaved refrain from emotional outbursts or enervating displays of grief. It simplifies the job of the funeral director if clients respect the "appropriate" sequence of events at this time and do not commence mourning until funeral arrangements have been set into motion. Stone believed that the organization of the ritual should take priority at this time.

> Let's get it done and over with then you can start to grieve. It's quite difficult sometimes dealing with people who are grieving and in a way that they won't listen to you. It's just the English sort of stiff upper lip—you've got to get it done so why not go to the man and get it done. It's unpleasant, but get it over with.

For bereaved people this is often a period of emotional trauma which manifests itself in a variety of forms. Some weep, while others may display feelings of bitterness, resentment, or anger. John, a director from Fry's funeral company, explained that undertakers often had to bear the brunt of these sentiments. The funeral company's desire to "get it over and done with," was not always shared by clients.

> I was asked to decide on details immediately whereas I felt that this could have been left until the following day when I was not so upset [2, p. 45].

The emotional distress of bereavement is frequently cited as an explanation for lavish expenditure on funerals and undertakers are often accused of persuading their clients to overspend. All the funeral directors with whom I was acquainted pointed out that such practice would not be in their own long-term interests as it would inevitably lose customers.[3] The receptionists must carefully gauge the mood of the funeral arranger and respond accordingly. John spoke of the difficulties.

> Once you've sat down and had a general chat with people you can pretty well sort out who's sitting in front of you and really decide the way you're gonna bat. Everybody's totally different but it's just experience. . . . Everyone who comes in is a different person. Some people are bloody awkward. I mean some people come in and they've just lost somebody and can be very bitter. When they come

---

[3] There is a brief discussion of this viewpoint later in this chapter under the heading "The Coffin or Casket," p. 125.

in here they can be quite aggressive. Other people come in laughing and joking.

Experience teaches undertakers skillful handling of the bereaved. By reinforcing the view that arrangers should defer to expert authority in ritual matters and desist from demonstrating their grief, undertakers are able to determine the nature and boundaries of the discourse. If the interview is conducted in a "professional manner" the parties can proceed with speed and "dignity" to a business agreement. Three mechanisms can be traced which serve to sustain this definition of the situation: the funeral director's *personal front* [3]; the *spatial organization* of the public office, and the *communication format* employed. Each will be dealt with in turn.

PERSONAL FRONT:
THE UNDERTAKER'S APPEARANCE AND MANNER

Goffman used the term "personal front" to refer to a performer's appearance and manner.

> "Appearance" may be taken to refer to those stimuli which function at the time to tell us of the performer's social statuses. These stimuli also tell us of the individual's temporary ritual state: that is, whether he is engaging in formal social activity, work, or informal recreation.... "Manner" may be taken to refer to those stimuli which function at the time to warn us of the interaction role the performer will expect to play in the oncoming situation [3, pp. 34-35].

Morticians manage their personal front as a means of emphasizing similarities or differences between themselves and others. In Chapter 4 it was shown that in attempting to "pass as normal" funeral workers tend to dress and behave in a manner which stresses their similarity with those outside the industry.

In the formal setting of the funeral home, however, directors conduct their appearance and manner in order to separate themselves from their clients. Having rejected the sombre black attire of their predecessors, so harsh and suggestive of death, many have now adopted a dress design which emulates the professionals.

> The funeral director must study to make himself in his manner and appearance acceptable to the functions which he has to perform. The idea that he should diffuse a permanent aura of deep mourning in dress and voice is wholly outmoded. . . .

> . . . Mourning clothing is much less common than it was and it is
> suggested that a black tie and a black jacket are not merely
> unnecessary, but undesirable, as they emphasize the intrusion of
> death into a household. . . . It is not suggested that excessive infor-
> mality of dress, or heartiness of manner, is desirable but rather an
> everyday professional note. A plain dark suit, cleaned and well
> pressed, such as many doctors and solicitors choose, with a grey or
> other suitable tie, combined with a businesslike, but unhurried,
> manner and a sympathetic interest in the problem in hand, is felt
> to be acceptable to most . . [4, pp. 2-3].

Their manner is consistent with their apparel. Business people must
exude confidence in the service they offer, their composed demeanor
producing a calming effect on those who consult them. If the bereaved
are to feel secure and justified in relinquishing control of this important farewell ritual, funeral directors' appearance and manner must
reassure them of their proficiency. This is achieved by framing the
encounter as professional and as one in which experts make specialist
knowledge available to customers via a contractual relationship.

SPATIAL ORGANIZATION

Acknowledging his debt to Kenneth Burke [5], Goffman builds on
the ideal type personal front.

> In addition to the expected consistency between appearance and
> manner, we expect, of course, some coherence among setting,
> appearance, and manner [3, p. 35].

Setting is part of the social front which combines with the actor's
personal front to produce a coherent definition of the situation. Personal front management permits funeral directors to define the
encounter as a meeting between professional and client. Power
relationships implicit in the interaction are enhanced through the
spatial organization of objects and bodies in the setting of the public
office.

The front office at Stone's where arrangements interviews were
conducted was dominated by a large, yet barely utilized, desk behind
which was seated the funeral director or Roberta, his receptionist. The
bereaved (who were summoned to the office rather than interviewed in
their homes) were settled on chairs, positioned on the other side of the
desk. There are numerous commercial and professional agencies which
employ this "over-the-desk" [6] arrangement when interviewing

clients. Solicitors and hospital doctors are two examples. Furthermore, this mode is assumed by most organizations for particular kinds of interaction, most notably those which involve a meeting between higher and lower ranks. A job interview, consultation with a supervisor or manager, or discussion with the head of school, are all likely to employ this spatial formula. Facing a less knowledgable person across a rather imposing desk assists in realizing a projection of power. The interviewee inevitably experiences a sense of ineptitude in relation to the interviewer. Formal situations which do not institute this method of organization are ordinarily attempting to create an informal atmosphere.

Embracing a conventionally formal setting establishes funeral directors as controllers of the dialogue. They are the experts who ask the questions and steer the exchange according to their knowledge of ritual requirements. As the inexperienced beneficiary of their wisdom, the next-of-kin can only respond and never really lead or structure the communication. Moreover, viewing the setting as formal, encourages the customer to maintain an equally formal approach. Feeling relatively ill at ease has the effect of hastening the pace of decision making and, again, guards against unchecked emotional display which (in a more relaxed environment) might detract from the efficiency of the interview.

The remaining furnishings and decor in Stone's front office supported the representation of the room as a formal and professional setting. Seating himself below photographs of his ancestors, the director conveyed an air of reliability and continuity of purpose. Having been established in the nineteenth century and surviving five generations implied that the service was traditional and of high quality. There was little other furnishing of the room. An ancient filing cabinet, free-standing safe, and a carriage clock[4] were the most conspicuous items. All were consistent with the image of the setting as professional and as such were not dissimilar from those which may be found in the office of any business professional.

STRUCTURING THE COMMUNICATION FORMAT

When Adrian Stone conducted an arrangements interview the line of questioning was always the same. "Follow the order on the form and

---

[4] Clocks have traditionally been used as *memento-mori* to remind people that time is short.

you can't go wrong," he advised, producing a copy of the standard invoice used by the company. He wrote the script.

> I designed the form with the idea that you start from the top and work down to the bottom and that's your idiot guide to the information you require.

The questions, printed in black ink against a pink background, had been arranged to facilitate the decision-making process. Each question flows "naturally" from the previous one. "Easy" choices, such as burial or cremation were made early in the interaction, leaving more sensitive ones, like embalming, closer to the end. Designing a form with which to control the delivery and receipt of information keeps the professional firmly in command. Indeed, clients expect those they consult to have expert knowledge and to take initiatory roles in the communication [7]. The interaction with the funeral director assumed an interview format in which he asked the questions and the arranger responded. Whenever the latter lacked the knowledge to make a decision, the director initiated a change of footing [8] from "Interview Format" to "Information Delivery" [9]. In other words, by adjusting the communication format, the undertaker alternated his personal front between one in which he was an inquirer and one in which he was a provider of information, or adviser aiding the decision-making process.

Indeed, undertakers see one of their most important roles as that of adviser. Controlling the communication format projects the impression that they are uniquely qualified to advise on all practical considerations relating to the funeral. They may, for example, be asked to explain the procedure for purchasing a new grave or for the reopening of an old one; to suggest the appropriate number of vehicles to comfortably accommodate a set number of mourners or for information about how to respond to the coroner or medical examiner's investigation. Furthermore, Illich [1] and Johnson [10] argue that the nature of professional authority is disabling to clients and therefore it is not unusual for consumers to request advice or defer to the judgment of the expert. Indeed, Stone was frequently consulted on matters of protocol or was tapped as a source for ideas concerning the most appropriate method of dealing with unusual problems. The following dialogue between Adrian Stone and one of his clients illustrates power relations in the discourse.

> Mr. A: One of the queries I did have was that we want Dad buried near to mother. My son thought his inscription should be on her grave with hers—which I thought was a good idea. I don't know how you felt about that?

AS: Well, I've no grievance either way. Would father have wanted the inscription to go on the grave with mum?

Mr. A: Well, that's what we thought. I mean all along I've been thinking "what did he want?" But I can't remember exactly how much room there is on the stone or how it's laid out or anything.

AS: We could add a little bible to the grave if you want—if there's not enough space. It's no worry to me where we put the inscription so long as it's not on somebody else's grave! We could just put, "And also Peter Joseph buried nearby."

Mr. A: Yes, yes, that's fine. Good, OK.

In the discussion between the two men the son of the deceased was unsure how to proceed. He sought guidance on matters of practice and was happy to defer to the undertaker's experience. In suggesting alternatives the funeral director made certain assumptions and introduced values which the arranger should 1) hold and/or 2) be aware of. Mr. A was quick to comply with what appeared to be "good" advice. The idea, for example, of adding a bible-shaped stone to the grave, whether the bereaved is a church-goer or not, assumes an acceptance of religious protocol. The format in which the recommendation was transmitted, however, with the funeral director oscillating from the role of inquirer to that of adviser may have had greater significance for the final decision than the nature of his counsel.

A completely detached professional role is unsuitable for this type of interaction as it is important for undertakers to appear to be caring toward their client and the deceased. They must, therefore, embrace a style of questioning which extracts choices in a relatively informal manner. Throughout the meeting they are careful that customers do not consider themselves subjected to rigid interrogation.

> Answers to questions should still be obtained by using a conversational approach. The interview must in no way resemble a third degree examination or the completing of a Government Form. It is an intimate family affair and the funeral director's attitude must be that of a friendly adviser [4, pp. 14-15].

An interview which employs a mode of questioning reminiscent of government form-filling is thought to be inappropriate because it does not foster a sense of care or trust. Such an approach alienates and disables [10] the respondent. Despite having designed a document enabling him to structure and control the discussion, Stone pursued turn-taking procedures [11] which lent the communication a quasi-conversational [12, pp. 51-52] quality. This, he hoped, gave the interview a personal and unique feel rather than a sense of one in which the interaction is strictly defined and predetermined. Undertakers publicly stress that their client's wishes are paramount. Illich [1] refers to this as "charismatic authority" and he notes that every professional appeals to "some supreme interest of his clients that not only outranks conscience but sometimes even the *raison d'état*" [1, pp. 17-18]. Funeral directors are keen to be seen to offer an individual service based on the needs and desires of each customer. (The discussion later in this chapter which examines the basis of the "tailor-made" funeral expands this point.)

THE CLOSED NETWORK

Before looking in detail at the arrangements interview and the choices made, the relationship between some elements of the after-death network should be considered.

Funeral directors assume that by contacting them, the bereaved wish to abdicate responsibility for disposal preparations. Furthermore, the price they feel justified in extracting for ensuring that this service is available 365 days of the year and for every hour of each day, is that of monopolizing the products and services of related organizations. Many commercial deathwork agencies, such as coffin manufacturers, shroud makers, cemetery and crematoria staff, have an exclusive alliance with funeral companies. The association conforms to the pattern of a "closed network." Here the concept of the closed network builds on Whyte's definition of the "network," which he describes as,

> . . . a set of individuals who do not belong to the same group or organisation and rarely if ever all get together at the same place, but who nevertheless initiate action for each other in pursuit of a shared objective [13, p. 249].

Individuals and organizations whose services revolve around those of undertakers—by virtue of their role as agents of the bereaved and possessors of the corpse—are precisely such a network. That those involved deal *exclusively* with one another in pursuit of these arrangements makes this system a *closed* network. In preparing services and manufacturing goods for the funeral, these agencies deal exclusively with funeral directors and have little or no contact with the general public.[5]

---

[5] Cemetery or crematoria staff may occupy a large part of their day dealing with requests from the bereaved for ashes, remembrance services, purchase of slots in the Garden of Remembrance, niches in columbaria or erection of memorial plaques. Each of these services, however, is concerned with post-funeral requirements.

EFFECT OF THE CLOSED NETWORK

One obvious consequence of the closed network is the mystification of the bureaucratic process and the maintenance of funeral directors' monopoly over "necessary" goods and services. Their relationship with other deathwork agencies is symbiotic. For example, a particularly favored cemetery is more likely to be recommended to next of kin who have not already chosen a disposal site. Furthermore, communication between organizations who share a set of beliefs, language and objectives can substantially reduce the time and effort involved in executing even the most complex of tasks. Maintaining undertakers as the sole purveyor of the funeral ritual results in one specialist agency dealing with another. Efficiency and expertise can be expected of the service. Bureaucratic procedures are understood and mistakes minimized: errors may be easily repaired or rectified, shorthand terminology is used to accelerate communication, and prompt payment of fees can be assured. Stationed as the intermediary between the agent and the public, funeral directors accept a large part of the responsibility for ensuring that papers are in order, goods are of a satisfactory standard, timing is adhered to, mourners behave "appropriately," and the whole funeral process is smoothly and expertly accomplished.

Media reports of the difficulties encountered by those wishing to arrange funerals without the aid of an undertaker attest the strength of the closed network. Few manufacturers will agree to sell *one* coffin on a retail basis, cemeteries and crematoria generally take bookings only from undertakers, hospitals release bodies to funeral assistants rather than relatives, overnight body storage facilities in public mortuaries are not readily available, the "self-drive" hearse does not yet exist, and priests are loathe to agree to perform a religious service without the assurance that chapels and times have been prearranged by fellow "professionals" in the undertaking business.

At present, few bereaved people appear to have an active desire to handle all the arrangements for the disposal of their dead. Although the modern reform movements have achieved publicity, most of their converts have been drawn from the more affluent sectors of society. This suggests that the majority of the populace accept the current system because it either indulges mourners' requirements or is tolerable because it guarantees the speedy and efficient service for which the expert is paid. Furthermore, because most communities in western society have been distanced from the after-death process, they are unaware of the "appropriate" requirements for the funeral and, therefore, need to consult an undertaker for advice. The network remains relatively unchallenged because there is a widespread reliance on experts. From the legal system to car maintenance, this involves the non-expert in the least disruption of time or lifestyle. In modern technological and bureaucratic society each industry or profession holds the knowledge to execute its function. Passing this information on to their patrons would be a time consuming and wasteful exercise burdening the clients with procedural data which they may never again consult. Moreover, retaining "expert knowledge" empowers the expert to define reality, determine client needs and "thereafter hand over a solution to the problem in terms of their own definition" [14, p. 137].

FUNDAMENTAL CHOICES

Whether the funeral is to be simple or elaborate, the next of kin are required to make three fundamental decisions: 1) choice of burial or cremation, 2) the type of coffin or casket to be used, and 3) the number of vehicles required for conveyancing to the grave.

Burial or Cremation?

Arrangements for the funeral cannot proceed until the funeral director has ascertained the choice between burial and cremation. With this information she/he can arrange details with the cemetery or crematorium, decide on metal or plastic fittings for the coffin, and press ahead with the necessary paperwork.

In the United States cremation is now gaining in popularity. Ten years ago only 10 percent of funeral arrangers opted for cremation; this has now increased to 15.2 percent and ranges from 55.8 percent in Nevada to 1.9 percent in Alabama [15]. Canada has a higher preference for cremation, at 27.3 percent, and Australia higher still with 48.6 percent of deceased cremated [15]. Since the mid-1960s, the English have preferred cremation to burial. The figures for inhumation in some cemeteries in the East End of London, however, do not reflect the national average of 70.5 percent cremations annually. For example, in Forest Avenue Cemetery, traditionally popular with East Enders, greater numbers favored inhumation. Of the 2,010 disposals handled in 1988, 1,060 (53%) were burials. There is no study to explain this discrepancy between national and local preferences. The greater incidence of tight-knit working-class family structures lacking extensive geographical and social mobility and inclining toward traditional rituals may go some way to accounting for this trend. There are also religious and ethnic minority groups in this area, such as Roman Catholics and Muslims, who object to the rapid destruction of mortal remains—although these are probably balanced by other groups such as Sikhs and Hindus who prefer cremation.

Many people decide their means of disposal in advance of death—some leave a clause in their will[6] and others have stated a preference to relatives. There is no financial incentive for British undertakers to favor one method over another. Payments for burial plots or cremation are due to the cemetery or crematorium authorities and any monies collected are passed on to them. The costs to the consumer, however, differ dramatically. Cremation is the less expensive option—the price for burial taking some account of land value. If the arranger is undecided, the funeral director will often prompt by urging the client to consider "what mum would have wanted." This may be the first of many encouragements to second guess the preferences of the dead. In so doing, the undertaker shifts the communication format from question and answer interview to a more informal, essentially counseling, style. Talking through memories of the deceased's words and actions personalizes the exchange and gains customer trust.

Funeral directors believe that as agents of the next of kin it is their place to mediate when there is dissension over choices of disposal within the family.

> If anyone does object to cremation and that's written on the form, then the Medical Referee at the crematorium would decide. But normally you get the family to sort it out. That's why we are the mediator as such. We're in the middle and I can sit there and say, "Come on be reasonable. Is what Uncle Fred thinks really that important? Is he that close a relative?"

Once the decision has been made, the bereaved must fill in the obligatory "application for cremation forms" and the director ensures that the copious paperwork is completed. Adrian described the procedure in England.

> The simple cremation, somebody having died in a hospital, the certificate of medical cause of death is signed by the doctor who attended the deceased during their last illness. That is then taken to the Town Hall and they inspect it and make sure it's correct and then issue the Certificate for Disposal and the Death Certificate.

---

[6] Whichever means of disposal was favored by the deceased, however, the decision to bury or cremate usually remains with the executor or next of kin—although in some states of America recent legislation has changed this.

The Death Certificate is the one that people take to their bank and insurance companies to prove that the death did occur. Then there's the Green Form that's issued to us for disposal—the Disposal Certificate—which is signed by the Registrar and brought in to us and then goes, at a later time, with other forms, to the Cremating Authority.

In the meantime we have to arrange the forms from the relative—because you must have a form signed by the relative that says you want a cremation to go ahead. Anybody can arrange a burial because that's the traditional way—it's no longer the normal way—but the form has to be signed by the closest relatives saying, "I wish to have the remains of so and so cremated."

There are then two forms signed by the doctors at the hospital which we arrange through the Registrar at the hospital. One doctor signs to say what the person died of and the second doctor has to sign confirming it.[7]

So you have the Green Disposal Certificate, the Form A—which is the application by the relatives, and the B and C Forms—which are the two doctors forms that go to the Cremating Authority.

At the crematorium there is yet another doctor—a medical referee—who inspects all of these forms and he will then sign the authority to cremate the body.

So you've actually got three doctors and a relative's signature before you can cremate a body.

Having ascertained the wishes of the bereaved regarding burial or cremation, the director would telephone the appointed cemetery or crematorium to check that the required facilities were available at the designated hour. Unless there was a query, for example, pertaining to grave ownership or depth of plot, the communication was short. The cemetery superintendent knows that she/he can rely on funeral directors to heed cemetery regulations. Arrival will be punctual, the cortège will be presented appropriately and waits its turn for the chapel in a "dignified" manner. The mourners will then spend no more than the statutory fifteen to twenty minutes within its walls[8] and the

---

[7] It is interesting to note that hospital doctors are paid a fee for this service, colloquially known in the medical world as "ash cash."

[8] It should be noted, however, that the length of time in the chapel can be extended by booking more than one "time slot."

undertakers will pay the correct rates of gratuities to cemetery employees who assist them in the prosecution of their duties.[9]

Given that the two parties to the contract are known to each other and have transacted similar business on myriad occasions, there is no necessity for the cemetery official to detail the intricacies of the paperwork and request that it is forwarded. Undertakers are familiar with the procedure for acquiring and dispatching the correctly completed documents. Their role as "middle person" between the bereaved and the crematorium is a prodigious advantage to the cemetery superintendent. Explaining the logistics of registration to each family would be formidable and time consuming. This may be one of the primary reasons why cemetery authorities recommend that the family contact an undertaker.

> The Cremation Regulations are still quite complicated and it is wisest to approach a funeral director immediately when death occurs and advise him that you desire to arrange for a cremation. Discuss with him how soon you wish the cremation to take place and whom you wish to officiate at the service, also the form of service. The funeral director will then do all that is needed to procure the necessary statutory forms for the cremation. You will need to sign the statutory Form A if you are the executor or the next of kin or are authorised by either to do so. The death will have to be registered and you will be advised how to do this.[10]

Only in exceptional cases is the cemetery superintendent willing to deal directly with the bereaved in allocating and preparing a grave plot.

The Coffin or Casket

The coffin or casket usually represents the single most expensive item on a funeral director's bill and its cost will vary according to whether the body is to be buried or cremated—the flammability of respective timbers being a factor. Adrian explained.

> We have a basic range—we're probably fairly similar to other people in the area. We've got veneer on chipboard with a couple of different colors so if something doesn't look too good to you then

---

[9] The undertaker pays gratuities to gravediggers and chapel attendants "on behalf of the mourners"; ministers receive their allotted fee at the chapel door before the entourage enter.

[10] Extract from leaflet, *The Manor Park Crematorium* (1987).

there's an alternative at a similar price. And there's a slightly more fancy one, veneered on chipboard and then there's the different shaped one—a coffin has shaped shoulders and a casket has square corners. Then we go right through to the American type of caskets with the all-singing, all-dancing hinged lids—which I think are horrible! But of course, some people do like them.

I still think you could not beat for actual practicalities, the solid oak coffin or the solid elm coffin—the traditional coffin.

Stone's did not have a showroom where customers could view and choose coffins. These are common in North America and becoming more popular in Britain, but there are few to be found in the East End of London. There are even fewer in small businesses because the practice demands that undertakers buy-in a variety of coffins which they are unable to sell as they must be kept for display purposes. As a relatively fixed asset it demands substantial financial outlay and, furthermore, space to exhibit. Instead, small businesses tend to rely on a glossy, full-color catalog to assist their customers. Leafing through this inventory and pointing to a casket, Adrian continued.

There's a casket that I don't reckon you can actually beat. It looks elegant without looking too dressy. You know, it's very smart lounge suit but not dinner jacket. And of course it's the linings and things like that, that you can do so much with as well—silks and satins.

And on another page,

That one's actually a solid oak coffin with a cut inside which proves it's solid wood—people never trust it—but that one (pointing to another) is just a veneered panel with a pressed side. And of course the difference in price is quite dramatic.

There's a solid elm coffin which will last you for years and years and years. I dug one of those out of the ground a couple of years ago, it had been there since 1957 and the lid was still on it—which is quite amazing!

But if you want to spend a lot of money, that's a nice casket. It's beautifully made, it's beautifully lined and you can have it in mahogany or oak. It's just a shame that they should stick it in the ground quite honestly because they are so expensive.

They're all very pretty, apart from the metal one—I had one of those a little while ago, horrible thing!

Apart from counseling on the suitability of coffins for cremation, undertakers are unlikely to offer any further advice on the purchase of this reliquary. The condemnation of their forebears, accused of encouraging excessive expenditure on funerals and especially among the poor, has resulted in a reluctance to extend unsolicited recommendations on coffin choice. With this in mind, East End undertakers are cautious not to advocate extravagance. Fry's, for example, viewed such tactics as having detrimental repercussions for the future.

> You've got to be a bit careful 'cos it's a very emotional time and it'd be very easy to sway people, to take advantage. It never does you any good. Mainly that's because later on they do reflect back on the way they've been treated. They do think back and it'll never do you any good. You have to be very careful at a time like that. It's like some people will come in and say, "Oh we want the best." You've got to be a bit careful because you know they can't afford it. So you've got to try and moderate people sometimes.

Adrian Stone expressed similar concerns.

> Of course there are people who wish to spend going up to £2000. Which is a lot of money. Although I must admit I do try and steer people away from that. I always say, "Well if you're having something like that buried, once you've buried all that money then you can't spend it on a memorial stone which you can see the day after." It's practical, isn't it? I would hate to have somebody come back to me and thinking, "Oh, what a pity we spent £1200 more than we needed to on the funeral when we could have had a really fantastic headstone."

As the supplier of both coffins and memorial stones, if the bereaved accept Stone's suggestion, they can of course place their order with him for a more permanent commemoration.

Whatever the cost, undertakers are at pains to point out that the price of the coffin includes the hire of two vehicles and the services of the funeral director and staff. They are keen to inform the public that whether the customer paid £200 or £1000 for "the box," on the day of the funeral the shining black vehicles will arrive promptly, the bearers' conduct will be impeccable, the conductor will direct with skill and poise, the arrangements and paperwork will have been efficiently concluded, the cemetery will be well prepared and, if requested, the priest will professionally commit the souls of the dead into the hands of God.

This practice of locating the coffin at the center of funeral provision was also noted by Habenstein in his study of the North American funeral director [16]. He described it as a method of compensating for "invisible" services (this might include laying-out) and slack periods. The coffin is chosen to support these costs as it is viewed as a prerequisite funeral accoutrement and one which is difficult for the public to price. The only other item charged separately and paid directly to the funeral director is the hire of additional vehicles. Given that most people are fairly familiar with the cost of running and maintaining a car, this is not an ideal unit on which other services may ride. Moreover, if the coffin is indispensable[11] then whosoever possesses the reliquary has custody of the body (without which the funeral cannot proceed). Herein lies the explanation for the undertakers' stress on retaining control over coffin distribution. One woman who attempted to organize her husband's funeral on a "do-it-yourself" basis described the attitude of the undertaking profession to her requests for a coffin.

> . . . I found there's a very, very strong undertakers' lobby. Not only was I refused, I was refused in terms of the most unctuous, sanctimonious cant . . . they all refused me a coffin without a full service [17].

Undertakers' monopoly of coffin retail is supported by the coffin manufacturer through the mechanism of the closed network. In return for loyalty the coffin maker sells exclusively to the undertaker.

The Vehicles

Stone's, like other funeral companies, provided a hearse and one mourning car as the minimum vehicle hire included in the price of the coffin. Clients may request more limousines and indeed, the undertaker may advise their hire once the arranger has estimated the number of "chief" mourners. Accompanying Gordon on one of the drives to a funeral, he told me of an undertaker who customarily advised his clients against the use of private cars unless they were black in color. "It makes the procession look like an outing to the seaside!" The alternative, of course, was the hire of his own mourning vehicles.[12]

---

[11]Although not a legal requirement, western custom usually dictates the use of a coffin. Some cemeteries in areas of Britain and Australia are now experimenting with shroud burials.

[12]There are clearly strong working class traditions associated with display at funerals and this has bearing on the fact that this strata are more likely than middle-class people to hire additional limousines. It is possible, however, that the rationale utilized by the undertaker cited here may also assist in explaining this class difference. Smaller budgets result in the purchase of poorer quality, or older, private cars which may be deemed unbefitting to participate in the cortège.

Charges increase with each additional car.[13] There is no reduction, however, if the funeral arranger chooses not to use the limousine. Inevitably, there are arrangers who insist that no mourning cars are required and who wish to meet the hearse at the crematorium rather than having it journey via the home. Nevertheless, whether desired or not, the bereaved must bear the unadjusted cost because, concomitant with the service accompanying the coffin, the mourning car must escort the hearse.

RELIGIOUS FUNERALS

Once material requirements for the funeral have been agreed upon, the interview turns to the question of religion. In Easton, various ethnic or religious groups, including Greek Orthodox, Hindu, Muslim, Christian Baptist, or Latter Day Saints, observed their own funeral rituals and customs. Stone's had customers from many of these communities and frequently provided funeral services held in the deceased's own style of religion and place of worship.

Regular church-goers of the Roman Catholic or Protestant faith customarily held the funeral mass or service in their church rather than the crematorium chapel. Adrian Stone was always mindful to acquaint himself with clergy new to the locality. If funeral organization was to run smoothly it was important for the bereaved to understand the relative importance of the undertaker *vis-a-vis* the priest.

Because the Catholic priest has been in contact so much before death, people tend to go to him and make the arrangements for the funeral. Then they come round here and say, "We've made arrangements with the priest for the church for such and such a day." I say, "Have you? Cemetery's full that day!" So basically, after a few false starts with an incoming priest you take him aside and slap him on the wrist! . . .

Now when people go round to Father Brown, he'll say, "Go and see (Stone) and he'll phone me up." So now we have a good relationship with them.

We get on very well, as we do with the local rector. It's a team ministry in this area. We get on very well with them. And they sort

---

[13]When a cremation is paid for by the State, the mourning car is still included in the price. Even when there are no mourners, theoretically, the car should accompany the hearse to the crematorium.

of say to people, "Don't talk to me sunshine, go round and see the man." And that's us.

Maintenance of harmonious relations can be advantageous to both parties. Stone illustrated one benefit for the clergy.

We help to make sure that Catholics in this area don't get buried on a Tuesday—Father's day off. He's entitled to a day off, he works Sunday! . . . You have to think of these things when you're arranging the funeral.

SECULAR FUNERALS

The majority of funerals are for people who nominally opt for a protestant or Church of England service. In everyday practice, however, they may have had little or no contact with the church. In similar fashion to the completion of statutory bureaucratic documents, for example, for hospital admittance or job application, respondents feel it appropriate to state some religious affiliation. For those who have grown to adulthood in traditional British communities, "C of E" is the most common option. Having stated a preference, they are asked if the funeral company should arrange for a minister to preside over the service. Whether or not the deceased was a practicing Christian, the response is usually affirmative.

It may be that the next of kin acquiesce with the employment of a minister as a form of "insurance policy" against the possible existence of an immortal soul. The Reverend Hogarth, a minister regularly engaged by Stone, believed that in bereavement "any religious stirring they had would be resurrected." It is also possible that agreeing to the presence of a cleric is simply because it is regarded as the acceptable or normal way to proceed, once again, the "done thing." In the absence of a satisfactory alternative, bereaved people are likely to default to the traditional protestant service. It was a religious minister who suggested to me that the relatives

. . . don't know what else to do. If you wanted a secular funeral you'd have to make a deliberate effort and most people don't know how. So although they don't really care about religion they'll take it as it comes.

Undertakers' questioning format certainly assumes a religious ceremony unless the client specifically requests a secular one. According to the British Humanist Association, 34 percent of Britons have no formal religious tendencies. In an increasingly secular society a number of clients do not require the archetypal religious ceremony. The under-taker's form, however, which sets the agenda for funeral arrange-ments, pointedly fails to address the issue of non-religious services. Mark Tyack, a funeral director interviewed by the *Sunday Observer,* explained this apparent oversight on the part of the funeral industry.

> I'd say about 90 per cent of the people we deal with have no connection with their local church. Nowadays, the significance of religion at a funeral is generally minimal, but it's the presentation they want.
>
> We don't actively promote non-religious funerals, he says, "because that would jeopardise our good relations with the clergy" [18, p. 56].

Consequently, the next of kin are quizzed on the religion *favored* by the deceased and not whether she/he *held* spiritual beliefs.

These factors together sustain ecclesiastical oligopoly of funeral rites, reinforcing the pattern, despite thriving secularity, that crises of death continue to attract the presence of the Church [19].

THE PROFESSIONAL FUNERAL MINISTER

Whatever denomination selected for the ceremony, funeral directors offer their clients a "made to order" service. Adrian described the cleric—referred to in local undertaking parlance as the "sky pilot"[14]—who would perform the ceremony.

> He's a sort of professional funeral service minister. He'll go anywhere to help me out when I need him. The team ministry in this area are very, very busy. And anyway, why should they take their time out to do something for which they don't get paid? Why should they go out and spend the best part of three hours talking to somebody who's not really listening to them anyway? Why not have the man—the professional. He will 'phone people the night before, have a ten to fifteen minute talk with them over the telephone, find out which bits to play up and which to play down. He's basically non-conformist. But people say he does give a lovely service. . . .

The employment of a minister on these terms has been found in other geographical areas [20]. Its incidence has led to popular criticism of the handling of the funeral ceremony [21, 22] castigating it as

---

[14]This is also military jargon used to refer to an Air Force padre.

depersonalizing. Time allocated in the crematorium chapel is a maximum of twenty minutes and therefore, it is contended, the obituary will inevitably be short and relatively hollow.[15] Furthermore, the probability of ministers spoiling the ceremonial performance by mistakenly referring to the deceased by the wrong name or placing too much stress on a trivial aspect of the deceased's personality are proportionately increased when the person was unknown to the them.

There are positive aspects of the arrangement, however, which may account for its persistence. First, for non-religious people who have no desire to seek spiritual solace, the arrangement allows the family to "set the pace." Hiring a minister for the duration of the ceremony allows them to indulge in this rite of passage without obligation to the church. The minister takes initial instructions from the undertaker and contact with the family is usually confined, first, to a short telephone call to ascertain salient information about the deceased and then a brief interaction during the funeral. The minister will not comment on the mourners' religious faith or sincerity nor prolong the relationship unless invited to do so. Another Church of England clergyman explained the procedure.

> You tend to be approached by an undertaker to go and do a service. He'll say, "I've got a funeral ten o'clock Wednesday, any chance of you being able to help us?"

> So you look at your diary and you say, "Yes that's all right. What's the name, age, who's the next of kin," and, if it was a woman, "was she married or not married."

> Now if people tell the undertaker that they want the clergyman to visit them or ring them or something then I'll do it. Normally, unless they want hymns and have particular hymns they want, people will leave the arrangements in the hands of the undertaker and the clergyman and the thing just follows its course. The vast majority just take the service as it comes and no more said.

> Unless a person was particularly connected with the church you normally only do any of those things by invitation of the family. If you haven't got that you just go and take the service. You turn up on the day, at the time, and the cortège will roll up and you conduct the service.

---

[15]Although, as noted earlier, it is possible to extend the time in the crematorium chapel by booking more than one twenty-minute period.

Second, for the undertaker it is simpler and more propitious to telephone the reliable "professional" who will take down the details of time, crematorium, name and telephone number of the bereaved, than it is to liaise with the local clergy to assess availability and deconflict their commitments. Moreover, the contract cleric is aware of the time restrictions imposed by the cemetery and will have a ready-prepared service of fifteen minutes length. In this the minister gains favor with the undertaker who is responsible to the cemetery and, furthermore, who is paid for the funeral and not by the hour. A *requiem* mass or its protestant equivalent demands more time but produces no greater financial reward.

Third, the undertaker's policy of circumventing the parish clergy wherever possible could potentially result in conflict between the two agencies. In practice, however, a church minister informed me that the team ministry tend to overlook the vast numbers of their dormant flock who elect not to avail themselves of their funeral services. This was because the non-church-goer was seen more as a liability in terms of time and effort than a possible convert.

> In the vast majority of cases the Church of England being what it is—that is, being the State Church—most funerals that one takes are for people that one doesn't know and doesn't get to know.

Fourth, for the "professional funeral minister" not on the Parish payroll, funeral fees are a source of income and may average £40-60 week—the charge in 1988 was £22 per service and was usually paid cash in hand. This payment to the clergy has interesting implications for their association with undertakers. Fees are paid in cash by undertakers when they arrive with the coffin and mourners at the chapel. This is traditional but the practice creates some disquiet among ministers. Their grievance is that the undertakers' means of payment is undignified and humiliating as they furtively deliver the cash into their hands, often in sight of the bereaved. One minister in particular, complained that an undertaker to whom he regularly contracted always insisted on taking him behind a gravestone to make the payment. This behavior, he interpreted as distasteful and sordid.

There are two principal explanations for the continuation of this apparently unwelcome practice, one connected with material gain and the other with the recognition of status. Many ministers commissioned by undertakers are retired or otherwise without a parish. "Cash in hand" is a "black economy" method of payment and leaves the choice of whether to pay tax and insurance premiums to the receiver. Despite feeling uncomfortable by the way money is transferred, the option of avoiding taxation may be more compelling to funeral ministers than their sense of injustice.

Status is affirmed in the following way. Undertakers' mien in handing over the money at the funeral resembles that with which they tip the gravedigger at the graveside. It effectively reverses the conventionally accepted stratification of the two occupational roles. It is normally the higher ranking individual who pays the less secure on a cash-in-hand basis [23]. Moreover, it firmly marks the undertakers' position of power in the relationship and communicates to all their omnipotent control of the funeral ritual.

TIMING

Having established the choice of burial or cremation, coffin, cars, and religious preference, at this juncture in the arrangements interview, funeral directors will ponder the question of timing. The day and time of the funeral must be decided before the crematorium or priest can be consulted. Collective memory of the shame of the paupers funeral meant that East Enders and their undertakers usually rejected an early start.

> Nobody wants the nine o'clock trot. That was the pauper's funeral—get it done and out of the way first thing in the morning. That is now known as the nine o'clock trot. There are many people in the East End of London still who will not start the most expensive funeral in the world at nine o'clock in the morning.

It might reasonably be supposed that it is the next of kin who decides the start time for the service. On the contrary, it is the funeral director who suggests, and seldom fails in allocating a specific time—one which is indubitably suited to business requirements.

> When we've worked out who's died, where they lived, where they died, age, date of death, and whether they're going to be buried or cremated and where they're going to start the funeral from, the question comes up, "Have you thought of a day? How about Friday? In the afternoon?"

> That's because I've already got one on that day and it saves me washing the cars twice. It's entirely a practical thing. Once you're out doing funerals, you may just as well carry on doing that. When you're in doing other things then . . . You can treat it as such as a production line but that's only so you can give people more time. . . .

PROVISION FOR PRIVATE GRIEF

"Dreaded issues" [9] are tackled late in the interview. This gives funeral directors the opportunity to build up rapport and confidence with the bereaved before tackling sensitive topics. Questioning people about whether they wish to view or embalm the body are delicate matters.

> By the time it comes to that question I think that they realize I'm their friend. I'm the only friend that they've actually had that day.

Forcing the next of kin to think once again about the body of the deceased threatens breakdown of emotional control. It is far easier to decide on burial or cremation, coffin, vehicles, and priest because, although primarily concerned with the fate of their loved one, they are nevertheless peripheral or abstracted from the body itself. In contrast, the choices of viewing and embalming directly concern the corpse and contact with it. Authorizing "restoration" work on the body or requesting to view can be particularly distressing for the bereaved. Synnott argues that secularization has produced a belief in the body, rather than the soul, as the site of the self [24]. The body, a mere shell to the religious, takes on greater significance and the way in which it is treated is understandably a source of anxiety for the family.

Interviewers are particularly aware of the need to maintain a business-like manner at this stage in the interaction. Emotional breakdown is seen by them as embarrassing for all parties. Reserving these issues until late in the exchange ensures that if the bereaved are unable to control their grief, the experience will be short as the interview is almost over.

Funeral directors offer their clients certain facilities which they ostensibly perceive as assisting them to "come to terms" with their grief. These facilities are incorporated in viewing and embalming. It is customary for the modern undertaker to provide a chapel or "rest room" where mourners may spend time in a final and personal farewell with their loved ones. Although illegal in the United States, in some funeral establishments in Britain the question of embalming does not arise in the arrangements interview because the company automatically embalms every body in its care. In these cases, if the bereaved did not wish the deceased to be embalmed, they would have to actively and forcefully request the mortician to desist from the practice. It is unlikely, however, that relatives would be sufficiently sure or firm about the issue. Furthermore, in many areas—and this is truer of North America than of Britain—the public are often under the impression that embalming is a legal requirement. In businesses where the bereaved are given a choice, it is during the arrangements interview that they are asked to state a preference for embalming and viewing the body.

TO VIEW OR NOT TO VIEW?

Class Factors

It is difficult to draw firm conclusions about the connection between social class and funeral preferences. In a reversal of the Victorian trend for extravagance among the wealthy, the more affluent classes and those of professional standing now tend toward less obtrusive rituals with minimum ceremony. In the funerals I attended in the course of this research it was the middle classes who generally avoided viewing, seeking instead to reduce their suffering by resolving the funeral ritual as quickly as possible. Some were of the opinion that viewing was ghoulish and perverse rather than therapeutic. On one occasion in particular when an aunt's funeral was being arranged by three young middle-class women domiciled in Oxford, they told Adrian Stone that they had no wish to view the body. They also requested that he refuse access to anyone else who wished to view.

> There's only neighbors who would want to come along to view and then it would be from morbid curiosity rather than anything else.

The Funeral Director's Professionalism

In the East End of London, as in many parts of North America, viewing is popular and is encouraged by the undertaker. Indeed, it is often cited as a form of grief therapy [25, 26]. Those close to the deceased are assisted in accepting the fact of death in so far as they are able to "pay their last respects" and to say farewell.

> Whether or not the bereaved person chooses to view the corpse is a very personal decision, and depends too on the circumstances of the death. . . . Generally, it helps survivors to accept the finality of death to see the body. Exceptions to this would be cases where the deceased did not die a natural death, and viewing the corpse would be harrowing for the bereaved. In such cases it is better to live with the memory of the deceased as he or she had been when alive [26, p. 241].

If the body is not to be displayed, the funeral director is divested of two key professional tasks incorporated in *decontaminating* and *humanizing* the body. Consequently, although the reduction in workload can accelerate the funeral procedure, loss of these functions is injurious to funeral directors' "professionalism": their skills and, arguably, their *raison d'être* are denied. Rather than providing an expert professional service which after removing the body cleanses, purifies and, through reconstructive work restores a semblance of "human dignity," undertakers are reduced to something akin to an agent of human disposal, merely collecting, packaging, and finally transporting the remains to the cemetery.

The long-term interests of professionalism are served if families agree to view, as funeral directors and embalmers are then able to demonstrate their skills in "resurrection" work. The purpose is to restore a measure of "human dignity" to the lifeless cadaver and in so doing to negate the power of the corpse as a signifier of death and contamination. The method is embalming and presentation which transform the dead into peaceful sleepers. Success is to some extent dependent on the choices made by the bereaved. A desire to view but not to embalm limits the tools of reconstruction to soap, water, brush and razor, clothing, and simple presentation skills. The skin of the deceased will retain a deathly pallor and lack elasticity, most noticeably in the folds of the face and hands.

During the arrangements interview, the questions of viewing and embalming are inextricably linked as the funeral director is unlikely to embalm if the body will not be seen. Stone estimated that nine out of every ten bodies to be viewed were also embalmed.

> Presentation is part of the job 'cos you have to pick up a sow's ear and make a silk purse. If we can plug him in—which is what it is, let's face it, basically raising an artery and just plugging into it—then he would look much, much better and much more pleasing.

If viewing is left until a few days after death, or if the person died violently, the sight of the corpse may disturb visitors. In such cases undertakers strongly advise "preservative" or "restorative treatment," in other words, embalming.

> I say, "Well, if you're seeing mum, maybe at the end of the week, would you like us to have the embalmer come in to present her at her best?" It does present people in a much better light and it's certainly a better coloring. It takes away any smell, which isn't too terribly important because a body that hasn't been moved for some

time doesn't smell anyway until it's been there for two or three days.

Some people think it's a good idea straight away, some people want to know a bit more and you either sell one or you don't. However, if I think they need it anyway I'll probably go on and do it—without charging—if they had no particular objections. It depends on the amount of time they're going to be in the chapel; what they looked like when they came in; whether they need a damned good clean up. Some people don't like the idea because if they've been in hospital they've been cut around so much they don't want them cut about any more.

There are clients who feel that embalming is otiose and undesirable. Customers who have not already considered having their relative embalmed, however, often come to accept the value of this service with little persuasion. The overriding reason may be that the majority do not understand the ramifications of their choice. Moreover, if it is presented to them in the language of preservation and hygiene (an approach recommended by funeral directors' associations) they are unlikely to dissent. The fact that few request an explanation is evidence that they have no desire to share in the knowledge of the deathworker. Their shyness is a form of self protection similar to that displayed in their unwillingness to enter the backstage regions of the funeral parlor.

Chapter 1 examined the way in which undertakers adopted embalming as a means of professionalizing their industry. Despite this, or perhaps as a consequence of it, modern funeral directors appear to be sincere in their belief that embalming is a means of protecting the bereaved and of extending the viewing service in order to mitigate the long-term trauma of grief.

When the body is to lie at the funeral director's private chapel, there are good reasons to justify the funeral director who encourages the family to visit his premises to view the remains. A well-embalmed body presented in a natural sleeping posture can be a more comforting memory than the last impression of their loved one affected by illness. . . .

No one should be afraid to visit a funeral director's premises to take a farewell look and pay their respects to a deceased relative. Yet in fact many people are fearful and much has been written about this psychological problem. Even so, the very natural desire to look for the last time at the deceased leads them to overcome their fear and visit with other members of the family [4, pp. 20, 63].

As discussed earlier, much bereavement literature maintains that viewing the body can have a cathartic effect. In bereavement, however, people do not expect to be shocked by the sight of the corpse. "They don't come here to see a video nasty," Adrian insisted, and so they require the services of an embalmer. The effect of this work (detailed in the next chapter) is to soften the harshness of death by presenting the mourners with a scene which is unreal, yet palatable. In offering embalming and reconstruction work, deathworkers, while pursuing their own financial and professional interests, stimulate a tacit demand for public protection from the brutality of death. It can be argued that they play a catalytic part, not simply in accommodating, but moreover, in moulding death taboos.

REPATRIATION AND EXHUMATION

In addition to the standard funeral service, undertakers can arrange for repatriation to another country and trade manuals list a formidable array of tasks which are the responsibility of the funeral company once they have agreed to accept instructions. These range from providing a certificate of embalming to ensuring that the relatives have procured a passport for the corpse if it is to travel to its destination via a third country.

On rare occasions undertakers are asked to secure an exhumation.[16] Procuring exhumation requires expertise and inside knowledge. Without the assistance of a deathworker, the uninitiated may flounder. Adrian Stone recalled an occasion when,

> . . . a solicitor who I happened to speak to had been trying to arrange an exhumation for some time. And of course, I made a few 'phone calls and because I knew exactly what to do it was on its way within two or three days.

> Obviously, if you read all the medical journals you wouldn't need a doctor but it's much better to send him to school for seven years and ask him to do it. Well it's the same with us.

---

[16]Exhumation is usually requested for one of the following reasons: to determine the identity of a body, to obtain papers buried in the coffin, to facilitate the widening of adjoining roads, to remove human remains from a Parish churchyard for reasons of public health.

PUBLIC DISPLAY

Final questions in the interview schedule are devoted to methods of disseminating news of the death and funeral and to the acquisition of floral tributes. Funeral companies will offer to contact the local press to organize a notice stating the time and place of the funeral. Indeed, several local newspapers refuse to accept notices from the bereaved as this leaves them vulnerable to the possibility of hoaxes.

The question of flowers is not simply an area where undertakers may offer aesthetic advice, it is also a means by which they can gauge the quantity of tributes likely to be received and so make provision for their transportation and display in the hearse and following vehicles.

At this stage the dialogue is almost at an end and by now the major decisions have been taken and the arrangers will shortly be released, having suffered and survived what is likely to be the final interview before the funeral. Stone was supremely confident that his customers appreciated being able to leave all the arrangements to him.

> They come to me for a job and they expect me to do my job. They're very relieved that this is generally the last place they come to and you then take everything away from them apart, maybe, from a little trot down to the florists.

THE END GAME

Before leaving the funeral premises, clients are usually presented with a card stating the details of their requirements for coffin, burial or cremation, vehicle hire, date, time, and place of the funeral. Items are priced,[17] the cost of disbursements noted and an estimate of the total given to the arranger. The price of funerals generates controversy in popular discussions of the industry. As indicated earlier, funeral directors are aware of the criticism they receive about the high charges of the funeral and are conscious that the bereaved should not overspend. The report of the Office of Population Censuses and Surveys [2] which formed the basis for the 1989 Office of Fair Trading (OFT) publication on *Funerals,* focused on the cost of funerals in Britain and highlighted the dissatisfaction of a substantial proportion of bereaved people whom they interviewed. Some, for example, thought that specific items or services were over priced:

---

[17]The funeral director's services are included in the price of the coffin and of the cars—the breakdown therefore, being invisible. Some companies include the cost of embalming under the heading of services. Stone's charged separately for this item which in 1988 they priced at £30.

Well, I thought the coffin was awfully expensive for a cremation. There were a lot of fittings on it that I felt a bit excessive.

I felt that I paid four times more for a following car than I would for a taxi.

I think it's very expensive for cremation where it's just a plain coffin needed.

A cold bare room and a bare coffin—I felt for this service it was over-priced.

I couldn't see why the clergy had to be paid that much for a five minute service—plus £100 for opening a grave we already had; it was ridiculous [2, pp. 43-44].

Others simply believed that the costs in general were exorbitant or that the bill should be clearly itemized.

In comparison with the cost of things in general I felt it could have been lower.

I think it's an awful lot of money just to bury someone, and you have to be buried.

I just think they take you for a ride. I am very sorry for people who just haven't the money.

I feel that we could have been shown a price list for the coffins or a brochure with the prices underneath each one, rather than just pictures and no prices [2, pp. 44, 46].

In view of this type of criticism the OFT report recommended that funeral directors should,

. . . allow all those who come into immediate contact with the recently bereaved, such as doctors, hospitals, and registrars, to hold a supply of their price lists. It follows from this that the Office (OFT) hopes that doctors, hospitals, and registrars will cooperate by making the information available, if they do not already do so. . . .

The Office also recommends that funeral directors themselves should make their price lists available to those with no immediate need of their services, if they do not already do so. They should also prominently display a price list. The NAFD should amend its code of practice to make this a requirement for its members. Funeral directors should also consider including some price information (for example, the cost of the basic simple funeral) in their advertisements in Yellow Pages, local newspapers and so on.

The Office therefore recommends that the code should require funeral directors' accounts to specify individually the charges at least for the following: the coffin (including its fittings), the hearse, following cars, care and removal of the body (including embalming if the client requires it), and attending to necessary arrangements [27, pp. 29-30].

Moreover, the OFT was eager to ensure that the funeral industry should offer a package of goods and services which, when combined, supply a "basic, simple funeral" to all those who require it.

The Price Commission found that "a recurring motif was the desire for simple funerals." It was to satisfy this desire that it recommended that funeral directors should provide a basic funeral, and the specification in the NAFD's code of practice follows closely the Price Commission's list of what such a funeral should include.

. . . In summary it comprises:

a coffin fitted and lined as is customary locally; conveyance of the deceased or delivery of a coffin; care of the deceased (which may include embalming) and use of the rest room; provision of a hearse and following car and necessary conductor and bearers; and attending to all necessary arrangements.

The Office has no doubt that a demand for the basic simple funeral still exists; three-quarters of the arrangers surveyed said that they had wanted one [27, pp. 30-31].

When arranging a funeral, although the NAFD code of practice and the OFT Report [27] both suggest that undertakers provide an itemized price list, in effect, apart from disbursements[18] the only items which appear on the bill relate to the price of the coffin, vehicles, and occasionally, embalming. If the latter is automatically carried out then that too will be included in the cost of the undertaker's services and will not appear as a separate charge.

---

[18]This includes money paid to outside agencies for services rendered by the funeral director on behalf of the family, for example, doctors' and priests' fee(s), cemetery/crematorium charges, gratuities.

THE TAILOR-MADE FUNERAL

For funeral directors, anxious though they may be to comply with the OFT guidelines, the "basic, simple funeral" undermines all their efforts to present the service and funeral as one which is unique to the individual and "tailor-made" to meet their requirements. Stone explained how this works.

> I get as much information as I can. Then you get people interested by asking the right questions—questions that they can answer—and you're talking about, "Where are you from? Where has the person died?" You can't do a burial the other side of Reading for the same price as you can in Forest Avenue. Once you've explained that there is a local cemetery which provides a public grave service so there's no need to go to the expense of a private grave there's a difference of £300.

> And so you're projecting the idea that you're tailor-making the funeral to their requirements and then you can give them a list of charges and how much that will cost in all. Roughly that's about £509.70 for a burial! And that's about the cheapest that we can do but that's providing every service that they require.

In reality, the arranger, whether she/he chooses a "basic package" or a more elaborate "custom-made" funeral, is bound by the strict limits set and reflected by undertakers and by local and ethnic customs and rituals. As "expert advisors," funeral directors suggest guidelines which the bereaved—deferential to the professional—are likely to accept. Any attempt to step outside of acceptable boundaries will result in the undertaker expressing reservations—or if the bereaved's request threatens the industry—an even strong condemnation may be elicited. Undertakers' attitudes to handling jewelry illustrates this point.

> I feel quite strongly about this sort of thing—jewelry being buried or cremated. And I will tell people straight. "I don't approve of it." If they can convince me that it was the old mum or dad's wish then fine. But they're going to have a bit of a time doing it. Because funnily enough when you get to jewelry you always hear the story that, three weeks later in the paper, there's a man from a crematorium seen selling a bit of gold here and there. It has happened. Like the one: "Do you actually burn the box?" "Well, yes we do!" Then they say, "Ah they don't always." I think it was actually proved back in 1921 that somebody didn't burn the box and nobody's ever forgotten it!

Finally, services offered to arrangers are bound up with the notions of "dignity and respect" which undertakers are reluctant to define, yet keen to encourage. Any requests made by the next of kin should also comply with the ethos of these precepts. After all, deathworkers, quite apart from their own perceived role as public servants, are salespeople and the quality and appearance of their product will serve to enhance or detract from their business. As one funeral director told me, "When you're out there you're very much aware that you're your own best advert."

Their objection to the basic simple funeral is not wholly due to its cost-cutting nature, but also that the basic package suggests "off-the-peg" rather than "tailor-made." To extend the clothing analogy, the sale of production line goods is less prestigious than unique designer items. The former are manufactured in bulk and require little in terms of human input, imagination, skill, and time. They do not require the labor of a professional or skilled operative. Funeral directors fervently aspire to professional status and in consequence are eager to be seen to provide a distinctive and quality service for each funeral.

The arrangements interview provides funeral directors with all the information they require to authorize them to prepare the body, organize, and execute the funeral. In presenting a professional front and structuring the interview in a manner which places them firmly in control, they set the agenda for the discourse and accelerate the process. Their aura of professionalism instills confidence in the bereaved that the body will be appropriately cared for and that it is safe to leave all arrangements in their hands. The plans for the "tailor-made" funeral which the undertaker and next of kin together design, empower the deathworker to begin work on humanizing the body—the focus of the next chapter.

REFERENCES

1. I. Illich, *Disabling Professions,* Marion Boyars, London, 1977.
2. OPCS, *A Survey of Funeral Arrangements 1987: The Report of a Survey carried out by Social Survey Division on behalf of the Office of Fair Trading,* K. Foster, Office of Population Censuses and Surveys, Social Survey Division, HMSO, London, 1989.
3. E. Goffman, *The Presentation of Self in Everyday Life,* Doubleday, New York, 1959.
4. National Association of Funeral Directors, *Manual of Funeral Directing,* National Association of Funeral Directors, London, 1988.

5. K. Burke, *A Grammar of Motives,* Prentice Hall, New York, 1945.
6. M. Cain, The General Practice Lawyer and the Client: Towards a Radical Conception, in *The Sociology of the Professions: Lawyers, Doctors, and Others,* R. Dingwall and P. Lewis (eds.), Macmillan, London, 1983.
7. T. Parsons, *The Social System,* Routledge & Kegan Paul, London, 1951.
8. E. Goffman, *Forms of Talk,* Basil Blackwell, Oxford, 1981.
9. A. Peräkylä and D. Silverman, Reinterpreting Speech-exchange Systems: Communication Formats in Aids Counselling, *Sociology, 25*:4, pp. 627-651, 1991.
10. T. J. Johnson, *Professions and Power,* Macmillan, London, 1972.
11. H. Sacks, E. A. Schegloff, and G. Jefferson, A Simplest Systematics of Turn-taking for Conversation, *Language, 50,* pp. 696-735, 1974.
12. J. Heritage and D. Greatbatch, On the Institutional Character of Institutional Talk: The Case of News Interviews, in *Discourse in Professional and Everyday Culture,* P. A. Forstorp (ed.), University of Linkoping, Studies in Communications, SIC 28, 1989.
13. W. F. Whyte, *Learning from the Field: A Guide from Experience,* Sage, Beverly Hills, 1984.
14. G. Mungham and P. A. Thomas, Solicitors and Clients: Altruism or Self-interest, in *The Sociology of the Professions: Lawyers, Doctors and Others,* R. Dingwall and P. Lewis (eds.), Macmillan, London, 1983.
15. T. Walter, Dust not Ashes, The American Preference for Burial, *Landscape, 32*:1, pp. 42-49, 1993.
16. R. W. Habenstein, *The American Funeral Director and the Sociology of Work,* unpublished Ph.D. thesis, University of Chicago, Chicago, 1954.
17. J. Spottiswood, quoted from BBC Radio 4, *Punters,* November 12, 1987.
18. *The Sunday Observer,* April 14, 1991.
19. W. S. F. Pickering, The Persistence of Rites of Passage: Towards an Explanation, *British Journal of Sociology, 25*:1, pp. 63-78, 1974.
20. M. Page, Grave Misgivings, *Religion Today, 2*:3, 1985.
21. T. Walter, *Funerals and How to Improve Them,* Hodder & Stoughton, London, 1990.
22. L. Pincus, *Death and the Family: The Importance of Mourning,* Faber and Faber, London, 1976.
23. S. Henry (ed.), *Can I Have it in Cash? A Study of Informal Institutions and Unorthodox Ways of Doing Things,* Astragal Books, London, 1981.
24. A. Synnot, Tomb, Temple, Machine and Self: The Social Construction of the Body, *British Journal of Sociology, 43*:1, pp. 79-110, March 1992.
25. J. Hinton, *Dying* (2nd Edition), Penguin, Harmondsworth, 1972.
26. W. Stroebe and M. S. Stroebe, *Bereavement and Health, The Psychological and Physical Consequences of Partner Loss,* Cambridge University Press, Cambridge, 1987.
27. Office of Fair Trading, *Funerals: A Report,* HMSO, London, January 1989.

CHAPTER 7

Humanizing the Body

Death without corruption removes the mortal half and gets as close
as possible to creating an Immortal who belongs in this world (as
opposed to the gods who really belong elsewhere) [1, p. 228].

In applying the term "humanization" I refer to the techniques
employed by embalmers who aim to restore "human-like" qualities to
the deceased. When the funeral director assumes custody of the corpse
it is contaminated in the sense that it is a receptacle for disease and a
symbol of mortality. If the bereaved wish to view the body and they
have no objection to it being embalmed, morticians use this technique
to attempt to revitalize characteristics of the corpse which they consider will enhance human-likeness, for example, facial color and elasticity of skin. The objective is to supply, not merely a representation,
but the physical presence of the individual. The desire to see the person
once more, "as s/he was in life" can then be fulfilled. This aspiration
celebrates individuality and in so doing hints at a form of immortality.
It is not a physical immortality, nor in increasing secular societies is it
spiritual, rather it is psychological, in the nature of "living on" in the
minds of survivors.

This chapter examines the humanization techniques employed by
the funeral company and considers their implications for both the
undertaker and the client. The utilization of theatrical strategies is
unavoidable if morticians are to breathe "life" into their subjects. They
begin the process by laying out and embalming the body. In this they
imitate the role of the medics, donning gown and gloves, not only for
protection and health, but also to add credence to the character. Having
restored color and elasticity to the skin of the corpse, the worker
becomes make-up artist and uses cosmetics to reform or highlight
facial features. Meanwhile funeral assistants are busy with coffin and
costumes preparing a fiction of sleep in which the departed will be the

central character, lying robed, often in nightclothes, in the cushioned coffin.

Pursuing the theatrical analogy further, the dramatic performance of the funeral ritual requires props, costumes, and make-up. The extent to which each participant dresses or rehearses for their role in the obsequies depends on the prominence of the character they are to play and the frequency with which the part is performed. For the death-workers who almost daily rehearse the funeral routine in costume replete with supporting characters and props, the unique task of each funeral is the preparation of the corpse. In life each person is distinctive. It is the duty of the mortician to ensure that in death the deceased retains, or rather, recovers this individuality.

CARING FOR THE BODY

The treatment which the body experiences in the hands of the funeral director can best be explained by reference to the notion of "care," discussed earlier. The majority of undertakers normally reserve "humanization" for those bodies that are to be viewed. It is horrifying for the bereaved to witness or even to contemplate putrefication. The humanization procedure is therefore administered because it is deemed beneficial for the bereaved. The family, as observed in Chapter 4, are keen to "do their best" for the deceased and this commonly entails purchasing goods and services which ensure "comfort" for their relative and enhance the impression of well-being when publicly displayed. In the funerals observed in Easton it was predominantly the "respectable" working class who chose to view the remains. That they subsequently selected embalming and thus received the complete package of humanization is entirely in keeping with a popular endeavor to be "clean and tidy" and to "keep up appearances." Employing the funeral director to present the body in its best possible light functions to rescue their loved one from the humiliation and indignity of a tarnished public appearance. The aphorism that one would not want to "be seen dead" wearing a particular item of clothing may have its roots in this desire for careful presentation of the corpse. Indeed, it is not dissimilar to the erstwhile practice of setting aside a best suit or dress for the purpose of burial. The finer the display and the more lifelike the departed appear—the closer the individual comes to immortality.

The dilemma facing the bereaved is that in the liminal phase [2] when life has been extinguished and corruption commenced, the corpse is not an individual object of desire but a source of contamination. Its profanity is demonstrated in two ways. First, it is defiling to those in close contact because it is both a physical pollutant and a symbolic reminder of the power of death. Second, the cadaver has lost the human quality of vitality. The body lacks vigor, the skin is discolored and slack, the hair limp, limbs are stiff and inactive and further deterioration is inevitable as decomposition rapidly erodes organs and tissues leaving only liquid putrescence and obnoxious odors in its wake. If the relics are to regain individuality and constitute the focus of death rites, the march of decay must be halted by temporary preservation and human features redeemed for the duration of the funeral ritual.

Employing an undertaker to deal with the arrangements for the funeral encourages the symbolic transformation of death into material goods and services. The dead body is the subject of these provisions. Deathworkers see their obligations to the living to be protection from pollution while enabling them to enjoy meaningful contact with the deceased. In order to succeed in this they must transform the defiling corpse into a life-like representation of its former self. Indeed, in contradiction to the bereavement counselor's encouragement to view the body because it will "emphasize beyond all doubt that the person is really dead" [3, p. 187], the illusion of the peacefully sleeping individual is sometimes so powerful that it may have the reverse effect. A widow who had found it especially difficult to come to terms with the death of her husband explained it in this way.

> But I still blame it onto the fact that I didn't mourn my husband properly. Well when he died he was so, he looked so, he was just asleep, that's all. Even in his coffin he didn't look dead. And he didn't. I'm not exaggerating that. Not at all.

THE "LIVING DEAD"

At the end of my first week at Stone's funeral company and after attending my second funeral, Adrian offered to allow me to view two "finished" bodies as they lay in the chapel of rest awaiting their public. He was clearly eager to demonstrate the results of his embalming work and to expound the value of this procedure. It was a late winter afternoon and the pathway to the chapel was dark. Once inside, he had to grope for the light switch. Although I felt apprehensive at the prospect of viewing the dead I was cheered by my guide's carefree attitude and unfailing sense of humor. He had a way of ridiculing common fears about death which exposed their irrational nature.

> People are always afraid when they come in here that something's going to jump out at them. But the thing that's in here is never going to jump out at anything because it's dead!

When the room was illuminated my eyes alighted on two coffins, one on either side of the entrance. Given that the chapel was small and the space at the far end taken by the altar, coffins were obliged to stand to either side. The boxes rested on trestles and, in lieu of a lid, each was draped with a purple velvet pall. In the one to my left I was immediately aware of a bump about half way along the underside of the cloth. The room was cold and unwelcoming and I felt concerned about the mysterious origins of this strange shape. The director quickly dispelled any fears beginning to take root in my imagination as he nonchalantly removed the cloth from the coffin. Underneath lay an elderly Greek man whose burial was scheduled for Christmas Eve. The bulge in the fabric had merely concealed his clasped hands clutching a golden crucifix which rested in a ridge about half way down the box.

Although struck by the tranquillity and silence of the corpse, nothing else about it was especially disturbing. The man had probably been in his sixties at the time of death. He had neatly brushed grey hair and a moustache and was clothed in a shirt and dark suit. The skin coloring appeared natural—not the grey pallor I had anticipated. Adrian Stone assured me that it was the embalming process that had given him this "fresh, natural" hue. I could see even from this cursory inspection how the undertaking trade could claim to be able to produce a "sleeping" deceased with the "human quality of dignity." By the time the body reaches the chapel it has successfully completed its journey through the funeral premises, attracting along the way the attention of the embalmer and presentation crew.

Adrian handled the body with the familiarity and dexterity of a surgeon demonstrating the results of his handiwork to a group of admiring students. He carefully unfastened the man's shirt collar and manipulated the head to reveal the embalmer's incision in the base of the neck.

> I always put something around the neck or make sure that there's a high collar. It wouldn't be nice for people to see the marks made by embalming. That's why if they are embalmed we don't let them view the body until it's been dressed and put in the coffin. It wouldn't do for them to notice the extra navel or anything like that.

Leaving the Greek uncovered to facilitate comparison he turned to the other box and pulled down the pall. Inside, lay an elderly woman in a pale gown. Her hair, although tidily arranged looked wispy and fragile. Her skin was yellow and soft and clung, precariously it seemed, to her face and hands. Her fingers, on which the skin hung languidly, were discolored and red at the tips—a sign, I later learned, that she had not been subjected to "preservative treatment."

> When somebody dies of a heart attack, the muscles and the skin, in trying to survive, take all the oxygen out of the blood. Then this redness appears which is from the veinal blood, the dark red blood. With embalming you can get rid of that.

The woman lacked the substance and latent vigor of her neighbor with whom she shared the quarter. Adrian was quick to attribute the differences in appearance to embalming, pointing out that the color and elasticity of the man's skin could easily have been reproduced in the woman. With the assistance of a little cosmetic work he was sure that she would have become far more "presentable" for the viewing relatives.

Having been shown the models of "before and after" to demonstrate the effects of embalming, I was next invited to witness the process itself. I accepted a ring-side seat and found myself early one morning in the garage workshop facing a sheet-covered corpse which lay outstretched on a wheeled trolley resembling the type used in hospital operating theaters. Unlike the two bodies I had previously observed, this one was "fresh" in that the only attention it had received since death was to be stripped of clothing, wrapped in a sheet, placed in the removal shell and transported to the premises where it had lain overnight.

ENVIRONMENT AND EQUIPMENT

Attired in the white coat of the expert, Stone prepared his equipment. Each item was neatly laid out in order of use: scalpel, clamps, tubing, container filled with formalin and complete with pump, sticking tape, needle and cord, razor and shaving foam, make-up box, and hairbrush. As shown in Chapter 4, morticians emphasize their similarity to surgeons or pathologists and so it is not surprising that aspiring professionals should adopt the trademarks of the groups they emulate. The protective clothing of the embalmer (a legal requirement in many parts of North America) resembles that worn by the surgeon. In the embalming theater, hygienic surroundings and protective clothing for the operative are paramount. Affluent or large scale companies commonly reserve a room which takes the style of the hospital operating theater and is specifically for the cleansing and preservation of the corpse.

> The chief function of the preparation room is as an embalming theatre and as such should be designed in line with the highest standards of hygiene.
>
> It should be spacious, light and well ventilated. The floor should be easily washable, for example terrazzo or tiles with coving at all wall skirtings. Walls also should be tiled or of some other washable surface.
>
> Equipment should include embalming table, . . . sink and slop-hopper, separate hand basin for embalmer's personal use, cupboards for embalmer's requirements and protective clothing [4, 18: p. 6].

In many smaller establishments which possess neither the space nor the finances to expand, embalming is carried out in less salubrious surroundings. Such was the case at G. R. Stone. The trolley on which the body lay had been positioned in the area between the parked funeral vehicles and the maintenance workbench. This space clearly fell below the NAFD guidelines for being "scrupulously clean" and "fit for inspection" [4, 18: p. 6]. In urging their members to maintain hygienic preparation rooms, professional associations are guarding the industry against scandal. They further recommend that if the bereaved were to peruse the embalming area they should not be shocked but "find everything seemly and hygienic" [4, 5: p. 5]. For this reason the mortuary (or its equivalent) is spatially separate from public areas and access effectively denied.

LOSS AND RESTORATION OF "HUMAN DIGNITY"

Stone's reconstruction operation on the corpse was executed with skill and precision and it was difficult to see how the work could have been more expertly performed in an hygienic, surgical, hospital-like environment.

A further NAFD recommendation is the admonishment to treat the body with dignity.

> When a family entrust the body of one they love to a funeral director, they charge him with what could be considered a sacred duty.
>
> In the many and varied tasks that comprise the working day of the funeral director and his staff they need continually to remind themselves of this responsibility. This may well be done if they

accept the principle that on all occasions when handling or attending to the body of the deceased they should conduct themselves as
they would if the next-of-kin were standing at their elbow, or act
as they would if the deceased were a member of their own family
[4, 5: p. 1].

In the practice that I observed and in reports by other researchers of
the funeral industry [5-7], the treatment counseled by the professional
associations is reserved for the finished product—the fully humanized
body. Adrian argued that the job of the mortician was to deal speedily
and efficiently with the preparation of the body. If this required that
the corpse be handled in private with only a minimum of delicacy then
so be it. Although the cadaver was never subjected to unnecessary
indignity, to facilitate cleaning and embalming it was sometimes
unceremoniously hauled from one place to another and turned and
rolled into uncompromising positions. This was all done in the interests
of recreating a human object and to this end the funeral director
justified a variety of operations including washing, shaving, cutting,
sewing, and even gluing, which in combination with carefully applied
make-up could produce an impression fit for the lead performer.

The corpse has value for the bereaved as they remain emotionally
attached to the body of their loved one. When preparatory work *begins,*
however, the physical body holds relatively little worth for the funeral
director. Its importance lies in its value as chattel for securing trade
and in the esteem with which it is regarded by the client. The methods
employed by deathworkers to enable them to cope with the unpleasant
tasks inherent in their trade continue to take precedence until their
labor is complete and human dignity reclaimed. As Stone remarked,

> . . . you cannot be dignified lying down in a plastic removal shell or
> a plastic stretcher. You can be neat and tidy but you can't be
> dignified. At that time people lose all their dignity. You give it them
> back when they have a nice shiny coffin and they've got people
> all stood there and properly dressed. That's O.K. They've got
> dignity then.

During the process of humanization, the corpse, in a sense, "came to
life" for the embalmer. Stone's first contact with the deceased was as a
cadaver and therefore he had no knowledge or memory of his charge in
human state. Before resurrection work began—in the preliminary,
highly contaminating period after death—the deceased was referred to
in private as "the job" or "the bod." As decontamination work
progressed through the stages of washing, shaving, brushing hair,
embalming, dressing, and presenting, the mortician, having labored on

the body, took pride in his achievement and started to acknowledge the human characteristics of his dependents. Witnessing the effect of his embalming skills in generating the illusion of life in the cold flesh and bones before him, he spoke, not of "the bod," but of "Mrs. Jones" or "Mr. Smith." His creation was then transferred from the depths of the workshop to the chapel of rest. The rhetoric and treatment were, of course, for the benefit of the bereaved but the pride with which the embalmer viewed his creation prompted him to bestow human privileges on the once debased cadaver.

STAGES IN THE HUMANIZATION PROCESS

The attention received by the cadaver was directly proportional to the bereaved's desire to view. If the body had already been laid-out and the relatives had no wish to see it again, it was dressed or placed in a shroud and sealed in the coffin. If relatives opted for viewing, the mortician embarked on the humanization process. There were seven stages in the restoration of the human body. All, or some combination of these were performed on each cadaver. They were laying-out, embalming, positioning, reconstruction work, cosmetology, clothing the body and finally, once the coffin had been prepared, presentation in the chapel of rest. Each will be discussed as I observed them in the back regions of Stone's funeral company.

My first encounter with the humanization process was with the body of a middle-aged woman. Her hair was dark but thick and wiry and showed no signs of the lifelessness which had overtaken the rest of her body. A slim torso and attractive face gave the impression that, dying in her middle years, she had managed until the end to hold on to some of the physical traits characteristic of youth. Whatever the cause of death there were no obvious signs of violence or of the type of suffering that one might expect after a long illness or sudden heart attack. Her skin was neither sagging nor yellowing and did not display areas of red patches where the blood had congealed. On the contrary her skin already had a firm appearance and retained a slightly olive tint which I assumed had been natural in life. It was difficult to see at this stage the extent to which embalming would be advantageous.

As each stage of bodily preparation commenced, Adrian Stone, in his role as embalmer, gave me prior warning of what to expect and chatted throughout about the skills and techniques required to achieve the desired results. His analysis of the process was peppered with anecdotes of previous cases—all presented as "success stories."

Laying-out: First and Last Offices

Before embalming, the body must be washed. Throughout the proceedings the woman's lower regions, from the groin downwards were covered with the sheet in which she had lain in the removal shell.[1] After a rather superficial wash with a wet flannel and soap this sheet was lifted briefly and a sanitary towel placed between the legs. The sheet was then replaced and the body ready for embalming. Being familiar with the instructions issued to hospital nurses for the laying-out procedure, I was surprised to witness the cursory nature of the undertaker's "last" or, in his case, "first" offices.

If the person has not been laid-out, it is the funeral director's responsibility to ensure that this is carried out. The funeral trade refers to this work as performing the "first offices" or "sanitary protection." Nurses, who traditionally accomplish these duties know them as "last offices." The discrepancy in terminology clearly derives from the fact that for the nurse, laying-out is the final deed on behalf of a patient. Although there is often some overlap between the duties of the nurse and those of the undertaker, the deathworker's responsibilities usually begin where the health worker's cease. Laying-out may be the first of many operations undergone by the corpse before it is released from the undertaker's custody.

Terminology apart, the mortician's version of laying-out is at variance with that of the hospital nurse. When death occurs in a hospital setting it is the job of the nurse to carry out the last offices. The body is washed in similar fashion to bed-bathing an immobile patient. Finger and toe nails are cut and cleaned. Men are shaved if appropriate. Rectum and vagina are then compacted with wool. Nostrils are also packed if there is discharge but care is taken not to alter the contours of the face and to ensure that the plugs are invisible. Feet are tied together with bandages at the ankles. Wounds are sealed and dressings renewed. The body is then placed in a shroud which is secured at the neck and wrists. Finally, the hair is brushed into the style usually worn. The corpse is laid in a clean sheet and is ready for removal to the mortuary from where it will be collected by the funeral assistants.

When undertakers perform the first offices, their emphasis is on the washing and positioning of the body. Orifices are not plugged but an absorbent cotton wool pad is placed between the legs. After cleansing

---

[1] Undertakers customarily place a cloth over the genitals of male and female bodies and this is known as the "modesty cloth." Its use appears to be associated with the notion of granting dignity to the deceased.

and shaving, care is taken to fix the body in a dignified posture. This may entail tying the feet and arms and introducing a chin rest to discourage the jaw from sagging. The NAFD manual is particularly mindful to stress that a number of practices—undoubtedly common among female layers-out in the nineteenth century—are to be strictly outlawed. These include tying the big toes together, securing arms and hands beneath the buttocks, and placing pennies over the eyes. These techniques are regarded as undignified and unsuitable for the modern "professional" funeral director.

Adrian Stone told that in his experience, hospital bodies had not always been laid-out.

> They're not I'm afraid and I really don't think many nurses today would actually know what to do. They're wrapped up clean and tidy. That's as good as I would like to ask for really. You may have weeping wounds and all sorts of things like that and they're all tied off. They don't do badly I must admit. Bearing in mind they've probably got another ten people on the ward who'll want their services immediately. . . . You really can't make them wrong.

That hospital laying-out falls short of the previously accepted standard does not coincide with the claims of the nurses.[2] Until evidence is available which sheds light on the extent to which bodies are laid-out before leaving the hospital, there is no way of ascertaining the validity of either claim. What is clear is that both groups have a vested interest in retaining authority over these essential functions. Nurses are trained to lay-out the body and it has traditionally been their duty to care for the final requirements of those in their charge. Relinquishing this task to the funeral director detracts from their vocation and, moreover, an accusation of failing to perform this final service may be interpreted as a slight on their professionalism.

Adrian Stone reported a "genuine sympathy for the plight of the nurses" whom he perceived as overworked and justifiably "more concerned with doing what they can for the living rather than worrying over the dead." Other funeral directors with whom I spoke informed me that collecting a body which had not been laid-out was unproblematic. Furthermore, they believed that as custodian of the body, the task was legitimately their responsibility. When, earlier this century, the midwife and neighborhood layer-out were banished from the undertaking trade, the hospital nurse was to become the only agent to retain control over an essential aspect of the treatment of the corpse. In this,

---

[2] I am grateful to Nicky James for bringing this to my attention.

nurses may pose a threat to the funeral industry; bereaved families may have lost the skill or inclination to lay-out their dead, but if the nurse is still able to perform the job then the laying-out services of the undertaker need not be patronized.

"Preservative Treatment" or Embalming

Watching Adrian Stone advance toward the corpse wielding a length of tubing with a sharp metal attachment on one end, I questioned my ability to remain to the finish. In this, my experience resembled that of medical students observing their first dissection or *post-mortem* examination [8-11]. My senses recoiled as he unflinchingly thrust the metal into the lower abdomen, twisting and turning the rod until the body fluids began to flow through the tubing and into the drain beside the trolley. The next step was to replenish the emptying blood vessels with the preserving chemical, formalin.

To do this he made a small incision at the base of the neck in search of the carotid artery. Once located, he coaxed it into life by plugging in the nozzle of the container holding the embalming fluid and activating the pump. When the speed at which the body ejected its natural fluids reduced, the vigorous pumping on which Adrian was engaged increased the rate of exit. At regular intervals he arrested the action to monitor the effect on the body. Gently slapping and massaging the fingers and lower extremities of the limbs assisted the movement of blood and chemical around the body, not only changing the color of the skin but also endowing it with the artificial elasticity and hence the "life-like" qualities which are the hallmark of the preserving process.

In some funeral establishments embalming is an automatic procedure which is only omitted by the specific veto of the bereaved. In others, as at G. R. Stone, the arranger is asked to decide. Embalming is the morticians' most powerful weapon as, in the interests of humanization, they battle against the corruption of the body. This practice, with its promise of "restoring a life-like appearance" in the corpse, is said to afford both psychological and physical protection to undertakers and their clients as it temporarily preserves the human tissue. Rationalization for the use of embalming is three-fold.

The first and second objectives issue from the public health discourse of the nineteenth century. Both are concerned with the potential dangers which the decaying body holds for the public.

> . . . the treatment prevents nuisance from purging and leaking fluids, and overcomes any risk of obnoxious smells [4, 5: p. 7].

Furthermore, the industry claims that,

> . . . (s)ince the treatment destroys all pathogenic bacteria, there is
> little danger of infection or contagion from an embalmed body [4, 5:
> p. 7].

Having been subjected to the venom of the nineteenth-century reform
movements and compelled to reappraise their practice, funeral directors have appropriated the discourse of the early reformers, expound-
ing the doctrine of hygiene, sanitation, and protection as their own.
Nowhere is this more clearly demonstrated than in their justification
for custody and treatment of the body.

The third explanation for the practice of embalming is that, while
physically protecting the bereaved from the ravages of death pollution,
it enables them to view their dead *as though they were alive.*

> This is perhaps the most valuable aspect of the treatment. The
> change effected is truly remarkable—gone is the deathly pallor and
> the discoloration of the lower features. Instead the family sees a
> life-like presentation of their loved one appearing as though peace-
> fully sleeping. This result is a source of great comfort and has a
> decided psychological value [4, 5: p. 7].

That the profession is able to claim psychological merit for the
process, stems from the popular conviction among psychologists that
viewing the body is beneficial to the bereaved. This defense is repeated
by funeral directors throughout Britain and North America. A report in
The Independent newspaper echoed these sentiments.

> What we do is for the living, so they have a positive picture of their
> loved ones. . . . Once they see they're all right, so to speak, then the
> process of grieving can begin [12].

Positioning the Body

In cases where there had been no physical damage and no repair
was required, initial phases of body preparation took roughly fifteen
minutes, with a further ten minutes to remove equipment and seal,
each with a small stitch, the wounds in the abdomen and neck.
Throughout the operation the woman's head lay propped on an iron
"head rest" resembling a cobbler's last. The effect—apart from giving
the impression of discomfort—was to lift the head sufficiently to force
the chin to rest lightly on the upper chest. When the iron was removed
the lower jaw was released and the lips of the corpse parted as the

mouth fell open. Now began the stage in which the mortician controlled the "undignified" demeanor of the flesh. To close the unsightly gaping mouth, Adrian Stone resorted to surgeon's needle and thread. Holding them firmly together he deftly connected the upper and lower lips. In the style of accounting which I have referred to as "professionalizing," he commented as he worked that, "surgeons do this sort of thing everyday. At least my patients never feel it!" The result of this minor operation was a rather tight-lipped appearance which the director promptly mellowed by gently massaging the skin around the mouth.

A variety of similarly secreted supports served to embellish the human form. The tying together of feet enhances the "natural" poise of the deceased. Packing cotton wool beneath the eyelids avoids a sunken appearance. The manual of funeral directing advises on matters of positioning.

> There is no need for the nose to be meticulously centred and point-ing to the ceiling. The setting of the mouth is more than simply propping up the chin. The dentures must be properly seated and the lips smoothed into a natural relaxed position. The eyes need expert attention too, a wafer of cotton wool spread gently over the eyeball will serve to support the eyelid when the substance of the eyeball shrinks as it inevitably does after death. The lids should be set in natural sleep. . . .

> The hands themselves need careful attention. How often one sees them left with the fingers stiff and straight! The fingers should be bent to a natural pose; this may need a little pressure on the wrist and knuckles, but a little patience will bring the right result and make a wonderful difference [4, 5: p. 6].

Reconstruction Work or Damage Limitation

There are frequent occasions when more extensive repairs are demanded. Funeral directors believe that although their clients are blissfully ignorant of the intricacies of preparing a cadaver, they are aware that the result is artificial. Customers are perceived as desiring the effect because it removes the physical damage imposed by death. In cases of considerable disfigurement, where even the bereavement experts advise the bereaved not to view, the mortician can restore the deceased to a former dignity. Embalmers are proud, and relatives usually grateful, of their accomplishments. On one occasion Adrian had worked for many hours on the face of a woman who, prior to death, had been in an accident with a lorry. Her injuries had not originally been diagnosed as fatal and in the hospital she had received stitching to a deep wound which ran from the hairline to the nose. Her family, visiting her immediately before death could not fail to notice the hideous scar. When she arrived in Stone's workshop the director resolved to restore her to her former state.

> After she was embalmed and the skin had dried a bit I stuck the skin together with superglue and then removed the stitches. I carefully shaved off the surplus glue and filled in the cracks. I spent a couple of hours blending in the color and putting back the lines and the pores. And the granddaughter came and said, "That's not my grandmother she's got stitches all down her face." The daughter said, "Yes of course it is."—She was over the moon!

The extent to which reconstruction work is required depends on the appearance of the deceased. Extensive physical damage requires potentially lengthy and intricate work whereas death from "natural" causes may necessitate only revitalizing cosmetics. If the deceased met a violent death, the funeral director may be asked, or may offer, to attempt a "full reconstruction." Stone proudly related the tale of a case where the parents of a suicide victim had requested him to use his skills to repair the outward signs of damage.

> A young black girl had climbed out of a first floor window and landed on her face. When I asked the relatives about viewing they said, "We'd like to, but we saw her in the hospital and oooh!" And so I just said, "Well leave it to me."

> I built up the damaged side of her face—spent a day on it. But when I charged them for it I charged what I would for somebody I'd spent an hour on. But that one job, time taken completely out of it, I probably lost money. I think I started at ten o'clock one morning and finished at seven o'clock at night. Not bad for £32!

> But the woman was over the moon. She always says to me, "You made her look beautiful." They knew it was artificial but it took away the damage and made her complete again.

Cosmetology

In a theatrical environment, make-up techniques can wholly transform the face of the subject. In the case of the young black woman her countenance was reconstructed with wax filler and cosmetics. For the majority of cases—elderly people dying of "natural" causes—the mortician simply relies on cosmetics to add color and vivacity to the face of the deceased. In Britain the application of cosmetics is rather conservative and morticians use a standard mixture of tints and colors in their pallet. This custom contrasts with the practice of funeral directors in North America where it is not unusual for women who are close to death to be anxious that a friend or relative is able to locate their make-up kit for *post-mortem* presentation. For example, a colleague from the United States reported the words of her aging aunt in declaring that, after death she would ". . . just hate to be seen wearing the wrong shade of lipstick!" In England, perhaps largely due to public unwillingness to acknowledge and discuss the minutia of after-death procedures, the choice of style and shade is left to the cosmetician. Morticians try hard to achieve a pleasing and accurate result, but as they can only guess at the shades favored by the deceased, they are not always successful.

> I try not to go the American way and go over the top. Every now and then you get it all wrong—wrong color make-up. You can usually tell whether somebody wore make-up or not. You can usually tell how people looked but sometimes the relatives let you know that you've got it terribly, terribly, wrong.[3]

If restoration work is likely to necessitate substantial cosmetology, morticians may request a photograph of the deceased to assist them in their quest for accuracy and perfection. One such case was reported by a listener to a radio "chat show." Her mother-in-law had been washed-down in the local mortuary and consequently suffered terrible physical distortion. The caller telephoned the radio to report her absolute delight with the cosmetic skills displayed by her local funeral company.

> I know my mother-in-law was treated well by the undertaker. . . . She died of a heart attack and went to a mortuary and they hosed her down—which I didn't realise they did. Then they took her to the chapel of rest and she didn't look like my mother-in-law. . . . Her hair was flat, everything. And the undertaker was a great guy. I said, "You know, can you do something?" He said, "Well we don't know what she looks like in life. You bring us a picture, we'll get somebody in to do it."
>
> I gave him a picture and he actually got somebody in and made her better than the mortuary left her [13].

---

[3] One can only guess at the number of relatives who *do not* advise when the funeral director gets it wrong.

A photograph, however, is rarely necessary. In the final analysis, accuracy and the replication of the living individual is only secondary to the dramatic effect. The mortician interprets the bereaved as desiring an undamaged, serene and life-like body and it is this perception that dictates mortuary practice. The viewers do not primarily come to see the body as it was in life but rather to witness its transformation from cold permanent death to a less threatening state of slumber which, while hinting at immortality, lauds individuality.

The Finishing Touches

Once the central character has been washed, "plugged," embalmed, shaved, made-up and had hair brushed and neatly arranged, she/he is clothed and presented in the coffin for private viewing and for the public ceremony of the funeral. The two features which supply the finishing touches to the embalmer's work are dressing and coffin assembly. Both tasks are the responsibility of funeral assistants. "Making a box" (assembling a coffin) is time consuming but requires little thought or skill and always conforms to a routine model. In contrast, "dressing a person" is regarded by workers as a rather tricky job demanding practice and forethought.

Clothing the Body: Pyjamas and Designer Sets

The costume worn by the deceased in the coffin or casket is chosen by the relatives. In Easton there were still people who had reserved an item of clothing, or had one made specially for this purpose. It was not unusual for relatives to request that the body was dressed in a favorite garment or in nightwear belonging to the deceased. An alternative was for the arranger to select a burial gown or shroud from the undertaker's catalog. These fabrics are designed to blend with coffin linings and are color-coordinated so that the final impact is designer matched. The long gowns, which are open at the back to facilitate dressing, are made of pastel-tinted satin and each is supplied with a matching "pillow case" and face cloth. The latter is intended to veil the face when not in view. In practice this tulle is seldom used because it detracts from the impression of sleep.

> The customary final touch is to place a face-cover over the features. The reason for this is most difficult to understand . . . it is probably better to leave the face uncovered as would be the case with anyone resting in bed in life. This again follows the principle of letting the presentation be as natural as possible [4, 5: p. 9].

Allowing the bereaved to select clothing overcomes the possibility of attiring the body in a gown or color which may be regarded as offensive. A large percentage of customers do prefer the corpse to be dressed in everyday clothes and this may be because it amplifies the memory and individuality of the deceased in life.

> We took his favorite shirt and trousers to the funeral director and he used those. It's what he would have chosen himself. It was much more *him* than one of those apricot colored nightshirts we were shown.

Furthermore, if pyjamas or nightdress were selected this had the effect of making the person appear normal but with an added bonus in that it gave perfect expression and excuse for the subject's unresponsive or "slumbering" state.

Dressing a Body

Although the use of specially designed shrouds simplifies the operation, the act of clothing the corpse remains an exacting task. Peter explained.

> If a person brings in clothes you was taught to dress the body—which is a bit awkward until you really know how to do it. Basically, if you see someone who's been doing it all the time you think it's entirely easy. But if you don't know how to do it and someone said to you, "Dress that person," you would have a job. . . .
>
> If someone had said to me, "Here's a person, dress it," I'd have got in a bit of a state. Obviously, if they're dead you would start lifting the person up. You'd start lifting them from the back, which basically, you'll never do it. But if you see a person do it it's like any job—the more you do it, the better you get at it. There is a certain way to do all sorts of things in the funeral trade. Don't matter what it is, from the word go to the word finish, there's a certain way and if you do it properly it should be alright.

Adrian Stone, who was an expert dresser, explained that struggling with a shirt or jacket was far more difficult than putting on trousers. The latter, however, also had its problems.

> This is achieved by reaching over the body and rolling the hips toward you with one hand while pulling trousers up with the other hand, then walking round the other side of the body and repeating the process until the waistband is up to the waist.

The easiest way to dress the arms of the corpse was to use a gown manufactured for the purpose. Stone's were regularly asked to fit shrouds which had been made to order by a local seamstress. These were described as being, "the easiest things to fit and always looked the best."

My first experience of dressing a body was for a woman whose relatives had supplied what appeared to be a set of white "bridal" garments. Assisting Adrian I admired the dexterity with which (despite hindrance from myself) he maneuvered the woman and installed her in the white dress, jacket, and shoes with apparently little effort. He then produced a minute pair of white net gloves. I recalled wearing a similar pair when, as a child I attended a Confirmation ceremony at church. I remembered how difficult it had been to coax my fingers, one by one, into the correct shafts instead of continually through the holes in the net! The director and I each took a shrunken glove and spent what seemed to be an age, painstakingly adding this final touch to the woman with the cold and clammy hands who was being prepared for her final religious rite of passage.

Stone went on to explain that families often provided an item of clothing either wholly unsuitable in style or simply ill-fitting. The dresser was then forced to adopt various techniques to ensure that presentation did not suffer. A written account of the trials and tribulations of undertaking illustrates this problem.

> When people die, they have usually been ill for some period of time . . . with usually, a not inconsiderable loss of weight. When the Sunday suit turns up large enough for two of the old boy. Whilst this is better than the other way about, it still takes some artistic license to hide the excess folds of clothing so that the result does not look as if it has just escaped from Oxfam. . . .
>
> On the other side of the coin the undertaker will make his preparations as normal (only) to be presented with clothing that will go nowhere near doing its duty. This presents much more of a problem than the opposite and a degree of tailoring would be useful. Threads and strings underneath to body are used to hold clothing together that has been cut at the back in order to look right at the front. We would always hope that nothing would show or break revealing trade secrets [14, pp. 50-51].

Fortunately for funeral companies the bereaved remain oblivious to their struggles.

The final task for the dresser is to check the appearance of the clothed corpse. Whatever attire is chosen, the garments,

. . . must be fitted carefully to appear to be comfortably worn by the deceased. This may seem to be an obvious statement but it is by no means easy to achieve. The fitting round the collar and over the shoulders can often look awkward and the sleeves may be left looking very stiff and formal. Again, stand back and check to see if a natural appearance has been attained [4, 5: p. 9].

All that remained to achieve the complete humanization of the body was its presentation in the coffin.

Assembling the "Box"

In Easton, undertakers continued to craft coffins well into this century—some persisted in this practice until the 1960s. G. R. Stone, whose predecessors were carpenters, produced their last "box" in 1961. Today, coffins are typically produced *en-masse* by a manufacturer who supplies local businesses with easy-assembly kits. These boxes are constructed by the funeral assistants while the embalmer prepares the corpse.

In the illusory trades of theater and funeral company, the technicians who create props for the show have a variety of tactics and artifacts to assist them in the production of the fantasy. At Stone's the construction of the coffin highlighted some of the strategies employed.

Unless relatives had decided to spend a great deal of money on the coffin, the box itself was likely to be made of lightweight chipboard with a veneered finish imitating oak, mahogany, or some other high quality wood. The boxes were manufactured in standard lengths and widths according to the average sizes of the population. After measuring the length of the body the worker selected the one to be used. Unless the deceased had exceptionally broad shoulders or hips, the standard box chosen by length also fitted by width. Peter and Barry then placed the shell of the coffin on a trestle and work began.

First, handles and "belltops" were affixed to the sides and lid. Each coffin was provided with handles although these are now for adornment rather than use. When transported, the coffin is lifted or shouldered from below—workers never rely on the handles to support the weight of the body. "Belltops"—furnishings which serve the dual purposes of ornamentation and the disguise of nails and screws—were attached to the lid. It is rare for these to be of metal composition (as was once the case), plastic being more suitable for cremation. These traditional embellishments, whose only practical purpose today is either as screwcover or wreath holder, reach the undertaker in sets—handles in packs of four or six according to local practice. Stone's routinely appended four handles and two belltops to each coffin. With an eye for correct positioning, Peter and Barry lined up each handle and tapped them into place with small tacks. The pieces for the lid, positioned above and below the name-plate were also held in with tacks.

Peter talked through the next stage of the operation.

> Now you put in the plastic sheeting because that lines the box and makes sure you don't get any leakage through the joints.

He produced a large roll of white plastic from which rough lengths were cut and stapled onto the base and sides of the coffin. The ample excess was neatly folded and secured in place at the corners and edges.

> Once you've done that you have to cut off the extra so that you've got a neat edge and you can start putting in the sheets and frills.

In this case the coffin was to house a woman whose relatives had chosen apricot colored satin sheets and frills. The side-sheets were clearly shorter than the depth of the box. Peter explained.

> Once the body's in it'll fill most of the box so you're not going to see anymore than the sides and top. So there's no need to cover anywhere else.

Peter held the material while Barry stapled it to the sides of the box. Working together the job was soon complete and they turned their attention to the frill. This was a long piece of smocking, machine embroidered and designed to fit along the top edge of the coffin. It was intended to afford a "luxurious" finish to the linings but, like most practices in the undertaking business, served another function, that of hiding any rough edges or plastic sheeting which had not been covered.

The insertion of a "pillow" sustains the impression of slumber. The men recycled waste from the workbenches around them to constitute the filling for the pillow. Into this "environmentally friendly pillow" they stuffed scraps of cardboard, sawdust, and offcuts of plastic sheeting. The search was simple because this area of the garage boasted a wealth of debris.

Presentation of the Body: The "Unreality Principle"

Reaching this, the ultimate stage of humanization, the body has completed the process of decontamination. Arriving in the funeral director's workshop in a defiled condition it has been subjected to numerous purification techniques. In suppressing or draining polluting body fluids the corpse is rendered harmless to the bereaved and made safe for viewing. During this process it has progressed from the bowels of the premises through to the chapel of rest for viewing and in anticipation of departure for the funeral celebration.

All that remains is the final preening of the body once ensconced in the surrounds of the coffin. Rather like the window dresser who is at pains to display goods in the most attractive fashion, undertakers seek to present their product in the most benign light. The trade manual gives explicit instructions on the achievement of this aim. Having earlier fixed the position of the head and its features, the emphasis is on the way in which the body should lie in the coffin.

> The aim of the funeral director or his assistant should be to attain a natural restful posture (with) the head resting on pillows of just the right height, possibly inclined a little to one side.

> The posing of the arms and hands is also worthy of careful attention for hands can be most expressive. . . . The funeral director must use his judgement as to what is most natural for the subject. It will certainly not be straight down each side. Maybe the right hand folds naturally over the left or vice versa, maybe one hand rests naturally over the other wrist, maybe one hand will rest on the breast and the other loll nearly straight down, maybe the family will request the hands folded on the breast. . . . Whatever the position chosen ensure that it looks natural. . . .

> A coverlet is supplied so that the finished result is . . . that of the deceased lying on a divan or bed. The judicious use of wadding to pack the arms in position can help retain a natural restful posture [4, 5: p. 6, 9].

VIETNAMESE PREPARATIONS

When funeral directors are charged with the preparation of the body they stress the humanization techniques. There are, however, ethnic minority communities who, although they may surrender the body into the undertaker's custody, prefer to exercise personal control of the laying-out and coffining of their dead. They wish to observe their own cultural rites rather than conform to those prescribed by the local undertaker. The Vietnamese community in Easton was one such group. In choosing a characteristically Vietnamese style of ritual, however, they recruited the assistance of the funeral director. This is distinctive from some other ethnic minority groups, for example Sikhs, who prefer to lay-out the body in the privacy of the chapel of rest but without the aid of the undertaker. Adrian Stone recounted the laying-out of the body of a Vietnamese woman.

> It took about twenty minutes. They asked me to do things and helped where they thought they could. They knew what they wanted to do and I did it the way I know how. I did all the washing—I don't think they wanted to touch her. They didn't seem to mind helping but they didn't want to do it.

It is pertinent to note that in requesting the funeral director's corpse-handling skills, the relatives were adopting a similar strategy to that observed of the rural Cantonese [15]. Although there is a specific ritual process for washing and laying-out, the bereaved's fear of pollution minimizes the family's physical contact with the deceased. Rather than handling the body themselves, they enlist the aid of an expert more accustomed to performing the dirty and dangerous tasks demanded. In this case, the Easton funeral director elevated the menial role he was asked to play by accounting for it in terms of his expert knowledge and the family's lack of ability—"they knew what they wanted to do," he told me, "and *I did it* in the way that *I know how*."

The ritual progressed with Adrian being instructed to wash and dress the body.

> I washed the body in *sake* and then dressed it in two shrouds and a sort of calico undergarment and then this yellow satin thing on top. Torn up bits of paper which represented money were then pinned to the sheet.

The body was coffined and kept in the chapel of rest where it was viewed by mourners both before and during the funeral service. Although the director had no knowledge of the spiritual beliefs of his clients, he was nevertheless able to perform a service which provided them with the essential elements of their own death rituals. For their part, the bereaved had clearly adapted some of their traditional customs to life in Easton and this was demonstrated by the use of the undertaker's premises for preparation, and later, for the ceremony. Because this potentially threatened an unhappy juxtaposition of control and subordination, both the undertaker and his customers were circumspect in their handling of the situation.

CONCLUSION

When funeral directors have absolute control over the preparation of the body and its environment their objectives accord with the principle of "naturalness." This goal, because it is an illusory device, requires substantial effort to produce. In common with the theater, props and artifacts are carefully chosen and meticulously prepared to create the artificial condition. Designed to *resemble* rather than *become* the genuine article, materials and techniques are enlisted that reflect the temporary nature of their use. In the theater, scenery is constructed from lightweight, pliable materials. Walls and doors are constructed of hardboard or even cardboard and are fixed in place by wedges, hoists, and invisible strings. If an outdoor set is required, bushes may appear with hollow stems and paper leaves; boulders—although grey, dirty, and pock-marked—will probably weigh little and have all the other properties of polystyrene. This enables the technicians and stagehands to rearrange and replace pieces where appropriate and to continually renew the fictional themes. The audience not only expect that what they view will be unreal but, moreover, this is essentially what they desire to see. They pay to be transported from the drudgery or monotony of everyday reality into a realm of fantasy where little or nothing is real but everything is infused with the potential to be so.

In many ways the funeral industry's commitment to visual effect stems from similar principles. Undertakers believe that because the reality of death is an unpleasant one, few wish to meet it head-on. One of the roles that they, therefore, assume is the manufacture of the death mask and its environment. When mourners come to view the body they anticipate an image of the deceased that conveys serenity and peace. The presentation of the individual in a posture of sleep, with head resting on a satin pillow and gently wrapped in satin sheets and surrounds, is a spectacle all parties ultimately acknowledge as unreal. Through the successful production of the "memory picture," however, image and reality are blurred and mourners leave the funeral parlor with a lasting mental photograph which accords more with a fantasy of death than with its realities.

REFERENCES

1. M. Bloch, Death, Women and Power, in *Death and the Regeneration of Life,* M. Bloch and J. Parry (eds.), Cambridge University Press, Cambridge, 1982.

2. R. Hertz, *Death and the Right Hand,* R. Needham and C. Needham (trans.), Cohen & West, London, 1960.
3. J. Hinton, *Dying* (2nd Edition), Penguin, Harmondsworth, 1972.
4. National Association of Funeral Directors, *Manual of Funeral Directing,* National Association of Funeral Directors, London, 1988.
5. R. E. Turner and C. Edgley, Death as Theatre: A Dramaturgical Analysis of the American Funeral, *Sociology and Social Research, 60*:4, pp. 377-392, 1976.
6. D. Unruh, Doing Funeral Directing: Managing Sources of Risk in Funeralization, *Urban Life, 8,* pp. 247-263, 1979.
7. S. R. Barley, The Codes of the Dead: The Semiotics of Funeral Work, *Urban Life, 12*:1, pp. 3-31, 1983.
8. H. I. Lief and R. Fox, The Medical Student's Training for Detached Concern, in *The Psychological Basis of Medical Practice,* H. I. Lief et al. (eds.), Harper & Row, New York, 1964.
9. H. S. Becker et al., *Boys in White: Student Culture in Medical School,* University of Chicago Press, Chicago, 1961.
10. P. Atkinson, Professional Segmentation and Student's Experience in a Scottish Medical School, *Scottish Journal of Sociology, 2,* pp. 71-85, 1977.
11. M. Millman, *The Unkindest Cut: Life in the Backrooms of Medicine,* M. Morrow, New York, 1976.
12. A. Puxley, embalmer, quoted in *The Independent* newspaper, December 15, 1991.
13. Louise, called to *LBC* Radio, February 8, 1988.
14. J. M. Watson, *So Far, So What: Tales from Beside the Grave—An Undertaker's View,* unpublished paper, 1991.
15. J. L. Watson, Of Flesh and Bones: The Management of Death Pollution in Cantonese Society, in *Death and the Regeneration of Life,* M. Bloch and J. Parry (eds.), Cambridge University Press, Cambridge, 1982.

CHAPTER 8

The Funeral Ceremony

After taking possession of the corpse and having gone to considerable lengths to humanize it, funeral directors assume full responsibility for the funeral ceremony. In the course of fieldwork in Easton I attended the final rites of passage of various ethnic and religious groups. Some communities provided their own deathworkers (usually Jews and Muslims); the remainder contracted the services of a local undertaker. Funeral companies are largely able to meet mourners demands by providing everyone with the same basic service, enhanced and adjusted according to the requirements of the bereaved. As Adrian Stone explained.

> Although it's necessary to know the rites of many different religions, all funeral services conform to a basic pattern.

It is this "basic pattern" that forms the focus of this chapter.

Funeral ceremonies are dramatic displays of human disposal. An understanding of the ritual from the undertakers' point of view requires investigation into their theatrical practices. Like the medical and legal professions who deal with the public in times of crisis, the funeral director routinely handles situations that are emotionally traumatic for clients. Dramatizing the rites adds weight and significance for the mourners for whom the funeral director behaves as though this were the only death of any consequence. Furthermore, the use of theatrical techniques and the embellishment of ritual, enable the undertaker to avoid making mistakes. There is no second opportunity to get it right and so they must make certain that the performance is as near perfect as possible. To do this they employ stringent criteria for checking vehicles and arrangements. Moreover they design new, or adapt existing rituals to assist them in meeting deadlines and guarding against spoiled performances.

Every occupation guards against mistakes at work [1]. Controlling the drama of a rite of passage such as death demands a successful first time performance. There is no room for error as this will not only detract from the ceremony but may result in loss of business. Mechanisms are employed to ensure that blunders are rare and can be rectified quickly. Dominating the funeral ceremony, the director is particularly vulnerable to mistakes and incorporates defense mechanisms into all aspects of the ritual. Dealing with people who are emotionally distressed and, moreover, who are expected to participate without prior rehearsal, intensifies the difficulties of the role. Fluency is only accomplished if workers and clients comprehend the funeral director's cues to behavior. Cues must be clear and precise if they are to be effective. Furthermore, the fact that the funeral is a routine occurrence for the directors (although it means that they are well rehearsed) can result in miscalculation. Their familiarity with the ritual may cause them to misinterpret the requirements of the bereaved, expecting them to conform to ceremonial ways of conduct without giving them the opportunity for innovation or the necessary guidance for conformity.

Knowledge of the "basic pattern" of the funeral means that undertakers are always one step ahead of their clients whom they ritually disable by dramatizing and mystifying the ceremony—withholding information yet requiring adherence from the mourners.

This chapter provides an examination of the funeral and begins with the final preparations on the funeral company's premises. It then goes through the various stages of the ritual, taking the reader on the last journey of the deceased: traveling in the cortège from the shop to the home and on to the cemetery, arriving at the chapel and disembarking for service and disposal. Post-funeral rituals are then observed as the mourners gather around floral tributes—the last remaining symbols of death—and finally return to the cars for the journey homeward. Throughout, the discussion will address issues of ceremonial control and power, mechanisms for ensuring a successful performance, the timing of the drama and the giving and taking of cues, the use of mortuary symbols to confer status and reinforce hierarchy, and the centrality of the family and the reassertion of social order. The following investigation takes a "standard" white working class, "C of E" funeral as its core—ethnic and religious deviations from these rituals are discussed where appropriate.

FINAL PREPARATIONS FOR THE FUNERAL

In the funeral director's premises in Easton, the first funeral of the day did not leave before nine o'clock. Working class memories of the humiliation of the pauper funeral, which due to its early start was nicknamed the "nine o'clock trot," guaranteed a relatively leisurely start for the funeral operatives. If the bereaved were local and did not expect mourners from out of town, the director may have suggested that a morning funeral would bring an early end to the whole business. By lunchtime the deceased would have been "laid to rest" and mourners could resume some semblance of normality. Furthermore, if left until the afternoon, chief mourners may spend the early part of the day anxiously contemplating the ritual and waiting nervously for the arrival of guests, flowers, and funeral director.

The funeral of Mr. Wright had been booked into the crematorium chapel for a quarter to ten in the morning and was therefore set to leave the shop at nine o'clock. Shortly after a quarter past eight the instruction came from Adrian Stone to load up the cars and Peter and Barry retreated backstage to comply with his orders. The coffin was transferred from the chapel of rest to the rear of the hearse that was standing, engine running, in preparation for the journey.

The hearse and cars are indispensable to the ceremony and their appearance and efficiency checked and re-checked. The funeral assistants were required to make a daily inspection of the engine, examining items such as oil, water, and battery fluid levels against a printed list. They were also compelled to run the engine each day to guard against mechanical failure. Stone was proud of his fleet of vehicles and this was particularly noticeable when they were on display. A large proportion of his employees' time was devoted to cleaning and polishing bodywork and interior to a meticulous standard.

> The vehicles are checked every day and cleaned inside and out so that they are always ready to go. There are very few people who can actually clean a car as far as I'm concerned. Once they've worked with me for a little while they suddenly find out that there's more to it than they thought.

There are two primary reasons for the fastidious care given to the vehicles. The first stems from the undertaker's attempts to guard against spoiled performances, and the second is connected with the need to advertise services.

Vehicle breakdown was one of the funeral director's nightmare scenarios. Given that the cars spend most of their working lives running at an average speed of ten to fifteen miles per hour, engines were prone to malfunction and were carefully tended in pursuit of reliability. The director was quite vociferous about the possibilities of breakdown.

> My hearse only does funerals, so half the time its out on a funeral—
> and half the time it's coming back from one. So, therefore, prob-
> ability is that at least one in three breakdowns must happen on a
> funeral. Of course, you try your hardest for things not to go wrong
> but they do. They do break down. You do get punctures. You do
> have idiots who forget to fuel it up.

Consequently, aside from daily audits, the engines were started and
left to run on the morning of the funeral.

A further protection against spoiled performances was linked to the
ritual of the cortège. Once the coffin had been loaded, Peter, the driver
of the hearse, led the vehicles out through the rear of Stone's premises
and drove with them in ritual procession to the front of the shop where
floral tributes were placed in and around the coffin. The flowers could
easily have been loaded in the rear workshop and the cortège commenced its journey from the back of the premises. The ritual of driving
from the rear to the front of the shop effectively acted as a practice run
and gave the director warning of faulty vehicles.

> It may sound stupid but if the cars are going to break down they're
> going to do it in the first little run around the corner. And they do
> break down.

Loading up early and driving to the front with plenty of time to spare
before departure gave the director time to organize a substitute hearse
or car if one was defective.

An additional explanation for this ritual was that it furnished the
undertaker with good cause to display his fleet at the entrance to his
premises. Concern for the appearance of funeral vehicles is related to
the fact that they reflect the quality of the company's services. In the
British industry where publicity is frowned upon and high-powered
selling methods seen as distasteful, displaying the hearse and mourning cars is one of the few means of advertising. Once the gleaming black
Rolls-Royce hearse and shiny limousines were parked in the High
Street in front of G. R. Stone's premises, they remained—sometimes for
as long as fifteen minutes. The lengthier the stay the greater the
number of people to view them.

While flowers were loaded the funeral director checked details with
Roberta. A final rehearsal of the next of kin's name and address,
relationship to the deceased, time at chapel and any special requests
were repeated before he took charge of the proceedings.

THE FUNERAL CORTÈGE

If the vehicles were functioning and the coffin and flowers present and correct, the cortège was ready to leave. The funeral conductor took with him a minimum of three coffin bearers. In a procession constituting hearse and at least two mourning cars the manpower requirements were met because in the small funeral company drivers also provided a "shoulder" for the coffin.

Before attending my first funeral as an observer, Adrian advised me of appropriate dress for such occasions—"black skirt, white blouse, black coat." Insisting that I was attired in black meant being recognized by all as part of the undertaker's entourage. The use of personal front in the form of costumes and manner performs the function of defining the professional's exercise of power and control over the ritual. The funeral workers wore a uniform of black trousers, white shirt, black tie, and black overcoat in winter—black jacket in summer. Shoes were also black and polished to military standards. Black has traditionally been associated with funerals and mourning and in Easton was still regarded by funeral directors as essential to a display of respect for the dead. Furthermore, in similar fashion to other occupational roles such as nurses [2] and the police [3], the deathworker's costume is a device of social visibility. It circumscribes a role for the wearer and differentiates him/her from others in the drama. In other geographical areas, funeral workers favored grey uniforms as they considered black to be too dismal and somber. This fashion may in part be a response to the changed mode of attire among mourners. During my attendance at funerals it was not uncommon to see mourners in black or dark colored coats but, other than this, many did not appear to have made a special effort to wear the dark clothing once *de rigueur* at funerals. Indeed, for many ethnic minority communities, the wearing of black mourning garb has never been part of their funeral customs.

The care and attention given to appearance and manner is— irrespective of mourners beliefs—regarded by the industry as a reflection of the care and dignity afforded to the deceased and their relatives. The National Association of Funeral Directors' words on this matter are enlightening.

> All staff should turn out in clean, well pressed clothes, and should have clean hands. . . . Smoking on funeral vehicles or by staff waiting outside a church or chapel should be forbidden. Loud talk or laughter must be checked. Staff must be made to realise that they are "on parade" every moment of the duration of the funeral.

> In general, funeral staff should at all times give quiet, dignified
> service as unobtrusively as possible. Whenever they are not
> required to act they should make themselves inconspicuous but
> available and alert. The art of moving quickly and quietly, in
> particular walking silently, must be mastered. No speech among
> the staff should ever be above a whisper. Courtesy must also be
> stressed at all times [4, p. 73].

From the beginning of the funeral ceremony, the director, his men
and equipment were front of stage. Some of the players in the drama,
however, had a more prominent role than others. The conductor spent
the greater part of the ritual in front stage solo performances—leading,
directing, and cueing the behavior of others. His dominion over the
performance was personified by wearing a silk top hat. This headgear,
traditional among English undertakers, has declined in use in most
other localities. In the East End of London it lingers as a mortuary
symbol which grants ceremonial power to its wearer. "The man in the
hat," as Peter explained, has the power to control the whole enterprise
and is responsible for any mistakes.

> When you go on a funeral, it doesn't matter what your job, the
> funeral director will tell you everything. So if you watch that man,
> if there's any rickets that's his fault—that's if you do your job
> properly. I've done lots of rickets—my fault because I wasn't watch-
> ing him. That man knows where he's going, which route he's
> taking, what time he's got to be there, when he's actually got to be
> in the chapel, when it comes out of the chapel and when it's going
> into the ground. He has to work all that out. But that doesn't
> concern me because I'm not a director.

Once Adrian Stone donned his "silk" (as it is known in the industry),
his funeral assistants were aware that he was in command. Like
the members of an orchestra they looked to him for correct timing
and performance and he was entitled to expect conformity to his
instructions. Although workers were familiar with the structure of
the well-rehearsed ceremony, the need to guide, and to some extent
respond to, the actions of the bereaved meant that each funeral
was distinct and therefore required orchestration. Stone illustrated
this point.

> I suppose every time Michael Crawford gets out to go on the stage
> at the "Phantom of the Opera" he's got a different audience. It's the
> same with me. He plays it probably very different every day. I could
> never tell you how I'm going to handle a funeral, circumstances
> help you.

In addition to controlling his assistants, the hat gave mourners a focus among the funeral director's men and they turned to the conductor for cues to behavior and deportment. The "silk" was worn in the hearse as Adrian Stone directed the proceedings from the passenger seat, navigating and overseeing the progress of the cortège through the streets. When the procession reached the home of the deceased, the hat was removed as he entered the house, first, as a traditional mark of respect and second, to grant front stage action to the relatively minor roles of the bereaved family. On leaving the home he replaced the hat to signal departure. It was removed at the cemetery and not worn again for the remainder of the performance as the coffin was transferred into the chapel and control delegated to the priest.

COLLECTING THE MOURNERS: OBSERVING FAMILY HIERARCHY

Leaving the office at nine o'clock the cortège traveled slowly to the house of the deceased to collect the mourners. This was a time-honored practice and entirely logical and rational behavior in an era when most people died, and remained at home, until the funeral. In the late 1980s it was regarded by funeral directors in the East End as a dignified and ceremonial farewell from the community—returning the deceased to the place they knew as home was "only right and proper." On one particular occasion Adrian explained that a detour made by the cortège had been specifically designed to visit an earlier home of the deceased.

> I wanted to go past the old house—you know, where they used to live; where the husband and wife first lived when they were married. They do want to go past that sort of place. They'd moved into an old people's home and that was fine but they wanted to go past the old home. So we did.

Indeed, it was often the case that when the vehicles and coffin arrived at the home people were waiting in the street to witness the spectacle. Mr. Wright's home had been a flat in a pre-war council block and a small assembly of people had anticipated the arrival—removing hats and, later, murmuring farewells as the cortège left. This practice is perhaps now unusual as the ritual visit has been discarded and mourners either present themselves at the funeral director's premises or alternatively, make their own way to cemetery or crematorium and so dispense with the official mourning cars. From my observations and discussions with people bereaved in other parts of the metropolis, it would seem that erosion of this once practical, and now symbolic, ritual is proceeding apace in more affluent regions. Its persistence in Easton may reflect the strength of working class and ethnic minority communities in the East End of London. As Pickering noted in his discussion of the persistence of rites of passage,

> ... in areas where families are associated with closely knit social networks, and where kinship culture and traditions are strong, greater use will be made of rites of passage than in sections of society where families are set within loosely knit social networks [5, p. 77].

Timing is a constant cause for concern for the conductor and this is brought into greater focus later in the chapter. For most funerals within the white, working class community, he allowed between twenty and thirty minutes to arrive, collect and load flowers, and seat the mourners. For other religious and ethnic minority groups requiring some form of ceremony at the home this allocation must be extended. For example, Sikhs usually hold a short service and allow members of the community the opportunity to view the deceased before the funeral. A period of thirty to forty-five minutes may be set aside for time at the home before the cortège can leave for the temple. Although the funeral director allows ample time, arranging and organizing flowers and mourners can be a protracted affair.

The drive to Mr. Wright's home was a short one. The flat was located in a cul-de-sac and in order to facilitate our exit the drivers backed their vehicles into the street in reverse order so that the hearse would be the first to leave. The coffin remained in the hearse as the assistants followed the director up the stairs to the home to collect the remainder of the flowers. After a few minutes they returned clutching blooms which were placed among those already surrounding the coffin.

Floral tributes in the East End are many and varied. The more unusual pieces encountered during fieldwork were constructed in animal shapes, for example, one of a dog and another a parrot. More common was the heart-shaped pillow and the "empty chair." A funeral director has, rather humorously described the problem of securing the popular chair in the hearse.

> The chair as a floral tribute is the worst to handle of the normal pieces—usually brought by a close relative and required to take its correct place in the hierarchy of proximity to the coffin. It is too tall to stand up in the hearse window, too deep to stand at the head of the coffin on the deck and too flimsy to be strapped down on the top of the hearse and survive the journey to the cemetery in view of the

imminent raging storm. The normal way around this is to hope that there is another chair or gate of heaven that can be strapped back to back! [6, p. 36].

Worthy of note in the choice of flowers was their predominantly secular nature. Barring wreaths and bouquets, most pieces were designed to draw attention to an interest held by the deceased in life, for example, a dog, a chess piece. Alternatively, they signified the great loss felt by a loved one and this explained the popularity of the empty chair. Although religious symbolism in the form of the cross and the occasional "gate of heaven" did appear among tributes they were by no means conspicuous. A further interesting aspect of the use of floral tributes was the way in which those chosen by ethnic minority groups often took familiar East End themes. On one occasion, arriving at the home for a Sikh funeral, the flowers had been delivered by the florists and left on display in the front garden. Among the blooms were heart-shaped pillows and others which formed the words "Grandad" and "Dad." The extent to which either of these floral details was evidence of secularization, westernization, or simply lack of choice at the florists, is open to conjecture.

The arrangement of flowers was a source of concern for the funeral director as he tried to ensure that tributes were grouped on and around the coffin according to the donor's relationship with the deceased. Placing a wreath from a relatively unimportant well-wisher in a prime location on the coffin could cause acrimony among the bereaved. Correct arrangement of the floral jigsaw was not an easy task as the varying shapes and sizes of the pieces were either more or less appropriate to this or that position in the hearse. Some were strapped to the roof of the vehicle and, if there was an abundance of flowers, others may be placed in mourning cars or even require the provision of a separate floral hearse. Stone highlighted some of the problems.

The closest relative's flowers obviously go next to the coffin but that has to be practical as well. Florists listen to relatives who do the silliest things. You've seen these things with large sized lettering—if they write grandfather it's longer than the car! Fine, very nice, but what are we supposed to do with it?

The other thing is that you have to guess how many flowers there are going to be. If the relatives have said there's going to be a lot of flowers and you haven't got many following cars you might have a floral hearse—which is another hearse without the body in it and just decorated with flowers. That's fine, but you'd look very silly providing a floral hearse if there's very little to go on it. I mean you

> look daft. Oh you do, yes. So you load the flowers and you hope it's
> all nice and that you get all the relatives' close enough to the coffin
> and that you don't have to think about cutting some in half!

A fundamental element of the undertaker's work at the home was the recognition and demonstration of hierarchy in relation to the deceased. Parallel to the strict ordinal mores governing the presentation of floral tributes was the seating of mourners in the cars. Leading the bereaved from the home, the funeral director was aware that, like the flowers, he must rank them according to their relationship to the deceased: next of kin and immediate family seated in the first mourning car, more distant relatives positioned behind, those with the most remote ties relegated to the rear of the procession. Some funeral directors ask the next of kin to supply a list of people to be allocated to each car and this delivers them from the intractable and delicate task of assessing the grief status of each mourner. Others felt this practice unnecessarily bureaucratic and instead organized the mourners themselves.

This scene in the funeral ritual, where the hierarchy of the mourners was determined, was significant in reasserting the primacy of the family. This was true whoever ranked the mourners because in either case the bereaved were forced to consider and categorize one another in hierarchical terms. In western society the family is regarded as a fundamental unit. In this final rite of passage it is celebrated above all others. That the last journey of the deceased should travel via the home is an implicit veneration of family structure. Furthermore, ranking and seating the mourners according to family position played a reinforcing role in the ideology of family supremacy. Several cases of gay bereavement have been publicized in which the partner had not been invited to the funeral. This underlines the practice of "putting the family first." When it occurs there may be a homophobic prejudice on the part of the family against the nature of the erstwhile relationship. That similar complaints of exclusion have been voiced by girlfriends or boyfriends of dead youths point to the pervasive power of the family as the source of their distress.

On this occasion Adrian Stone was followed into the street by the widow, her two daughters and two sons, all of whom he guided to the chief mourning car where the driver was standing to attention with the door open. A handful were similarly ushered into the second car and the others made their way to private vehicles. The cortège cannot begin its journey to the cemetery or crematorium until the funeral director is certain that all private cars are ready to join the procession. When everyone was prepared with engines idling, the conductor took his place as master of ceremonies. Poised at the head of the retinue he ceremonially placed the "silk" on his head and walked slowly out into the road. This was the cue for the procession to depart.

"WALKING" THE CORTÈGE

"Walking" the cortège away from the home was the most highly dramatized act of the show and the funeral director basked in the glory of the solo performance. For him, the climax of the production was the journey from the home to the cemetery, the pinnacle of which was the initial walk. This is the only time during the ritual that he has exclusive charge of practically the entire cast of players and props—all immaculately presented and on stage. Leading the cortège on foot for a short distance allowed the director an opportunity to demonstrate the quality of his business. If the cortège was particularly large or the flowers especially abundant and striking, the distance walked may be extended. The conductor *en grande tenue* resembled a military commander who, on parade at the head of his troops, proudly led them in an exhibition of funereal regalia and pomp. The dramatic sight of a lavish funeral procession, ritually led at walking pace, halting traffic and pedestrians in its wake, is intended to generate awe in those who witness it.

Traditionally the cavalcade would have been walked to the outskirts of the deceased's neighborhood and this may have been a considerable distance. In the days of the horse-drawn hearse there was less traffic congestion or anxiety about maintaining speed on the roads. In the funerals I observed, the edge of the neighborhood was deemed to be a few yards or the end of the street—whichever was the shorter. Originally intended as a mark of respect, the custom was linked to the philosophy of enabling the community to bid farewell to an erstwhile member. Although ostensibly these explanations hold sway there were more pragmatic reasons for the conductor to indulge the practice, not least of which was that earlier alluded to—the opportunity to advertise business.

A further explanation was that walking often provided a method of turning into a busy main road or of negotiating a difficult crossing.

> You walk off and you make sure you've got all the private cars behind you. And I do try to let as many people clear and out of the way as I possibly can. But you do get the people who try to cut you up! There's always the driver whose recognized what you're doing

and who's coming roaring down the road and not stopping for you at all. And you walk out in front of him and he realizes that he's either going to squash you or he has to do a lot of braking. And when he's stopped and everyone's staring down at him, you very politely say, "Thank you very much."

Confidently stepping out in his striking costume and top hat, the conductor commanded the attention of other road users, halting the traffic sufficiently for the parade to effect its maneuver.

Linked to this, but more frivolous, was that walking was occasionally used as a method of retaliation against irate drivers. During one drive to the cemetery I was aware that Adrian had walked a considerable distance from the home. When later questioned he explained that having gained entry to a large roundabout, another road user had sounded his horn in annoyance at the delay.

As we had plenty of time in hand before we were due in the chapel I decided that he could suffer another quarter of mile for being impatient!

The final explanation for the walk derived from the need for perfect timing. In the theater the stage entrances and exits of thespians are carefully timed to correspond with the plot and to give cues for the performance of others. Undertakers are similarly bound by strict deadlines and have to make prompt appearances at the cemetery. Being early would spoil the performance as mourners would be forced to endure a barren waiting period, interrupting the ritual and detracting from the drama. Furthermore, witnessing the arrival and departure of other funeral parties while waiting, would have lost the sense of individuality and of their ritual as being of paramount significance—a sentiment which the funeral director has meticulously cultivated since taking custody of the body. If the cortège was late, the party would lose their place in the chapel and be forced to wait for a lull in funerals before the service could proceed. Experienced conductors were aware of the distances, short cuts, time required, and expected traffic flows between their area and the local cemeteries and crematoria. If the business at the house takes less time than expected the director may walk the cortège for a considerable distance. In so doing he not only advertises his business but, furthermore, believes that the slow pace is regarded by his customers as a tangible embellishment to the dignity of the ritual.

TIMING THE CORTÈGE

When the conductor decided that his walk was over he gracefully boarded the slow moving hearse, stationing himself in the passenger seat and firmly at the head of the cortège. He continued to dictate the speed of the procession, instructing the driver to accelerate or decelerate according to the time available and the progress of the private mourning cars at the rear of the cortège. It was the job of the director to ensure that all private cars arrived at the correct cemetery. This was far from easy as having no visible connection with the undertaker's vehicles other road users failed to recognize the private car's claim to right of way. Before leaving the home Stone had taken time to note the number and type of cars attaching themselves to the procession. On two occasions during the journey to the cemetery he was obliged to halt along the route to allow these vehicles to recover their positions.

Although successful driving required practice and concentration, the responsibility for overall command lay with the director. Peter explained.

> When you go on a funeral and you're a driver, if you drive a lim' or a hearse doesn't matter, what you do is watch the funeral director. You watch him and you shouldn't go wrong. That man's got it all down and he knows everything about the funeral. I don't know which route the funeral's going until that man tells me where to go. That's what he's there for.

Furthermore, expected to arrive promptly at the crematorium, the conductor made constant assessments of progress and adjusted the speed of travel accordingly. The conductor's management of the cavalcade was considered skillful by his assistants, Peter and Barry.

> B: That's where you get your speed variations as you run 'cos he'll be checking his watch and he'll think, "Oh we're two or three minutes early," or two or three minutes late. And so you jump from eighteen to twenty-five or from eighteen down to ten to get there at the specific time.
>
> P: But nine times out of ten you'll find that a good director doesn't have to go fast or slow. He can tell that from A to B it's gonna take half an hour and he knows his route. He's done it so often he knows how the traffic is on that route and barring an accident he near enough knows how long it takes. And my gov'ner he'll go into a church and he'll look at his watch and he'll say

this'll be over at such a time. And it is! Whereas I could go in there and I wouldn't know that—no-one would.

DRIVING SKILLS

The funeral industry maintains close links with the world of car hire and this reflects its origins in that many nineteenth- and early twentieth-century funeral companies began their days as carriage-masters. Livery men pride their skills and this has been inherited by the driver of the funeral vehicle. At Stone's, Peter drove the hearse and Barry chauffeured the lead mourning car. Gordon, as owner of the second limousine, was always contracted to drive when the vehicle was required. When not working for the funeral company he was actively engaged in the car hire business. Considering himself as the only true livery man he decried the inadequacy of funeral operatives who lacked the faculty to assist and seat passengers in the most supportive fashion. Although the funeral assistants were generally responsible for low-grade tasks and dirty work, driving was one aspect of their work of which they were proud, perceiving it as requiring a high level of skill and proficiency. Barry was eager to describe the challenge of driving a funeral vehicle.

> Peter's been driving for thirty years. So have I, but you've got to forget everything you know 'cos it's like an advanced driving test. I was a bit nervous to start with 'cos of the size of the vehicle. I mean, it's between eighteen and twenty foot long and it's about eight and half foot wide—which is about the width of a normal single decker bus. Threading that through the traffic was a bit nervy to start with.

Driving in the funeral procession demanded a new set of skills as, contrary to normal road practice, the aim of the exercise was to drive as slowly and as closely together as possible. The distance between cars was important and drivers viewed the ability to maintain a few inches between their vehicle and the one in front as the mark of an experienced and accomplished operative.

Once again there were symbolic and practical reasons for the perpetuation of an apparently absurd custom. The spectacle of the funeral parade was indeed impressive. Its splendor was amplified and symbolic value enhanced if it resembled an unbroken chain of black polished vehicles menacingly crawling through hurried streets and constituting a theatrical throw-back to an earlier time when *memento-mori* were more familiar. Furthermore, as already noted, the slow pace and proximity between the vehicles was considered by the trade to import dignity. The cortège bore the deceased on the final journey of this world. A marked lack of urgency was regarded as a sign of respect for the dead and an indication of the sympathy extended to the bereaved.

Maintaining a few inches between each vehicle ensured that the cavalcade was not divided. Other road users whose path was impeded by the crawling procession were often tempted to "leap frog" their way ahead. Barry was incensed by the behavior of some drivers.

> You do get the occasional one who acts as though the world's gonna end and they've gotta get there. What happens is people in private cars realize that funerals will hold them up so if they can't get in front of you they've gotta stick behind. And they'll try everything in the book to try and overtake you and they take liberties, absolute diabolical liberties.

Apart from the physical perils wrought by a cavalier motorist the effect on the visual impression of the cortège was ruinous. The procession was separated and the spell broken once an intruder had breached the ranks.

On a practical level it was important for the cars to remain closely positioned in order to travel as one articulated vehicle through modern traffic conditions: negotiating roundabouts, crossing road junctions, and going through traffic lights. Closer proximity increased the likelihood that when a light turned to red all the vehicles would be able to cross without dislocation. Losing limousines was potentially embarrassing if the driver was unaware of the destination. Although there were three East London cemeteries in the vicinity regularly used by this company, conveying mourners to the wrong one would be a significant error. To arrive at the correct destination ahead of the hearse would be equally damning. Strict protocol governed the order of the procession. The hearse, transporting the lead character in the funeral drama was always at the forefront.

CHAPEL SERVICES

As the cortège approached the cemetery gates it slowed to a crawl and the director disembarked to check with cemetery officials that the funeral could proceed as planned. Resuming his seat after a few minutes the procession advanced the final yards to the chapel. Pulling up along the side of the building we glided to a halt and Adrian again disembarked to ensure that the party was expected.

Arrival at the chapel was a junction where the funeral performance was potentially at risk. Most frequently, problems arose from the need for precise timing of the ceremonies. If the previous funeral was running late there was a knock-on delay for all others. More disconcerting were the rare occasions when the priest failed to arrive. Many contingencies could give rise to this including communication breakdown and transport problems. Whatever the cause, the repercussions were immutable and the undertaker invariably deemed culpable. This happened on one occasion during fieldwork. Gordon described the incident and its implications for the funeral company.

> We got to the chapel only to discover the minister hadn't turned up. It turned out later that he'd got the wrong crem'—silly idiot! Well anyway, it doesn't go down well for us because of course, everyone thinks it's your fault and it's no good trying to explain because they just think you're making excuses.

> I reckon we lost a lot of business there because they won't come back to us and also they tell their friends and relatives and we lose out.

Mourners do not have to be devoutly religious to be dismayed when the priest they are expecting to administer their service fails to attend. Without someone to preside over the ritual the performance is grossly flawed. Unless a priest or someone equally authorized can immediately step into the breech the disposal will pass either without ceremony or with a perfunctory substitute. The incidents when the priest did not arrive shed some light on the reasons for the popular retention of religious rites of passage. In circumstances such as these, if funeral directors are unable to swiftly recruit a minister they may arrange for music to be played or encourage the bereaved to say a few words about the deceased. Whatever ensues, the symbols used to substitute for religion are unfamiliar and the drama of the ceremony is lost. This leads to a meaningless ritual as the mourners' understanding of the alternative symbols does not conform to their cultural preconceptions of the funeral ceremony.

When our cortège arrived, the priest was waiting at the chapel door to receive the assembly. Approaching the familiar figure of the Reverend Hogarth, the funeral director extended his hand in greeting, surreptitiously transferring the cash payment for the service as he did so. A small gratuity for the chapel attendant together with a swift check that the previous funeral had left the building, meant that everything was ready. As all was in order the conductor gave the cue for the cars to be vacated and the coffin unloaded.

MINIMUM PARTICIPATION FOR THE BEREAVED

Previous chapters have noted that bereaved people collude with the undertaker in the dramatic construction of the funeral ritual—defending themselves against spoiled performances by refraining from behavior which violates the funeral parlor's backstage. The funeral ceremony is a further occasion where they sustain the theatrical production by allowing the conductor to escape from his public to check backstage props and characters.

> On arrival at the place of service the chief mourners should be kept in their cars if possible until everything is checked and absolutely ready [4, p. 76].

Having placed all responsibility for preparations in the hands of the undertaker, the bereaved lack the knowledge of protocol or the impetus to proceed alone. At no stage in the funeral ritual was it clearer to the observer how little control the bereaved had over this rite of passage. The director took a few minutes to verify that the chapel and priest were ready. Whether in private cars or those of the funeral company, mourners remained ensconced in their vehicles until instructed to move by the conductor. They placed themselves firmly in his hands for guidance throughout the ritual.

The funeral director considered minimal participation by the bereaved—leaving the mechanics of the performance to the experts—to be the most effective means of ensuring a successful ritual. Wherever his clients had insisted on taking an active part in the funeral, the director could point to damaging results. For example, on one occasion chief mourners had persisted in their desire to walk with the cortège for the full distance to the cemetery. Inevitably, the time slot in the chapel had been lost and the lengthy wait before an interval could be found was judged by the undertaker as chastisement for his customers. A more common request at burials was to be allowed to lower the coffin into the grave. This also exasperated the funeral director who maintained that failure to lower the box slowly and gradually meant that his assistance was required. In his view this merely complicated and prolonged the operation.

Another popular desire was for chief mourners—and usually male ones—to be allowed to act as coffin bearers. If Adrian Stone could not dissuade them he set about organizing and aiding the operation.

> You have various people standing there and you sort them all out into various height order. Then you say, "O.K. gentlemen, we're going to shoulder ourselves. Face the church, put your shoulder under the coffin and then come out backwards."
>
> That's quite simple I would have thought, but you have to turn at least half of them around. Then they might all turn round! You do get the situations that do go wrong. I'll sort of wander off to one side and speak to one of my blokes and say, "Did I say anything or not!" (laughs) It's the only way, otherwise you'd go mad.
>
> I have actually stood in front of people and said, "Right, who's not listening to me then?" And it's just partly ridicule to make them do it right. Then once you've got them right they're O.K. People will generally follow you behind and do exactly what you say.

The undertaker's drivers normally acted as bearers and shouldered the box ready for the procession into the chapel. Carrying the coffin in ceremonial fashion was cited by them as further evidence of skilled work.

> P: There's a certain way to do all sorts of things in the funeral trade. I mean if you've never shouldered a person it is awkward.
> B: That's right. I was scared of it coming off my shoulder, even though it couldn't. And Adrian kept saying to me, "It can't come off!" But you felt so insecure. And you're not supposed to hold the coffin at all.
> P: It should be in your shoulder, well tucked into your shoulder and it won't come off.
> B: But you feel so insecure at the start when you think about it. You think, "Oh God it's gonna come off!" And if you go up a step or anything like that you think it's gonna slide off.

The impact of a coffin falling from the shoulders of the undertaker's men would have been horrifying for the bereaved and unquestionably detrimental for the company.

Certain cultural traditions are nurtured by the trade. One such custom was conveying the corpse feet first. Consequently, of the three bearers required, one was stationed at the front (or foot) of the box, the remaining two supporting the rear (or head). Although funeral assistants were chosen for their aptitude for the work and not their physique, height was nevertheless important. In a group of three the two at the rear should be of similar stature. The shortest person would take the front so that the box would lean forward. This not only eased the burden but improved the deportment spectacle and was rather more dignified than a precarious backward recline.

The notion of limiting the role of the bereaved (voiced by the funeral director) was echoed by the priest conducting the funeral service. One Anglican minister explained that he preferred only minimal audience participation.

> I don't have them standing during the service. I work on the basis that unless I've been asked to the contrary I have minimum audience participation. They may say "Amen" whenever they choose. You get the odd ejaculation, people will sometimes say things. The only thing I ask them to join in is the Lord's Prayer—and they don't always. I get them to stand at the committal. So I minimize audience participation—it makes it easier. That's why I don't direct them to the prayer book. If I ask them to look at the book I've got to talk about page numbers and miss this bit and miss that bit . . . I don't feel that's a terribly dignified thing to do.

When challenged to justify reduction in their involvement, this minister rationalized his approach by reference, first, to the mourner's lack of familiarity with religious ritual and, second, to the debilitating effects of grief.

> I mean if you had a group that you knew all belonged to a church you might say a psalm together. But most people don't want to. They're sad. I mean it's like the people who choose hymns and then they don't want to sing them when they actually get there because they're too sad.

Whatever the basis for restraint, both funeral directors and ministers effectively sacrifice the participation of the bereaved in pursuit of the drama and presentation of the funeral performance. This phenomenon is symptomatic of the professionalization of death. Throughout this study the way the bereaved have been physically separated from the deceased and excluded from most funeral preparations has been annotated and their collusion acknowledged. Allowing customers to determine the length and style of the funeral would bring unscripted drama to complicate the performances of the undertaker and priest and chaos to the well-ordered timetables of cemeteries and crematoria. At present all participating experts understand, and strive to meet each other's requirements to maintain occupational regularity and predictability.

There were, however, ceremonies in which the mourners exercised a greater degree of involvement. These tended to be rituals, first, which did not require the use of the crematorium chapel and second, burials rather than cremations. I shall consider each in turn.

Not all religious services were held in the crematorium chapel. The majority of non-conformist burials were held in the deceased's own place of worship whether a Catholic church, Baptist meeting hall, or, on rarer occasions, the undertaker's chapel. Avoiding the crematorium chapel resulted in fewer restrictions for the mourners as they did not have to adhere so strictly to timetabling demands. This in turn reduced the necessity for undertaker control. In practice, however, unless the funeral director was aware that the party had "strong cultural traditions" he attempted to organize and direct them according to his basic funeral formula. For example, Irish Catholics in Easton usually held the requiem mass in their local church where the body was kept overnight. Apart from these deviations to the funeral director's routine, little else changed. The conductor collected the mourners; kept them in the cars until the church and priest were ready; insisted on a prompt finish to the ceremony and transported coffin, mourners, and priest in cortège for a short graveside committal at the cemetery.

By contrast, Chinese funerals were regarded by Stone as "strange" and unusual. His lack of knowledge and familiarity with their customs forced him to play a relatively minor role in the performance, responding to the requests of the bereaved rather than guiding their behavior. In the case of the Vietnamese funeral (the preparations for which were discussed in the previous chapter), the service was held in the funeral home. The following dialog between the director and myself highlights the latter's subdued role in the rituals.

AS: We had the service in our chapel here.

GH: Was the coffin still open for the service and so people presumably viewed as well?

AS: That's right. They went in and burnt many joss-sticks, waved various things about and they all dressed in white cotton robes with hats on—white cotton hats.

GH: And were you actually present in the chapel?

AS: No, not inside the chapel, no.

GH: So how long did the ceremony last?

AS: About twenty minutes. They were quicker than I thought. They came early, quicker than I thought. And I had to change the time at the cemetery. . . . When they'd finished they asked me to seal the coffin and they put three strips of writing on it. They stuck one, almost like a sealing strip at the head. . . . I don't know whether they meant to stick it to the top and the side so that if the lid was removed it would show?

It is clear from Adrian Stone's description of the mourners' dress and behavior that he lacked insight into the meanings of their funeral ritual. Miscalculating the time required for the ceremony and forced to rearrange the appointment at the cemetery revealed diminished control over the proceedings.

Where burial was the chosen method of disposal, the mourners appeared to have greater capacity for independent thought during the ritual. Funeral company vehicles were parked as close as possible to the grave and for Roman Catholic or Anglican funerals the priest led the procession ahead of the conductor and coffin. Burial was the preferred choice of the Roman Catholic, Afro-Caribbean, Greek, Muslim, and Chinese communities. Distinct graveyards were maintained for those of the Catholic faith but other ethnic and religious groups who opted for interment usually shared the cemetery, although some, for example, Muslims, elected for plots on non-consecrated ground separate from the main burial area.

If there is an element of truth abiding in the stereotype of the British as people who readily submit to authority and are reluctant to challenge instructions for fear of causing embarrassment, this may provide a clue to the almost blanket acceptance of the funeral director's control over the overwhelming majority of English funerals. That those who select burial appeared to exert greater ritual control than the cremationists, may derive from the fact that cremation is now the most popular choice of disposal—68.5 percent of all deaths in England and Wales in 1988 ended in cremation [7]. Those who chose burial are to some degree indulging in deviant behavior. The statistics demonstrate this, but more significantly, there is now a broad consensus that cremation is the norm. Opting for a minority method of disposal suggests strong cultural or religious traditions with correspondingly explicit rituals.

That cremation should effectively disable the bereaved derives from the novel and technical mechanisms it utilizes. Interment, until the mid-twentieth century the customary method of disposal in Britain, was surrounded by a wealth of rituals which conferred meaning and value for the participants. The slow procession to the grave, the dignified lowering of the coffin, the pregnant silence before the handful of earth is symbolically cast into the grave, all augment the sense of moment and the implacable realization that the deceased has truly departed this world. Cremation, by comparison, is a modern phenomenon which has not acquired equality of theatrical impact for the mourners in spite of attempts to dramatize the ritual with techniques such as the spontaneous closing of the curtains. Critics of the way in which cremation is performed point to the meaninglessness and anomie of the ceremony and to dissatisfaction among the bereaved

[8, 9]. The mechanical nature of the disposal—relying on machinery to lower the coffin into the chambers below the chapel—and the production line to the furnace, remove the human aspect of disposal. Many less industrialized cultures surrender their dead to the funeral pyre, but this avoids the technological mechanisms of contemporary crematoria. Furthermore, it involves a "hands on" approach in which mourners may kindle the fire and stay to witness the transformation to ashes. The extent to which adherents of modern western funeral culture would welcome this extensive participation is debatable. Although viewing chambers have now been constructed in most British crematoria to allow chief mourners at Sikh and Hindu funerals to see the coffin as it is placed in the cremator, this concession to the cultural rituals of ethnic minorities is not offered to culturally "mainstream" clients. The lack of bereaved participation in British cremation rites, however, does not stem from the callous inclinations of deathworkers or from a conspiracy to divest mourners of control, but to the modern proclivity to be hostage to mechanical techniques and exigencies of bureaucracy.

While the degree of participation by the bereaved differed between groups it was notable during fieldwork that burial parties had greater autonomy. In the case of Irish Roman Catholic funerals—a substantial proportion of Stone's clients—this may be linked to the mourners' view that the priest should take a leading role in the ceremony. Participants tended to look to him for guidance rather than to the undertaker who consequently had to work much harder to assert his authority. In most West Indian and Chinese funerals there was no question of the funeral director commanding the proceedings and once the bereaved had reached the cemetery he overtly relinquished control to his clients.

Describing the Vietnamese funeral, Adrian Stone noted that apart from the performance of physical tasks, the mourners took overall charge of the ceremony at the graveside.

> We went straight to the graveside. We put the coffin on the side of the grave all webbed-up and they wanted to wait. And they threw flowers into the grave and also blessed it with joss-sticks and stood joss-sticks all round the grave burning. . . . (Later) we lowered it into the grave and then they stayed for about another ten minutes. Then they all stood up and said, "We can go home now." Throughout the whole thing they knew what they wanted—they told us to wait or go ahead all the time . . . they were sort of actively doing the bit as opposed to the people today who go along to see what the priest has to say.

When such groups eschewed a service in the chapel and brought their own priest, the autonomy they were granted did not disrupt the smooth running of the cemetery. More pertinent for the undertaker, it did not detract from his performance at all, as, having supervised the departure from his premises and maintained command during transit,[1] he was only relinquishing the control which he would ordinarily have delegated to the priest at the crematorium chapel.

DELEGATING CONTROL

When the mourners at Mr. Wright's funeral alighted from the cars they were ready to be led into the chapel. It is at this stage in the proceedings that the conductor prepares to delegate control to the priest.[2] The relationship between priest and undertaker in western culture has been defined by some as one of conflict [10-12]. Tensions derives from the blurred boundaries between the professions in respect of their work with the bereaved. The clergy are portrayed as accusing funeral directors of showing either too much, or too little concern for the spiritual care of their customers. Undertakers believe that priests overestimate their role in human disposal and consequently inflate the importance of their own interaction with the bereaved. The upshot was that the minister made preparations for the ceremony without liaising with the funeral service. During my fieldwork in Easton I perceived little conflict between the two occupational roles. Both organizations endeavored to maintain a reasonable working relationship. The potential for conflict, however, was demonstrated during the funeral ritual in the negotiation of control between the conductor and the priest.

A strict order of entry into the chapel was determined, first, by the degree of control exerted over the ceremony and second, by rank according to relationship to the deceased. It is traditional for the clergy to lead the coffin into the church and in former times the priest would have met the corpse and mourners at the lych gate. The conductor arranged the mourners in line behind the coffin. This was a relatively simple task as he kept the ranking adopted earlier for seating in the

---

[1] Of interest here is that despite the meaninglessness for the Vietnamese mourners, the undertaker "walked" the cortège away from his premises as he would have done for any other funeral. This evidences the assertion that the practical purpose of the ritual has superseded the symbolic one.

[2] Exceptions to this rule are non-religious funerals where the conductor has offered to officiate or ceremonies for people of the Brethren faith who consider no one privileged enough to conduct a funeral service and each takes an equal part in verbally commemorating the life of the deceased.

vehicles. Having instructed the mourners to follow on behind the coffin he positioned himself to the rear of the priest but ahead of the remainder of the entourage. The practical implication for this sequence of entry into the crematorium chapel was that the conductor, by preceding the mourners, was *in situ* and able to act as usher. Allowing the priest to lead the procession into the chapel symbolically transferred control into his hands for the duration of the funeral service. Retaining a position ahead of the coffin enabled the undertaker to assert his powerful status in the ritual as a whole. As the coffin bearers reached the catafalque the conductor stepped aside to let them pass. Mourners were seated as the bearers performed a dignified bow before the coffin and the conductor and his men exited by the rear of the chapel leaving the stage to the priest.[3]

ATHEIST FUNERALS

Not all funerals appeal to religious formulae and occasionally Stone organized the final rites for families who specifically requested no religious ceremony. I attended one such funeral in the early days of fieldwork. The widow of a confirmed atheist had rejected Adrian's offer of a minister. Unsure of the "appropriate" substitute and unaware of the availability of a humanist funeral, she had acceded to the director's suggestion that he play a piece of classical music in the crematorium chapel. Criticisms from undertakers, and more commonly from the clergy, that the ceremony degenerates when people choose popular music for funerals, may account for Stone's stipulation of classical music. As discussed earlier, bias questioning of this sort during the arrangements interview effectively limits funeral practice as clients are reluctant to assert themselves in professional settings [13]. Adrian Stone later afforded an insight into his choice of music on this occasion.

> We had a gent' down the road here, ever such a nice man, he looked like a church-goer. And his wife died and he said, "I'm not going to be a hypocrite, we're atheists. Is there any way we can just play a piece of music?" So I said, "Yes, surely. But do you have a special piece of classical music that you rather like?" And he said, "No, not really."

---

[3] The ceremony itself is not the concern of this study because here we are dealing with the experiences of funeral directors. The way in which the clergy handle the bereaved and the content and purpose of the funeral service have been dealt with at length by other researchers. See especially [11, 14-17].

So I started racking my brains and putting bits on tape recorders and things. But then I realized there's only one piece and that's from Edward G. and Charlton Heston in the film "Soylent Green"— it actually has a little place where in the film they close the curtains around the coffin. It's also nine minutes long so you're well within the time at the chapel!

During the ceremony I'll just take a chair and I'll sit there and bow my head for a few minutes. And then here it comes, and I can see the bit in the film of Soylent Green and that's the time to press the button.[4] And the music carries on for another minute and a half.

Although he felt that this piece of music was particularly apt, the director reported being wary about offering it to clients for fear of creating a substitute for the clergy.

I leave it to their own choice because if I don't then it's me who's standing up there and I'm supposed to be their friend.

His caution did not stem from circumspection about the clergy but a reluctance to *be seen* to restrict choice. Concern not to proselytize musical preference further augments the explanation for his aversion to offering an alternative to the religious ceremony.

Yes, I will do it for anyone but I would hate to think that if you didn't want an anglican service, or the church type service, that you had to have that piece of music. I wouldn't like to think that I was actually forcing this music on somebody because it's right for me.

PREPARING FOR THE NEXT ACT

The service in the chapel usually lasts between fifteen and twenty minutes. Keeping the ceremony short enhances the esteem of the priest in the eyes of the chapel attendant since the latter has to clear and tidy the room before the arrival of the next customers. If the method of disposal was cremation, the undertaker and his assistants utilized these few minutes to reset the scene and prepare the stage for the next act.[5] Once the mourners were securely established in the chapel the

---

[4] The person who officiates in the chapel ceremony is responsible for pressing the button to close the curtain around the coffin. This is usually the priest who, like the undertaker here, chooses a moment which he considers to be dramatically fitting.

[5] If it was burial there was nothing to be done but to wait for the mourners to emerge from the chapel.

flowers were unloaded and positioned next to the building in the area designated for their display. The significance of this viewing area will be dealt with shortly.

The other important task for the conductor was to organize the departure of the hearse. In the case of cremation the vehicle is no longer required as the coffin will remain in the chapel until removed to the cremation chambers below. For a burial the hearse would quietly disappear during the committal service. In practical terms there was no reason for the hearse to linger. Moreover, symbolically, it was important that the vehicle had withdrawn before the mourners left the chapel. Disposal of the remains was an essential task which on completion, undertakers' believed, gave the bereaved a sense of relief. When the ceremony was over, however, the body was no longer the concern of the bereaved, whether behind the curtain in the chapel or six feet deep in the ground, the deceased was lost to them and their world. The presence of the hearse would have been an impertinent reminder, creating dissonance and leaving the assembly with a perception of ritual incompleteness. Stage managing the departure of the hearse to coincide with the disposal of the corpse sustained the orderly practical and symbolic exit of both.

POST-SERVICE RITUAL

At the conclusion of the service the conductor entered the chapel to regain control and lead the mourners out to the flower area. The custom of viewing floral tributes after the service has been devised as a mechanism to replace the natural interlude which once followed burial. Following a committal service, mourners tended to step back slightly from the grave to admire the flowers and exchange sentiments. When the cremation service is over, however, mourners are swiftly ushered out of the chapel to make way for the next funeral. Loading them immediately into the cars would not only appear to be insensitive haste but, furthermore, would deny them the opportunity to talk (albeit briefly) immediately after the committal and so to mark the significance of the aftermath of the funeral. Instead, the funeral conductor shepherded them to the flower display where they could approach the chief mourners to express their sympathy, comment on the funeral ceremony and meet the priest. As Adrian noted:

> ... after the service, when the minister's pressed the button and the curtains have come, it's an excuse to take them across to see the flowers. It gives them time to breathe, talk to other relatives and

have a good cry. And then that's the time when they realize, that's over now and tomorrow's another day.

Apart from granting the mourners a short "recovery time" after the service, these moments promoted an appreciation of the new hierarchy in the family order. In assisting to restructure family position, the effect of this flower ritual is akin to that noted by Gittings [18] of the funeral rituals of the aristocracy in Medieval England. The conductors responsiveness to the next of kin and head of family serves to sustain and reinforce its integrity.

After no more than ten minutes (for fear of clashing with the next party) the conductor, appearing to take his cue from the chief mourner, ushered the assembly back into the cars for the journey home. The pace of travel is substantially increased and there is no imperative for the vehicles to remain articulated. Consequently post-funeral transit is only minimally ritualized and this reflects the assertion that the significance of the funeral lies with the body and its disposal. Once the deceased is no longer present—the perceived need for dignity and respect and the formal explanation for the slow ritual pace—the cortège can recommence a more everyday speed.

When the ritual is over all that remains for the funeral director is to return clients to the home or other place for the funeral tea. Before the performance is truly complete, however, the problem of liminality needs to be resolved. In tandem with the deceased, the relatives undergo a period between death and disposal during which they experience marginal personal and social status. The funeral, endorsing the awareness of the final disposal of their loved one, assists them to resolve their ambiguous position. Indeed, the ritual is regarded by funeral directors as a decisive stage in mourning. They believe it marks the end of the first phase of grief and the beginning of the healing process.

If viewing the flowers gave mourners the opportunity for private reflection and public acknowledgment of changes to the family group or community, it was during the homeward journey that Adrian hoped his clients would resume "normal" behavior.

> Usually on the way back, when you've taken people out to the flower area and they've had a bit of a stretch and a chat, they get back in the car and it's over. On the way home they'll all be sitting there glum and somebody'll say something like, "Uncle Fred would be laughing his socks off at us lot sitting here all glum—he was never glum and he used to go on about how you'll all miss me when I'm gone." And they'll all burst out laughing—you can hear it.

Funeral parties which failed to accept the modification to the group
were usually those where death had been tragic. In those cases the
undertaker faced the problem of how to take his leave of clients when
the ritual was over. The loss of a child was particularly difficult and
Stone related the tale of one memorable occasion when he had been
concerned that the funeral would not be properly concluded.

> There was the funeral of this young kiddy and we came back and
> there wasn't a peep from anyone, not a peep. And I was thinking,
> how do you leave people like this? What do you say to them? How
> can you leave them? You have to say something. You can stand
> there and talk to them because people do want to talk to you and
> they can go on for ages. And I just didn't know how I was going to
> leave this lot.

The undertaker's concern was that although the disposal ritual was
complete his job was not over because the bereaved were trapped in
the liminal phase by the magnitude of their tragedy. The funeral had
failed to return them to a state of "normality." In the event it was
humor—the director's salve for all ills—which provided the solution to
his disquiet.

> We did the funeral and we came back across Easton Marshes. And
> down by the marshes is a camping area. And there's a little slope
> and a stile and there were three people going over the bar with
> packs on their backs. The last bloke got over the bar and as he was
> lifting the pack up on his shoulders it took over and he went
> roly-poly-poly down the slope. And I whispered to the driver, "Did
> you see that? I think that's the funniest thing I've ever seen in
> my life!"
>
> And you have to bite your cheeks and you daren't look at the driver
> and don't whatever you do look at me! And then, of course, what
> happened was I heard someone in the back say, "Did you see that?"
> And they all burst out laughing. And there was this huge black
> limousine laughing its way up the road at the top of its voice all the
> way back. Thank God we didn't have far to go.
>
> I wanted to go back and give the guy a fiver and say would he please
> be there on similar occasions in the future! But that's great! That's
> my job. That's what I do. I take the funeral from the beginning to
> the end and, as I said, life continues.

CONCLUSION

In this chapter I have taken the funeral director's concept of the "basic pattern" and used it to examine the funeral ceremony. The funeral in the East End of London is not, as John Fry argued of other areas, simply a minor disposal service. Traditional rituals, such as bowing to the coffin and walking the cortège, have been retained by the industry and are regarded by them as bestowing dignity on the deceased and meaning for the bereaved. There are also practical aspects to many customs and some are embellished and reinforced as a means of averting failed performances for the funeral director. Floral tributes and ranked seating in funeral vehicles convey mourners' relationship to the deceased and disclose their status in the family hierarchy.

The role of funeral conductors in controlling the ceremony and their delegation of power to the priest for the duration of the religious service, are telling aspects of this rite of passage. This juxtaposition of professional authority effectively excludes the bereaved and results in limiting the mourners' role to participation in the liturgy. Furthermore, dramatizing the funeral and thereby mystifying the ceremony ritually disables clients. I have argued that customers who do not use the crematorium chapel and those who opt for interment rather than cremation enjoy a greater degree of involvement in the disposal service. Post-service activity, which in the case of cremation is organized around viewing the flowers, is regarded by the undertaker as allowing mourners a few moments to accept their loss before they return to life's normal activities. On a societal level, death of an individual signifies the destruction of one atom of that community's make-up; the social group has changed irrevocably. If the balance within the whole is to be restored and the role performed by that member reallocated or eliminated, survivors must stress their separation from the dead and only when they are able to do this has the drama of the funeral ritual been truly successful.

REFERENCES

1. E. C. Hughes, *Men and Their Work,* The Free Press, New York, 1958.
2. H. O. Mauksch, Becoming a Nurse: A Selective View, *The Annals of the American Academy of Political & Social Science, 346,* pp. 88-98, March 1963.
3. A. Niederhoffer, *Behind the Shield: The Police in Urban Society,* Doubleday, New York, 1969.
4. National Association of Funeral Directors, *Manual of Funeral Directing,* National Association of Funeral Directors, London, 1988.

5. W. S. F. Pickering, The Persistence of Rites of Passage: Towards an Explanation, *British Journal of Sociology, 25*:1, pp. 63-78, 1974.
6. J. M. Watson, *So Far, So What: Tales from Beside the Grave—An Undertaker's View,* unpublished, 1991.
7. The Cremation Society of Great Britain, *Pharos International, 55*:2, Summer 1989.
8. T. Walter, *Funerals and How to Improve Them,* Hodder & Stoughton, London, 1990.
9. L. Pincus, *Death and the Family: The Importance of Mourning,* Faber and Faber, London, 1976.
10. R. L. Fulton, The Clergyman and the Funeral Director: A Study in Role Conflict, *Social Forces, 39*:4, pp. 317-323, 1961.
11. J. Wood, The Structure of Concern: The Ministry in Death-related Situations, *Urban Life, 4*:3, pp. 369-384, 1975.
12. M. Page, *Funeral Rituals in a Northern City,* unpublished Ph.D. thesis, University of Leeds, 1989.
13. G. Mungham and P. A. Thomas, Solicitors and Clients: Altruism or Self-interest, in *The Sociology of the Professions: Lawyers, Doctors and Others,* R. Dingwall and P. Lewis (eds.), Macmillan, London, 1983.
14. J. Spottiswoode, *Undertaken with Love,* Robert Hale, London, 1991.
15. M. Page, Grave Misgivings, *Religion Today, 2*:3, 1985.
16. R. Grainger, *The Unburied,* Churchman Publishing, Worthing, West Sussex, 1988.
17. J. Hockey, The Acceptable Face of Human Grieving? The Clergy's Role in Managing Emotional Expression during Funerals, in *The Sociology of Death,* D. Clark (ed.), Blackwell, Oxford, 1993.
18. C. Gittings, *Death, Burial and the Individual in Early Modern England,* Croom Helm, London, 1984.

Conclusion:
The Undertaker:
Past, Present, and Future

The aim of this conclusion is to recapitulate and bring together the salient points of this book, and in so doing to present an overview of the occupational role of the modern funeral director.

THE DEVELOPMENT OF
UNDERTAKING

The undertaking trade that emerged in late seventeenth-century Britain—the ancestor of both the British and North American funeral industries today—modeled funeral goods and rituals on the earlier practice of the heralds who dictated the final rites of passage of the aristocracy. There were three primary reasons for this. First, the heralds were the forerunners of undertakers in that they organized and controlled the funeral. They therefore provided an example of what the entrepreneur deathworker wished to achieve. Second, and linked to this, was the undertakers' aspiration to conduct the funerals of the wealthy. When these tradesmen first appeared it was only the upper and middle social strata who contracted an outside agency to organize interment. The poorer sectors of society were unable to afford the service and, initially at least, may have regarded it as unnecessary and ill-befitting their more simple requirements. Third, as the aristocracy came to rebel against the stringent demands of the heralds they increasingly turned to the undertaker. Substituting for the College of Arms it was natural that undertakers should attempt to provide their clients with a familiar, if less expensive, ritual.

During the eighteenth century, undertakers fully usurped heraldic power and began to regulate funerals, initially, for the middle classes, and later, when burial insurance made it possible, for those of the respectable poor. By the mid-nineteenth century, deathworkers in Europe and North America had become powerful groups prescribing the amount and nature of funeral trappings according to a code of social status. In Britain, the stigma of the pauper funeral and the real fear of dissection at the hands of the surgeon or anatomist encouraged the poor to strive for a "decent" burial. Furnishing them with the lavish funeral, long enjoyed by the wealthier members of society, resulted in the undertaker plying a profitable trade from all sectors of the community irrespective of social class. The halcyon days of the undertaker were, however, short-lived.

One effect of industrialization in expanding and overcrowding the urban centers, was a Victorian preoccupation with the need to sanitize towns. The novels of Charles Dickens, for example, are absorbed with the social and physical degradation of the London urban poor. The depiction of undertakers as greedy profiteers extracting an unscrupulous profit from the misfortunes of others was a popular contemporary stereotype. The miasmatic theory of dirt and disease led to reforming legislation such as The Metropolitan Interments Act of 1850 which ruled that urban churchyards were no longer to be used for burial. This Act forced the removal of the cemetery to the outskirts of the city. One consequence, in concert with the work of vocal reformers such as Walker, Chadwick, and Dickens, was to curb the extravagance of funerals and the power of the undertaker.

At the turn of the twentieth century, although flamboyant rituals continued to be desired by the urban working class, the wealthy—for whom demographic factors were making death less familiar—were coming to reject the pomp of earlier obsequies. The growing preference for simple funerals among those who had the most to spend heralded a natural shrinkage in the undertaking industry. In order to survive, those who remained recognized the need to form associations to combat competition from part-time workers. Part of the drive for survival was the turn to professionalism and this, I have argued, is the key to understanding the work of undertakers throughout the twentieth century.

In striving to become a profession, the motives and working practices of the funeral industry have been transformed. Deathworkers have appropriated the discourse of the reformers and transformed their occupation from one with an overt desire for profit, to one concerned with providing a public service. Their emphasis has been on the roles of caretaker of public health and protector of the bereaved from the contaminated corpse. In the early decades of the twentieth century they emulated the professionalism of the clergy, removing grave goods from window displays and replacing them with religious icons. By the end of the Second World War this mood of traditional religiosity, declining throughout the western world, was being eroded and replaced by science. The chapel of rest, for example, lost its Christian status and by the late 1980s in most funeral homes it had become simply a "rest room."

THE MODERN FUNERAL DIRECTOR

Four central elements of the work of modern funeral directors illustrate their professional aspirations. First, the bureaucratization of the funeral; second, their possession of the body; third, the use of scientific "humanization" techniques such as embalming; and fourth, undertakers' overall control of the funeral ceremony.

Bureaucratization of the Funeral

Since the introduction of death registration the after-death system has become steadily bureaucratized. Death certificates require a doctor's signature (two doctors in the case of cremation). Coroners or Medical Examiners are obliged to launch an investigation into the cause of any unexpected death. This may involve other agencies, including the police and the hospital and inevitably multiplies administrative requirements. Undertakers and crematorium staff demand that customers produce official authority to dispose of the corpse and this is provided by the Registrar of Deaths. Signatures of the next of kin and a statement that there are no dissenting family members are required before cremation can take place.

The result is that the procedures for the registration of death and the disposal of remains are regarded by many as an intricate maze of form-filling and alienating officialdom. The advantages of hiring a guide to help them through the unfamiliar process are clear. Funeral directors, like professionals who deal with privileged knowledge, assume control over the proceedings. In so doing they promote a model of the bereaved as immobilized by grief and stricken with passivity by virtue of their distance from knowledge of death. Subject to the pressures of modern working life, mourners rely on undertakers as a source of expertise. Deathworkers are keen to encourage the bureaucratic process as it enhances mystification of their industry and allows them to define the parameters of deathwork.

Possession of the Body

In Britain during the 1920s, use of existing public mortuaries was encouraged as sanctuaries for the dead. Although justified in terms of public health these places were viewed with disgust by the populace and their use largely eschewed. Within fifteen years, however, funeral directors were providing a chapel of rest for clients who were beginning to accept this abode for their dead. The radical change in attitude can be traced to increasing public concern for health; the greater demands of modern industry; and, linked to this, an escalating propensity toward the distancing of death. After the Second World War there was a popular expectation that the urban undertaker would provide accommodation for the corpse.

Indeed, since the funeral cannot take place without the deceased, the modern funeral director's power hinges on *possession* of the body. The chapel of rest was a prerequisite for taking custody of the cadaver. Removing the body from the home, hospital, or public mortuary gives undertakers control over the after-death system. Lack of legal ownership and popular reluctance to deal with preparation of the polluting corpse reinforce the workers claim to control.

In stressing the vitiating aspects of their work, undertakers see themselves as providing a public service which protects the bereaved from the physical and psychological distress of proximity to the corpse. The effect of removal for the bereaved, however, is to *further alienate* them from death as they are estranged from the body and its ritual requirements. Their contact with the deceased is now limited to that sanctioned by the funeral director under the auspices of viewing. This unfamiliarity further mystifies deathwork procedures.

The Science of "Humanization"

Embalming extends the "protection" of the bereaved. Defining the process as "hygienic treatment," the embalmer uses the language of the reformers and operates within the parameters of their debate. Furthermore, since the 1960s, viewing the body has been regarded by bereavement "experts" as conducive to the grieving process. Preparing it for viewing in the chapel of rest ensures that the mortician is able to check any decomposition. It is possible for the worker to embalm in the home of the deceased but this would severely restrict working practice. Having the cadaver on the premises and using spatial boundaries to demarcate public from private regions, distances the relatives from the realities of mortality and further obscures deathwork procedures. Moreover, it facilitates the funeral director's purpose in preserving and presenting the loved-one in a manner perceived as acceptable to clients. Having prepared the body for viewing, undertakers control the ritual display. They interpret the wishes of the visitors as the desire to see peaceful, sleeping, life-like corpses. This enables them to exhibit embalming and presentation skills and furthers their professional and business objectives.

Controlling the Funeral Ceremony

The funeral ceremony is the climax of the after-death ritual. Once contracted by the bereaved to organize the funeral, undertakers consider themselves empowered to control the proceedings.

During the ritual they adopt responsibility for reestablishing the centrality of the family, utilizing the arrangement of floral tributes and seating plans to demonstrate the status of mourners in the family hierarchy. They can also be relied upon to assist chief mourners to renegotiate their social identity by directing them around the center stage, in and out of interaction with clergy, other family members, and supporting mourners.

Active participation of the bereaved in the funeral ritual is discouraged by both undertakers and clergy. Unless obsequies are unfamiliar to the conductor, as they may be in the case of ethnic minority funerals, ceremonial control is only delegated at one juncture and then it is to the priest. The power-base of the relationship between the funeral director and the cleric is made explicit through the physical transfer of money.

Funeral rites in the East End of London tend to be more traditional and flamboyant than those in other urban areas. This is partly accounted for by the requirements of the bereaved for an established ritual. Embellishing the ceremony is also employed by the funeral director as a method of guarding against spoiled performances. A further explanation for elaborate funerals is connected with a self perception of professionalism. Corresponding to the pattern instituted by the professions and in contrast to deathworkers in North America, funeral directors in Britain are unable to prominently advertise their services. The funeral cortège, therefore, provides a dramatic opportunity for the public exhibition of quality goods and services.

Rather than perishing at the hands of the nineteenth-century reform movement, undertakers have transformed the essence of their industry. The aims of the reformers were to reduce expenditure on mourning paraphernalia and ensure protection for the community from the dangers of decaying human material. The unintended consequences of their efforts were to *distance* death from society. Ironically, by removing the corpse from the home and by de-skilling those once responsible for laying-out and funeral arrangements, *greater* power has accrued to funeral directors. As coordinators of services related to the ritual disposal of human remains, they have been granted control over the after-death system.

In adopting the reform philosophy with its emphasis on sanitation, health, and protection from decay, undertakers have been instrumental in the transformation of the British way of death. This has changed from one of extravagance to a more detached, hygienic approach. In pursuing this image the trade has always maintained an awareness of public attitudes and the needs of bereaved people. Innovation has been rationalized in terms of client benefits. Hence, embalming *protects* customers from disease while *enabling* them to view their loved-one without shock or horror; removing the body to the chapel of rest *protects* the bereaved from disease by distancing them from the cadaver, and *enables* them to get on with the process of grieving without the intrusion of the body and by leaving all funeral organization to the professional.

THE FUTURE OF THE SMALL FAMILY BUSINESS

The closing decade of the twentieth century is witnessing the work of new reform movements dedicated to "rediscovering" death and to restoring control over dying and after-death rituals to those emotionally involved. The growth of the hospice movement, and more recently funeral reform groups, encourage the reassessment of hospital and funeral practice and devalue the need for the funeral director.

The funeral industry is again on the defensive but, more significantly, some undertakers are adapting their working style to complement the more caring and user-friendly approach to death demanded by their critics. Funeral companies are employing more women (especially in front stage activities), and premises with comfortable chairs, pink walls, and a "homely" atmosphere promote an image of the death-work as friend to the bereaved and facilitator of client wishes.

Some East End funeral directors would argue that their practice has always been caring and responsive to the requirements of the bereaved. The castigation of deathworkers as an alienating force by reformers is regarded by these workers as more applicable to the operation of larger funeral companies. The latter are viewed by many small family businesses as depersonalizing the ritual. In primary pursuit of profit and by dint of failure to tailor obsequies to the individual client, these funeral chains are branded as unprofessional.

The manager and staff of G. R. Stone upheld these beliefs. This small family firm in the East End of London, however, did not survive the financial trials of competition and take-over from a larger company.

Shortly after the completion of fieldwork the funeral director accepted an offer from Kenyon Securities, sold the business and left the industry. Of his staff, Peter and Barry took up employment with another local undertaker and so fulfilled their desire to remain in the trade. Gordon returned to full-time car hire. Ralf continued as a self-employed stonemason from other premises. Roberta sought receptionist duties elsewhere and Betty gave up her work as a cleaner. Within six months Bob, the former manager, had died. Adrian Stone returned from self-imposed exile to pay a final tribute to "dear old Uncle Bob" and conducted the funeral in the best style he knew.

The social world of the funeral company at the heart of this study has disappeared. In the East End of London, however, others remain in the belief that the professional funeral service they offer assists the bereaved to reconcile their loss. For as Adrian once told me,

> The service that we provide is complete—death to the grave. Sometimes on the outskirts it doesn't seem very far but it's a long, long journey for a lot of people.

Bibliography

Adams, S., A Gendered History of the Social Management of Death and Dying in Foleshill, Coventry during the Inter-War Years, in *The Sociology of Death,* D. Clark (ed.), Blackwell, Oxford, 1993.

Ariès, P., *Western Attitudes Toward Death: From the Middle Ages to the Present,* Open Forum Series, Marion Boyars, London, 1976.

Ariès, P., *The Hour of Our Death,* Penguin, Harmondsworth, 1981.

Ariès, P., Death Inside Out, in *Understanding Death and Dying: An Interdisciplinary Approach* (3rd Edition), S. Wilcox and M. Sutton (eds.), Mayfield, California, 1985.

Ariès, P., *Images of Man and Death,* Harvard University Press, Cambridge, Massachusetts, 1985.

Atkinson, P. et al., Medical Mystique, *Sociology of Work and Occupations, 4,* pp. 243-280, 1977.

Atkinson, P., *The Ethnographic Imagination: Textual Constructions of Reality,* Routledge, London, 1990.

Bailey, B., *Churchyards of England and Wales,* Robert Hale, London, 1987.

Barley, S. R., The Codes of the Dead: The Semiotics of Funeral Work, *Urban Life, 12*:1, pp. 3-31, April 1983.

Becker, E., *The Denial of Death,* Free Press, New York, 1973.

Becker, H. S. et al., *Boys in White: Student Culture in Medical School,* University of Chicago Press, Chicago, 1961.

Becker, H. S., *Outsiders,* Free Press, New York, 1963.

Becker, H. S., Problems of Inference and Proof in Participant Observation, in *Issues in Participant Observation,* G. J. McCall and J. L. Simmons (eds.), Addison-Wesley, Reading, Massachusetts, 1969.

Bennett, I., *Attitudes to Life and Death,* E. Hillman (ed.), conference paper, Report of North East London Polytechnic Seminar, 1978.

Berreman, G., *Behind Many Masks: Ethnography and Impression Management in a Himalayan Village,* Monograph 4, Society for Applied Anthropology, Cornell University Press, 1962.

Besant, W., *East London,* Chatto & Windus, London, 1903.

Blauner, R., Death and the Social Structure, *Psychiatry, 29*:4, November 1966.

Bloch, M., *Placing the Dead: Tombs, Ancestral Villages and Kinship Organization in Madagascar,* Seminar Press, London, 1971.

Bloch, M., Death, Women and Power, in *Death and the Regeneration of Life,* M. Bloch and J. Parry (eds.), Cambridge University Press, Cambridge, 1982.

Bloch, M. and J. Parry (eds.), *Death and the Regeneration of Life,* Cambridge University Press, Cambridge, 1982.

Bloch, M., *Ritual, History and Power: Selected Papers in Anthropology,* Athlone Press, London, 1989.

Bloom, S. W., The Process of Becoming a Physician, *The Annals of the American Academy of Political & Social Science, 346,* pp. 77-87, 1963.

Boston, S. and R. Trezise, *Merely Mortal: Coping with Dying, Death and Bereavement,* Methuen, London, in association with Channel Four Television Co., 1987.

Bowman, L., *The American Funeral: A Study in Guilt, Extravagance and Sublimity,* Public Affairs Press, Washington, D.C., 1959.

Burke, K., *A Grammar of Motives,* Prentice Hall, Englewood Cliffs, New Jersey, 1945.

Cannadine, D., War and Death, Grief and Mourning in Modern Britain, in *Mirrors of Mortality: Studies in the Social History of Death,* J. Whaley (ed.), Europa, London, 1981.

Carey, J. W., *Media, Myths and Narratives: Television and the Press,* Sage, Newbury Park, 1988.

Cassell's Household Guide, (1874) cited in J. Morley, *Death, Heaven and the Victorians,* Studio Vista, London, 1971.

Caudrey, A., A Solemn Bureaucracy, *New Society,* pp. 9-10, May 27, 1988.

Chadwick, E., *Report from the Select Committee on the Improvement of the Health of Towns—Effects of Interment of Bodies in Towns,* London, 1842.

Chadwick, E., *Supplementary Report on the Results of the Special Inquiry into the Practice of Interment in Towns,* London, 1843.

Curl, J. S., *The Victorian Celebration of Death,* David & Charles, Newton Abbot, 1972.

Danforth, L. M., *The Death Rituals of Rural Greece,* Princeton University Press, New Jersey, 1982.

Dingwall, R. and P. Lewis (eds.), *The Sociology of the Professions: Lawyers, Doctors and Others,* Macmillan, London, 1983.

Duvignaud, J., The Theatre in Society: Society in the Theatre, in *Sociology of Literature and Drama,* E. Burns and T. Burns (eds.), Penguin, Harmondsworth, 1973.

Douglas, M., *Purity and Danger: An Analysis of the Concepts of Pollution and Taboo,* Routledge, London, 1966.

Department of Social Security, *What To Do After a Death,* HMSO, London, 1987.

Durkheim, E., *The Elementary Forms of Religious Life,* J. W. Swain (trans.), Allen & Unwin, London, 1965.

Ettinger, R., *The Prospect of Immortality,* Sidgwick & Jackson, London, 1965.

Evans-Pritchard, E. E., *The Divine Kingship of the Shilluk of the Nilotic Sudan,* Cambridge University Press, Cambridge, 1948.

Farrell, J. L., *Inventing the American Way of Death 1830-1920*, Temple University Press, Philadelphia, 1980.

Feifel, H., Attitudes towards Death in Some Normal and Mentally Ill Populations, in *The Meaning of Death*, McGraw-Hill, New York, 1959.

Feifel, H. (ed.), *The Meaning of Death*, McGraw-Hill, New York, 1959.

Ferman, L. A. and L. E. Berndt, The Irregular Economy, in *Can I Have it in Cash? A Study of Informal Institutions and Unorthodox Ways of Doing Things*, S. Henry (ed.), Astragal Books, London, 1981.

Field, D., *Nursing the Dying*, Tavistock Routledge, London, 1989.

Firth, S., The Good Death: Approaches to Death, Dying and Bereavement among British Hindus, in *Perspectives on Death and Dying*, A. Berger (ed.), Charles Press, Philadelphia, 1989.

Frazer, J. G., *The Fear of the Dead in Primitive Religion*, Vol. II, Macmillan, London, 1934.

Freud, S., Thoughts for the Times on War and Death 1915, II. Our Attitude towards Death, in *The Standard Edition of the Complete Psychological Works of Sigmund Freud, Vol. XIV (1914-1916)*, J. Strachey and A. Freud (eds.), Hogarth Press, London, 1957.

Friedson, E., Medical Care and the Public: Case Study of a Medical Group, *The Annals of the American Academy of Political & Social Science, 346*, pp. 57-67, March 1963.

Fulton, R. L., The Clergyman and the Funeral Director: A Study in Role Conflict, *Social Forces, 39*:4, pp. 317-323, 1961.

Geertz, C., Ritual and Social Change: A Javanese Example, *American Anthropologist, 59*, pp. 32-54, 1973.

Giesey, R. E., *The Royal Funeral Ceremony in Renaissance France*, Librairie E. Droz, Genhve, 1960.

Gittings, C., *Death, Burial and the Individual in Early Modern England*, Croom Helm, London, 1984.

Glaser, B. G. and A. L. Strauss, *Awareness of Dying*, Aldine, Chicago, 1965.

Glaser, B. G. and A. L. Strauss, *The Discovery of Grounded Theory*, Aldine, Chicago, 1967.

Glaser, B. G. and A. L. Strauss, *Time for Dying*, Aldine, Chicago, 1968.

Goffman, E., *The Presentation of Self in Everyday Life*, Doubleday, New York, 1959.

Goffman, E., *Encounters: Two Studies in the Sociology of Interaction*, Bobbs-Merrill, Indianapolis, 1961.

Goffman, E., *Stigma, Notes on the Management of Spoiled Identity*, Prentice-Hall, Englewood Cliffs, New Jersey, 1963.

Goffman, E., *Forms of Talk*, Basil Blackwell, Oxford, 1981.

Goody, J., *Death, Property and the Ancestors: A Study of Mortuary Customs of LoDagaa of West Africa*, Tavistock, London, 1962.

Gorer, G., The Pornography of Death, 1955, reprinted in G. Gorer, *Death, Grief and Mourning in Contemporary Britain*, Cresset Press, London, 1965.

Gorer, G., *Death, Grief and Mourning in Contemporary Britain*, Cresset Press, London, 1965.

Grainger, R., *The Unburied*, Churchman Publishing, Worthing, West Sussex, 1988.

Griffin, G. and D. Tobin, *In the Midst of Life: The Australian Response to Death*, Melbourne University Press, Melbourne, 1984.

Habenstein, R. W., *The American Funeral Director and the Sociology of Work*, unpublished Ph.D. thesis, University of Chicago, 1954.

Habenstein, R. W., Sociology of Occupations: The Case of the American Funeral Director, in *Human Behaviour and Social Processes: An Interactionist Approach*, A. M. Rose (ed.), Routledge & Kegan Paul, London, 1962.

Habenstein, R. W., The Phoenix and the Ashes, in *Institutions and the Person: Papers Presented to Everett C. Hughes*, H. S. Becker et al. (eds.), Aldine, Chicago, 1968.

Habenstein, R. W., Occupational Uptake: Professionalizing, in *Pathways to Data: Field Methods for Studying Ongoing Social Organizations*, R. W. Habenstein (ed.), Aldine, Chicago, 1970.

Habenstein, R. W. and W. M. Lamers, *The History of American Funeral Directing*, Bulfin Press, Milwaukee, 1955.

Habenstein, R. W. and W. M. Lamers, The Patterns of Late Nineteenth-century Funerals, in *Passing: The Vision of Death in America*, C. O. Jackson (ed.), Greenwood, Westport, Connecticut, 1977.

Hammersley, M. and P. Atkinson, *Ethnography: Principles in Practice*, Tavistock, London, 1983.

Hennessy, P. J., *Families, Funerals and Finances, A Study of Funeral Expenses and How They are Paid*, Department of Health and Social Security Statistics and Research Division, Research Report No. 6, HMSO, London, 1980.

Henry, S. (ed.), *Can I Have it in Cash? A Study of Informal Institutions and Unorthodox Ways of Doing Things*, Astragal Books, London, 1981.

Heritage, J. and D. Greatbatch, On the Institutional Character of Institutional Talk: The Case of News Interviews, in *Discourse in Professional and Everyday Culture*, P. A. Forstorp (ed.), University of Linkoping, Studies in Communications, SIC 28, 1989, cited in A. Peräkylä and D. Silverman, *Sociology*, 25:4, November 1991.

Hertz, R., *Death and the Right Hand*, R. Needham and C. Needham (trans.), Cohen & West, London, 1960.

Heymowski, A., *I Samhällets Utkanter: om "Tattare" i Sverige*, Ingvar Svanberg, Chur, 1987.

Hinton, J., *Dying* (2nd Edition), Penguin, Harmondsworth, 1972.

Hockey, J., *Experiences of Death: An Anthropological Account*, Edinburgh University Press, Edinburgh, 1990.

Houlbrooke, R. (ed.), *Death, Ritual and Bereavement*, Routledge, London, 1989.

Howarth, G., Investigating Deathwork, in *The Sociology of Death*, D. Clark (ed.), Blackwell, Oxford, 1993.

Howe, E., *1981 Census: Word Profiles*, Research Note 6, Research and Intelligence Section, Chief Executives Office, London Borough of Hackney, 1983.

Hughes, E. C., *Men and Their Work,* The Free Press, New York, 1958.

Hughes, E. C., Good People and Dirty Work, in *The Other Side: Perspectives on Deviance,* The Free Press, New York, 1964.

Hughes, E. C., *The Sociological Eye,* Aldine, Chicago, 1971.

Humphreys, L., *Tearoom Trade: A Study of Homosexual Encounters in Public Places,* Aldine, Chicago, 1970.

Humphreys, S. C., *The Family, Women and Death: Comparative Studies,* Routledge & Kegan Paul, London, 1983.

Humphreys, S. C. and H. King (eds.), *Mortality and Immortality, the Anthropology and Archaeology of Death,* Academic Press, London, 1981.

Huntington, R. and P. Metcalf, *Celebrations of Death: The Anthropology of Mortuary Ritual,* Cambridge University Press, Cambridge, 1979.

Illich, I., *Disabling Professions,* Marion Boyars, London, 1977.

Jackson, C. O. (ed.), *Passing: The Vision of Death in America,* Greenwood, Westport, Connecticut, 1977.

Johnson, T. J., *Professions and Power,* Macmillan, London, 1972.

Jupp, P., *From Dust to Ashes: The Replacement of Burial by Cremation in England 1840-1967,* The Congregational Lecture, London, 1990.

Kantaris, S., A Dying Art, *Poems 1987,* Falmouth Poetry Group, unpublished collection, Falmouth, 1987.

Kastenbaum, R. and R. Aisenberg, *The Psychology of Death,* Springer, New York, 1972.

Kearl, M. C., *Endings: A Sociology of Death and Dying,* Oxford University Press, New York, 1989.

Kirchmeier-Andersen, S., *The Concept of Death in Danish Sermons,* unpublished MA thesis, University of Copenhagen, Copenhagen, 1987.

Kübler-Ross, E., *On Death and Dying,* Tavistock, London, 1970.

Laurence, A., Godly Grief: Individual Responses to Death in Seventeenth-century Britain, in *Death, Ritual and Bereavement,* R. Houlbrooke (ed.), Routledge, London, 1989.

Laws, S., *Issues of Blood: The Politics of Menstruation,* Macmillan, Basingstoke, 1990.

Lefebvre, H., *The Production of Space,* D. Nicholson-Smith (trans.), Basil Blackwell, Oxford, 1991.

LeGoff, J., *The Birth of Purgatory,* A. Goldhammer (trans.), Chicago University Press, Chicago, 1984.

Lief, H. I. and R. Fox, The Medical Student's Training for Detached Concern, in *The Psychological Basis of Medical Practice,* H. I. Lief et al. (eds.), Harper & Row, New York, 1964.

Litton, J., *The English Way of Death: The Common Funeral Since 1450,* Robert Hale, London, 1991.

Llewellyn, N., *The Art of Death,* Reaktion Books, London, 1991.

Lofland, J., Open and Concealed Dramaturgic Strategies: The Case of the State Execution, *Urban Life,* 4:3, pp. 272-295, October 1975.

McCray, L., The Good Death in Seventeenth-century England, in *Death, Ritual and Bereavement,* R. Houlbrooke (ed.), Routledge, London, 1989.

McManners, J., *Death and the Enlightenment: Changing Attitudes to Death Among Christians and Unbelievers in Eighteenth-Century France,* Oxford University Press, Oxford, 1981.

Mack, J. and S. Humphries, *London at War,* Sidgwick & Jackson, London, 1985.

Malinowski, B., *Magic, Science and Religion and Other Essays,* Doubleday, New York, 1954.

Marris, P., *Loss and Change* (revised Edition), Routledge & Kegan Paul, London, 1986.

Matza, D., *Becoming Deviant,* Prentice Hall, Englewood Cliffs, New Jersey, 1969.

Mauksch, H. O., Becoming a Nurse: A Selective View, *The Annals of the American Academy of Political & Social Science, 346,* pp. 88-98, March 1963.

Medcalf, L., *Law and Identity,* Sage, London, 1978.

Messinger, S. L. et al., Life as Theatre: Some Notes on the Dramaturgical Approach to Social Reality, *Sociometry, 25,* September 1962.

Metcalf, P. and R. Huntington, *Celebrations of Death: The Anthropology of Mortuary Ritual* (2nd Edition), Cambridge University Press, Cambridge, 1991.

Millerson, G., *The Qualifying Professions,* Routledge & Kegan Paul, London, 1964.

Millman, M., *The Unkindest Cut: Life in the Backrooms of Medicine,* M. Morrow, New York, 1976.

Mitchison, R., *British Population Change Since 1860,* Macmillan, London, 1977.

Mitford, J., *The American Way of Death,* Hutchinson, London, 1963.

Morley, J., *Death, Heaven and the Victorians,* Studio Vista, London, 1971.

Mungham, G. and P. A. Thomas, Solicitors and Clients: Altruism or Self-interest, *The Sociology of the Professions: Lawyers, Doctors and Others,* R. Dingwall and P. Lewis (eds.), Macmillan, London, 1983.

National Association of Funeral Directors, *Manual of Funeral Directing,* London, 1988.

Niederhoffer, A., *Behind the Shield: The Police in Urban Society,* Doubleday, New York, 1969.

Office of Fair Trading, *Funerals: A Report,* HMSO, London, January 1989.

OPCS, *A Survey of Funeral Arrangements 1987: The Report of a Survey carried out by Social Security Division on behalf of the Office of Fair Trading,* K. Foster, Office of Population Censuses and Surveys, Social Survey Division, HMSO, London, 1989.

O'Neill, E. H., An Experiment in Medical Education, *Medical Social Work, 2,* pp. 125-135, October 1953.

Osterweis, M., F. Solomon, and M. Green (eds.), *Bereavement: Reactions, Consequences and Care,* National Academy Press, Washington, D.C., 1984.

Page, M., Grave Misgivings, *Religion Today, 2:3,* 1985.

Page, M., *Funeral Rituals in a Northern City,* unpublished Ph.D. thesis, University of Leeds, 1989.

Palmer, A., *The East End,* John Murray, London, 1989.

Parkes, C. M., *Bereavement: Studies in Grief in Adult Life,* Tavistock, London, 1986.

Parkes, C. M., J. Stevenson-Hinde, and P. Marris, *Attachment Across the Life Cycle,* Tavistock/Routledge, London, 1991.

Parsons, T., *The Social System,* Routledge & Kegan Paul, London, 1951.

Parsons, T. and V. Lidz, Death in American Society, in *Essays in Self-Destruction,* E. Shneidman (ed.), Science House, New York, 1967.

Peräkylä, A. and D. Silverman, Reinterpreting Speech-exchange Systems: Communication Formats in Aids Counselling, *Sociology, 25*:4, pp. 627-651, November 1991.

Perinbanayagam, R. S., The Definition of the Situation: An Analysis of the Ethnomethodological and Dramaturgical View, *The Sociological Quarterly, 15,* Autumn 1974.

Pickering, W. S. F., The Persistence of Rites of Passage: Towards an Explanation, *British Journal of Sociology, 25*:1, pp. 63-78, March 1974.

Pincus, L., *Death and the Family,* Faber and Faber, London, 1976.

Pine, V. R., *Caretaker of the Dead: The American Funeral Director,* Irvington, New York, 1975.

Polson, C. J. and T. K. Marshall, *The Disposal of the Dead,* English Universities Press, London, 1975.

Porter, R., Death and Doctors in Georgian England, in *Death, Ritual and Bereavement,* R. Houlbrooke (ed.), Routledge, London, 1989.

Prior, L., Policing the Dead: A Sociology of the Mortuary, *Sociology, 21*:3, pp. 355-376, August 1987.

Prior, L., *The Social Organization of Death: Medical Discourse and Social Practices in Belfast,* Macmillan, Basingstoke, 1989.

Puckle, B. S., *Funeral Customs: Their Origin and Development,* L.T. Werner Laurie, London, 1926.

Reeves, P. M., *Round About a Pound a Week,* Virago, London, 1929.

Richardson, R., *Death, Dissection and the Destitute,* Routledge & Kegan Paul, London, 1987.

Riley, J. C., *Sickness, Recovery and Death: A History and Forecast of Ill Health,* Macmillan, Basingstoke, 1989.

Sacks, H., E. A. Schegloff, and G. Jefferson, A Simplest Systematics of Turn-taking for Conversation, *Language, 50,* pp. 696-735, 1974.

Sartre, J. P., *Being and Nothingness,* H. E. Barnes (trans.), Washington Square Press, Washington, 1966.

Schutz, A., The Stranger, in *Collected Papers, Vol. II,* Martinus Nijhoff, The Hague, 1964.

Simpson, M. A., *The Facts of Death: A Complete Guide for Being Prepared,* Prentice-Hall, Englewood Cliffs, New Jersey, 1972.

Smale, B., *Deathwork: A Sociological Analysis of Funeral Directing,* unpublished Ph.D. thesis, University of Surrey, Guildford, 1985.

Stannard, D. W., *The Puritan Way of Death: A Study in Religion, Culture and Social Change,* Oxford University Press, New York, 1977.

Stone, L., *The Family, Sex and Marriage in England 1500-1800,* (abridged Edition), Penguin, Harmondsworth, 1979.

Stroebe, W. and M. S. Stroebe, *Bereavement and Health, The Psychological and Physical Consequences of Partner Loss,* Cambridge University Press, Cambridge, 1987.

Sudnow, D., *Passing On: The Social Organization of Dying,* Prentice Hall, Englewood Cliffs, New Jersey, 1967.

Synnott, A., Tomb, Temple, Machine and Self: The Social Construction of the Body, *British Journal of Sociology, 43*:1, pp. 79-110, March 1992.

Turner, B. S., *The Body and Society: Explorations in Social Theory,* Basil Blackwell, Oxford, 1984.

Turner, R. E. and C. Edgley, Death as Theatre: A Dramaturgical Analysis of the American Funeral, *Sociology and Social Research, 60*:4, pp. 377-392, 1976.

Tylor, E. B., *Primitive·Culture: Researches into the Development of Mythology, Philosophy, Religion, Language, Art and Custom,* Vol. I (2nd Edition), Murray, London, 1891.

Ungerson, C., *Gender and Caring: Work and Welfare in Britain and Scandinavia,* Harvester Wheatsheaf, New York, 1990.

Unruh, D., Doing Funeral Directing: Managing Sources of Risk in Funeralization, *Urban Life, 8,* pp. 247-263, 1979.

van Gennep, A., *The Rites of Passage,* M. B. Vizedome and G. L. Caffee (trans.), Routledge & Kegan Paul, London, 1960.

Walker, G. A., *Gatherings from Grave-yards,* Longman, Green & Co., London, 1839.

Walker, G. A., *Burial Ground Incendiarism,* Longman, Green & Co., London, 1846.

Walter, T., *Funerals and How to Improve Them,* Hodder & Stoughton, London, 1990.

Walter, T., *The Revival of Death,* Routledge, London, 1994.

Watson, J. L., Of Flesh and Bones: The Management of Death Pollution in Cantonese Society, in *Death and the Regeneration of Life,* M. Bloch and J. Parry (eds.), Cambridge University Press, Cambridge, 1982.

Watson, J. M., *So Far, So What: Tales from Beside the Grave—An Undertaker's View,* unpublished paper, 1991.

Waugh, E., *The Loved One: An Anglo-American Tragedy,* Chapman & Hall, London, 1948.

Weinberg, M. S., Becoming a Nudist, in *Deviance: The Interactionist Perspective* (3rd Edition), E. Rubington and M. S. Weinberg (eds.), Macmillan, London, 1978.

Whaley, J. (ed.), *Mirrors of Mortality: Studies in the Social History of Death,* Europa, London, 1981.

Whyte, W. F., *Learning from the Field: A Guide from Experience,* Sage, Beverly Hills, 1984.

Widgery, D., *Some Lives! A GP's East End,* Sinclair-Stevenson, London, 1991.

Wilson, Sir A. T. and H. Levy, *Burial Reform and Funeral Costs,* Oxford University Press, Oxford, 1938.

Wilson, B. R., *Religion in Secular Society,* C. A. Watts & Co., London, 1966.

Winter, J. M. Some Aspects of the Demographic Consequences of the First World War in Britain, *Population Studies, XXX,* pp. 539-552, 1976.

Winter, J. M., Britain's "Lost Generation" of the First World War, *Population Studies, XXXI,* pp. 449-466, 1977.

Winter, J. M., Declining Mortality in Britain 1987-1950, in *Population and Society in Britain,* T. Barker and M. Drake (eds.), Batsford Academic & Educational, London, 1982.

Witz, A., *Professions and Patriarchy,* Routledge, London, 1992.

Wohl, R., *The Generation of 1914,* Weidenfeld & Nicolson, London, 1980.

Wolcott, H., Criteria for an Ethnographic Approach to Research in Schools, *Human Organization, 34*:2, Summer 1975.

Wood, J., The Structure of Concern: The Ministry in Death-related Situations, *Urban Life, 4*:3, pp. 369-384, October 1975.

Woodburn, J., Social Dimensions of Death in Four African Hunting and Gathering Societies, in *Death and the Regeneration of Life,* M. Bloch and J. Parry (eds.), Cambridge University Press, Cambridge, 1982.

Wright, M., *A Death in the Family,* Optima, London, 1987.

Index